Weeding Library Collections

Weeding Library Collections
Library Weeding Methods

Fourth Edition

Stanley J. Slote

LIBRARIES UNLIMITED, INC.
Englewood, Colorado
1997

LIBRARIES UNLIMITED, INC.
P.O. Box 6633
Englewood, CO 80155-6633
(800) 237-6124
www.lu.com

Production Editor: Kevin W. Perizzolo
Copy Editor: Curtis D. Holmes
Proofreader: Shannon Graff
Indexer: Christine J. Smith
Typesetter: Judy Gay Matthews

Library of Congress Cataloging-in-Publication Data

Slote, Stanley J.
    Weeding library collections : library weeding methods / Stanley J.
Slote. -- 4th ed.
    xxi, 240 p. 17x25 cm.
    Includes bibliographical references and index.
    ISBN 1-56308-511-9 (cloth).
    1. Discarding of books, periodicals, etc.--United States.
I. Title.
Z703.6.S55   1997
025.2'16--dc21   96-54865
                                                            CIP

"What are countless books to me, and libraries of which the owner in his whole life will scarcely read the titles?"
—Seneca 4 B.C.–65 A.D.

"If you want roome for modern books, it is easy to remove the less useful into a more remote place."
—Thomas Hollis, 1725
(quoted by Urquhart)

"A small collection of well chosen books is sufficient for the entertainment and instruction of any man, and all else are useless Lumber."
—Rev. Reginald Heber,
1787 (quoted by
Nicholas A. Basbanes)

Contents

Part 2
The Weeding Process for Circulating Collections

Part 3
The Weeding Process for Noncirculating Collections

Illustrations

Foreword to the Fourth Edition

At the time of the Library at Alexander, Egypt, it is estimated that there were a million different books in existence. (There were 700,000 in this one library.) Of these, only 400 titles have survived the barbarians, the Dark Ages, and the crumbling of ancient civilizations. In other words, 99.996 percent have disappeared. Some reappeared almost by magic; they were found on parchment manuscripts in which the old classic had been erased and replaced by religious works during the middle ages. Science managed to recover the original texts from these palimpsests.

Somehow, in 2,000 years, almost a million titles and several million volumes were "weeded out" and permanently disappeared. We modern librarian-barbarians, who currently are weeding libraries, have not reduced the number of titles in existence. There are now perhaps 60 million titles and none will disappear permanently because of us. But we are reluctant weeders because we do not want to destroy the heritage of mankind or reduce the ready availability of our books. This work is an attempt to overcome our natural reluctance to weed by making the process simpler, more objective, and more scientific.

Preface to the Fourth Edition

This book is based upon a number of research projects undertaken by the author over a period of 30 years, a careful study of the research undertaken by others, field observations, and discussions with librarians and computer specialists. It has been designed to be used for the following four distinct purposes:

1. As a comprehensive source summarizing the opinion, knowledge, and serious research in the field of weeding.

2. As a do-it-yourself guide for librarians wishing to weed their collections, with step-by-step procedures described in detail.

3. As a textbook for schools of librarianship. Deacquisition (weeding) and acquisition go hand-in-hand. Weeding is one of the best tools available for the long-range improvement of library collections.

4. As a stimulus to further study in the field. It is hoped that libraries using the recommended methods will measure and report their results.

By using the methods recommended in this volume, two distinct parts of a collection can be identified with confidence: the *core collection*, that part of the collection that is used, and a *weedable* part, which tends to remain on the shelves unused.

Much of the opposition to weeding has been generated by the fear that weeding will damage the collection and reduce use. Our findings should calm some of these fears. In all of our research, weeding by the suggested methods resulted in an increase in circulation. Fewer, selected volumes seemed to encourage more use.

The fourth edition has undergone a comprehensive revision and updating. It has also been edited in order to simplify certain chapters and reduce the quantity of less useful material. Among the major changes are:

1. A new chapter, Chapter 15, Weeding Reference Collections, has been added. For the first time, this book deals seriously with the noncirculating parts of the library collection. Unlike the rest of the book, this is based upon a literature and field study but no independent research by the author. It is now possible to use the weeding techniques suggested for circulating collections but modified for reference works.

2. Chapter 13, Computer Assisted Weeding, has been completely rewritten. The weeding process has been simplified. In the years since the third edition of this book, the computer has become faster, cheaper, and more pervasive in library procedures. It has also been a boon, since it preserves

much of the use-data formerly not recorded, unavailable, or difficult to reconstruct.

3.   All of the forms to be used for weeding have been redesigned. Each now includes specific instructions for use and makes it possible to weed a collection referring less often to the book itself.

4.   A major improvement has been made in all of our weeding methods because of new understanding of the relationship between in-library use and circulation use. A 1992 study by Selth, Koller, and Briscoe (page 71) has convinced this author that in-library use does *not* mirror circulation use. This has caused a dramatic change in our weeding techniques. We now recommend to all libraries that the in-library use of the volumes in the circulating collections be recorded. This means that patrons must be stopped from reshelving books and that the pages or clerks who do reshelve them must indicate the date of such usage before reshelving them.

   We also recommend that when sampling the collection to determine what cut-date should be used for weeding, both the books being charged out and the books simultaneously used in the library be sampled.

   However, these methods *should* be used by libraries which do not retain in-library use data. When in-library use is not recorded, the cut-dates for weeding can still be established with circulation data only and specific candidates for weeding identified. Then librarians must use their judgment to return to the shelves those volumes which might have experienced in-library use and not circulated.

5.   In the literature survey, most of the reports have been abridged, a few omitted, and significant new studies were added.

6.   The complete articles on weeding using the "Slote Method" have been omitted but can be found in the third edition of *Weeding Library Collections*. The articles are:

   Winche, E., and B. Molesworth. "Collection Weeding: York Regional Library," *APLA Bulletin* 44, no. 4 (January 1981): 38-39.

   McKee, Penelope. "Weeding the Forest Hill Branch of Toronto Public Library by the Slote Method: A Test Case," *Library Research* 3 (1981): 283-301.

   Williams, Roy. "Weeding an Academic Lending Library Using the Slote Method," *British Journal of Academic Librarianship* 1, no. 2 (Summer 1986): 147-159.

   Williams, Roy. "Choosing the Slote Method of Weeding Library Collections," in *Collection Development, Proceedings of a Conference of the Library and Information Research Group, University of Sheffield* (London: Taylor Graham, 1987): 88-94.

Acknowledgments

Special thanks are due Jane Hochman and Dr. Brien Weiner, who assisted with the literature search and the editing. They made numerous useful and constructive suggestions. Without their work this book would not have been written. Also to Dr. Loriene Roy, who sent me copies of her work that I had not found easily accessible; and to Ellen Emmett, head of the Library and Information Science Library, C. W. Post Campus, Long Island University. She not only gave me and the researchers free access to her fine library but assisted us in every way.

Thanks are due to the many people who provided me with their time, supplied me with copies of their records, and discussed, in detail, their weeding techniques and experiences. They were of particular help in the study of computer-assisted weeding and the weeding of reference collections. Included are Pamela C. Thornton of the Westchester (New York) Library System; Nancy Young and Barbara Blanchard of the White Plains (New York) Public Library; Drs. Mary Biggs and Patricia Butcher of the Trenton State College (New Jersey) Roscoe L. West Library; Myron Roochvarg of the Commack (New York) Public Library; Mary Jane Schmit and Lisa Abisognio of the Half Hollow Hills Library (Dix Hills, New York); Brenda Giovanneillo of the Nassau (New York) Library System; and George Trepp of the Long Beach (New York) Public Library.

For his work in editing and correcting the chapter on computers, I want to thank Kevin J. Johnson.

I also want to give special thanks to Jason Tirendi who assisted in creating the forms used for weeding and to Audrey Tirendi who not only worked on preparing the manuscript, but also encouraged me by helping to resolve the many challenges I faced.

Part 1
BACKGROUND AND
INTRODUCTION TO
WEEDING

1

Background to Weeding

Introduction

For many years, authors of library standards have been advising libraries to weed collections on a regular basis. For instance, "Standards for College Libraries, 1995" states

> The library collection should be continually evaluated . . . for purposes . . . of identifying for withdrawal those titles which have outlived their usefulness. No title should be retained for which a clear purpose is not evident in terms of academic programs or extra-curricular enrichment.[1]

This statement is typical of the dozens of such statements that recommend the removal of books from the collection. In addition, leading practitioners of librarianship have called for continuous and aggressive weeding of collections. Curley and Broderick endorse the "withdrawal of materials from the collection."[2] Evans states that "without an ongoing weeding program, a collection can quickly become obsolete."[3] Over the years librarians have been barraged by an almost endless stream of this sort of advice.

In spite of the advice, it has been observed and reported that too little weeding is being practiced, and that library shelves contain quantities of unused and unwanted materials. It is hard to find practicing librarians who feel that their collections have been weeded sufficiently.

Reasons for Weeding

To Save Space

In the face of rapidly growing collections, shortage of space, and the high cost of storing books on open stacks, there are potent reasons for vigorous weeding. Perhaps the strongest is the growing resistance to budget increases for new construction now being experienced by *all* types of libraries.

It should be noted that an increase in stack space is often the immediate cause of a much larger construction program. The real impact of expanding collections beyond their present library capacity must be related to the proper balance and functioning of the entire library. If one assumes that in the designing of new libraries an idealized relationship between book and nonbook space is achieved, then the addition of new books beyond the original capacity of a building has some very expensive implications.

In 1995, *Library Journal* reported that 99 new public library buildings had an average cost of $159.13 per square foot, or about $40.03 per volume of designed book capacity. Eight new academic libraries cost an average $123.63 per square foot. Public library additions cost $114.10 per square foot.[4] While most librarians seem aware of the high and ever increasing cost of books, the above report highlights the high cost of *housing* books. It is possible that high construction costs (and tight budgets) explain in part the drop in the number of new public libraries that have been built each year during the last five years.[5] Additionally, the true cost of housing a collection in a new library is even greater on a per book basis because new libraries are generally designed for expansion of the present collection and not all the designed book capacity is used immediately.

Two related aspects of these costs might be considered. In 1995, for instance, the costs of constructing eight new academic libraries[6] ranged from $27.50 to $127.92 per volume, with an average cost of $50.99. These figures indicate that a wide range of factors affect building costs, and that a new library may find itself spending considerably more or less than the $50.99 cost per volume. This observation calls for more study and analysis, with the goal of creating greater efficiency in the design of new facilities. The $50.99 average cost must be considered only as a point of departure when one estimates the cost of expansion.

The other aspect, rarely mentioned in the literature, is that the actual space taken up by books is a small part of a new library building. Fremont Rider mentioned that only 10 percent of the cubic area taken up by book stacks contains books.[7] Using the data in the 1995 *Library Journal* article on library construction costs, public libraries were found to have the designed capacity of approximately four volumes per square foot of enclosed space. This means that at full capacity a library actually uses about $\frac{1}{40}$th, or 2½ percent, of its enclosed area for books.[8] Thus it seems reasonable, when thinking of expanding collections, to think in terms of true needs—on an average every book added over the designed capacity of a library should ultimately require building expansion equal to 40 times the amount of space taken up by the actual book itself.

Computerization ultimately may reduce the need for more library buildings. CD-ROMs, the Internet, and computers with modems connecting users to the world are already found in many libraries. Perhaps centralized, computerized collections accessible to all will reduce the need for ever expanding library collections housed in ever expanding library buildings.

Other Advantages

There are many advantages in having a well-weeded library. Loriene Roy lists 27 reasons for weeding.[9] Essentially, weeding accomplishes the following:

1. *Increases book usage.* In 1911, Asa Wynkoop wrote, "It has been shown by experiment again and again that a collection of best books, when grouped by themselves, receive twice as much use as when scattered

among old and obsolete material."[10] Our findings have shown increased usage is one of the major benefits of weeding.

2. *Increases reader satisfaction.* With fewer volumes, the client not only saves time,[11] but also finds that the appearance of the collection has been improved and the collection revitalized.[12] A lack of weeding often results in tightly packed shelves and books stored in inconvenient locations, both of which tend to reduce user satisfaction.

3. *Saves staff time.* In a weeded collection, time is saved in shelving, reshelving, and taking inventory.[13] Retrieval becomes more efficient for both staff and users.

4. *Makes room for new technologies.* Computers, work stations, Internet access, plus the books, documents, and directories needed to support these technologies, require substantial blocks of space and seem to be expanding daily. Many new libraries have been designing such areas to handle their current and future needs.

Factors Discouraging Weeding

In view of the pressing space problem, it is difficult to understand why librarians have not weeded more aggressively. A number of factors have discouraged weeding.

Emphasis on numbers. The number of books in a library is often considered a criterion of the quality of a library. Thus librarians playing the numbers game may tend to keep obsolete books to be included in the official book count. While many librarians reject the validity of a number count as a sensible quality measure, the official reporting forms for years emphasized book counts in the data to be submitted to higher authorities.

Professional work pressures. Weeding has generally been considered a professional task. In many instances, work pressures have not left librarians much time to perform the tasks of weeding. Not only must weeding decisions be made, but the card or computer generated catalog, the shelf list, and other records must be maintained. Overworked librarians become intimidated by the tasks and the time required to do them. There is good reason for concern when using conventional weeding techniques. Danny Wallace reports that

> A reasonable estimate of an efficient weeding process might require twenty minutes of professional time for each item examined. . . . for a very small library of about 15,000 volumes it would require 4,950 person/hours equivalent to more than two years of professional level effort. For a library with some 98,000 items, . . . more than fifty-seven years of effort would be required.[14]

Public Displeasure. Generally, clients don't like to see a library weed its collection and find it "throwing out" books. In February 1991, the *Detroit Free Press* reported that some people were "appalled" at the Macomb County Library for "pitching" 20,000 volumes. Some public officials suggested that " . . . the county cut in half the library's $500,000 for new books."[15] Furthermore, Manley reports that, "Weeding is politically incorrect. Citizens go nuts when they find out that libraries discard thousands of books every year."[16]

Sacredness of collection. There are emotional and intellectual blocks against removing books from a collection. Many people consider books to be valuable records of human heritage and therefore almost sacred. In fact, historically there were sometimes religious laws prohibiting the discarding of books considered sacred. Johnson reports that for centuries ". . . prayer-books which were no longer usable . . . under Jewish law, could not be destroyed because they contained God's name."[17] For many librarians the removal of any book becomes painful. Such indiscriminate retention of books does not serve the public. Books that are not being used but that have historical value belong in a depository. A library that is serving its clientele properly needs to have a collection that is up-to-date and changing.

Conflicting criteria. Hard-to-apply and sometimes conflicting criteria have often made weeding an arduous and disturbing task. Weeders are torn between keeping the books people want and the "good" books. Librarians want balance, wide subject coverage, and quality. An attempt was made to apply these criteria when the volumes originally were selected. Then the weeder, frequently the person who selected the book in the first place, must make a subjective decision to discard a book previously judged worthy. This makes for difficult decision making.

The weeding process is not without risks. How many librarians have wished they had saved old telephone directories, mail-order catalogs, local newspapers, and a wide range of other items now sought after? Katz has pointed out that the vast majority of nineteenth-century local newspapers have been completely destroyed, "One of the most difficult research problems is to locate materials in local newspapers of the nineteenth century."[18] As anyone who has ever cleaned out an attic or basement knows, only a few days pass before a use is found for something just irretrievably discarded. In libraries, this risk must be minimized by some centralized responsibility for the collection of less-used materials.

While this study is unable to overcome the resistance caused by all of the above factors, it is aimed at making the physical and intellectual processes of weeding much simpler. If *objective* weeding criteria are used, weeding decisions are easier to make. Even clerical personnel, presumably more available than professionals, can be utilized for this work. With more certainty in weeding decisions, more extensive weeding could be done.

Collections Are Not Intact

Collections will change, however, in spite of efforts to keep them intact. What is available to the reader is *not* what has been so carefully selected and purchased. Access to the reader is reduced by:

1. *Theft and vandalism.* Collections do not consist of all the books which have been purchased. Losses due to theft and vandalism will change a

collection. Collections are routinely weeded of the newest and most wanted volumes by the patrons themselves. Thus the original collection, which was carefully selected, is not the collection that remains on the library's shelves. Libraries are extremely vulnerable to stealing since they operate on the trust system, making the books readily available to their clients. Stealing is a serious problem. Out of the thousands of documented cases of book theft, two stand out. In 1994, an Englishman, Duncan Charles Worsley Jevons, admitted to having stolen 42,000 books from libraries.[19] In 1995, an American, Stephen Carrie Blumberg, was convicted of stealing 23,000 volumes from 268 libraries, almost all of which were rare books housed in "secure" places.[20]

2. *Misshelved books.* A misshelved book generally no longer exists for readers. They are unlikely to have access to it either through the card catalog or through normal browsing in subject areas—two basic access points to a collection. Unless shelf-reading is constant, regular, and careful, a part of the collection has disappeared (for all practical purposes) just as surely as if the books had been stolen. Furthermore, especially in academic libraries, intentional misshelving is a common technique that a patron uses to assure temporary but easy access to a particular book. If this practice is not prevented, the working collection is considerably different from the collection originally acquired.

3. *Circulation.* Circulating collections are not intact since substantial segments are in the hands of the clients. It is not uncommon to have a fourth of a collection circulating at any given time. Of the volumes that are circulating, most will eventually be returned, but there are a certain number of books which, by virtue of being in demand, will almost always be out. Faculty loans in college and university libraries often are nonrecallable and therefore not part of the readily usable collection. As far as users are concerned, they are not dealing with the collection as originally established, but with a collection that is on the shelves at the moment they are in the library. Therefore, it is inconsistent to maintain that the collection acquired is identical to the collection available. An attack on weeding cannot be based on the concept of keeping the integrity, unity, and overall design of the collection. Such unity has already been destroyed.

Summary

It seems extremely timely that more attention be focused on weeding. Librarians are faced with economic pressures and demands for accountability for their expenditures. If ever there were a time for innovation in library services, attitudes, and operations, it is now. If by realistic thinning of collections librarians can reduce their requests for increased capital costs, and at the same time increase the services being rendered, they will be answering the challenge in a way most acceptable to society.

Notes

1. American Library Association, Association of College and Research Libraries, Standards Committee of ACRL's College Library Section, "Standards for College Libraries, 1995," *College & Research Libraries News* (April 1995): 245.

2. Arthur Curley and Dorothy Broderick, *Building Library Collections*, 6th ed. (Metuchen, NJ: Scarecrow Press, 1985), 308.

3. G. Edward Evans, *Developing Library and Information Center Collections*, 2d ed. (Littleton, CO: Libraries Unlimited, 1987), 291.

4. *Library Journal* 120, no. 20 (December 1995): 42-52.

5. Ibid., 52.

6. Ibid., 42.

7. Fremont Rider, *Compact Book Storage* (New York: Hadham Press, 1949), 8.

8. The computation for arriving at this figure uses 6 x 9 inches as the size of the average volume, a figure reported by Kilpatrick and Van Hoesen as the size of the median volume in their study, "The Heights of Three Hundred and Fifty Thousand Volumes," *Library Quarterly* (July 1935). By sampling a number of volumes, we estimate the average width of a volume to be $1\frac{2}{3}$ inches. This means that the average volume contains 90 cubic inches. Figuring the average library to have eight-foot ceilings, and therefore eight cubic feet of volume per square foot of floor space, and using four books per square feet, we find that the average new library has $\frac{1}{2}$ of a book (or 45 cubic inches) per cubic feet of enclosed area. This works out to about $2\frac{1}{2}$ percent of the 1,728 cubic inches in a cubic foot.

9. Loriene Roy, "Weeding," *Encyclopedia of Library and Information Science*, ed. Allen Kent, vol. 54, sup. 17 (1994): 368.

10. Asa Wynkoop, "Discarding Useless Material," *Wisconsin Library Bulletin* 7(1) (April 1911): 53.

11. Joseph P. Segal, *Evaluating and Weeding Collections in Small and Medium Sized Public Libraries—The Crew Method* (Chicago: American Library Association, 1980), 4.

12. Danny P. Wallace, "The Young and the Ageless: Obsolescence in Public Library Collections," *Public Libraries* 29 (March/April 1990): 103.

13. Roy, 11.

14. Danny Wallace et al., *Age Analysis for Public Library Collections: Final Report* (Baton Rouge: Louisiana State University, School of Library and Information Science, 1990): 12.

15. LeRoy Barnett, "The Enemy Is Us," *Collection Building* 11, no. 3 (1991): 25.

16. Will Manley, "The Manley Arts: If I Called This Column 'Weeding,' You Wouldn't Read It," *Booklist* 92, no. 13 (March 1996): 1108.

17. Paul Johnson, *A History of the Jews* (New York: Harper Perennial, 1988), 184.

18. William A. Katz, *Introduction to Reference Work, Vol. 1: Basic Information Sources* (New York: McGraw-Hill, 1987), 22.

19. Nicholas A. Basbanes, *A Gentle Madness* (New York: Henry Holt, 1995), 572.

20. Ibid., 567.

Current Weeding Practices

Conventional Guidelines to Weeding

While many authorities have recommended weeding, it should be emphasized that opinions on weeding have not been unanimous. Some have suggested either no weeding or weeding with great limitations. In addition, even those recommending it have stated a diversity of goals for this activity. Much of this diversity of opinion reflects the philosophies, concepts, attitudes, and prejudices of the writers. More often, the opinions are the results of practical problems facing administrators of ever-growing collections. The concept follows the need. All these influences can be seen in the range of the following goals.

1. *That all collections should be kept absolutely intact.* Books represent the accumulated recorded written heritage of civilization; therefore, wherever they may be, they should be preserved. This is the position of the anti-weeder. The removal of anything is considered profane. An extreme case reflecting this attitude occurred in Port Townsend, Washington, where a librarian lost her job after refusing to weed the library even though the library board had given her a direct order to do so.[1]

   A more common attitude is reported by Bonk and Williams. They state that there is a collection philosophy among academic librarians that "... research materials should be collected in advance of need and retained in perpetuity."[2]

2. *That collections may be weeded gingerly, by professionals only, using good judgment, not rules.* Only the experienced and trained librarian can perform this task. However, general guidelines for weeding can be established. The goal is to maintain a well-balanced collection that will match the needs and the wants of users, real and potential. Libraries attached to other institutions (schools, universities, or businesses) should have a further review of the books recommended for weeding, to be performed by members of the main institution (teachers, professors, researchers). Otherwise, "good" books or "useful" ones are likely to be removed.

   This position probably represents the majority opinion in the country today. It has been reinforced by unpleasant experiences when weeding has been handled by nonlibrarians. It has been generated by the alienation of members of faculties, for example, when weeding has occurred without their being consulted. In part, this position has been taught in library schools and represents an honest belief of some of the leaders in the profession. Truett reports that commonly in academic libraries, department heads or other librarian subject specialists did all or most of the weeding because of their specialized knowledge. Then the library frequently sought input from the faculty or academic departments library committees so that, after the preliminary weeding had been done, these specialists could examine the suggested weeds and return materials to the permanent collection.[3]

Faculty participation in the weeding process has been found to be disappointing. The benefit of involving the faculty seems to be more to prevent negative feelings rather than to improve the weeding process.[4]

3. *That collections should be so weeded that they are maintained at a predetermined physical size.* This aim, popular with some administrators, is an attempt to relieve the pressure for new construction caused by the ever-growing collections. Clark reports that weeding is often encouraged by ". . . Institutions confronted with growth of collections beyond existing housing capacity. . ."[5]

This approach, as with all others, is not without its critics. In 1944, Rider implied that the stabilization of the size of a collection is not feasible, and his opinion still retains a lot of its original validity. He maintained that as human knowledge grows, so must libraries. Just in one area, reference, the number of books gets larger each year. No college has succeeded in stabilizing collections. The continuations of periodicals, government documents, society transactions, etc., prevent stabilization.[6]

4. *That library stacks should be stocked with those volumes likely to give the library the greatest circulation.* This objective highlights the need for getting maximum usage out of social institutions and their resources. It also points up the conflict between two schools of librarianship: those who wish to give the user what he *wants*; and those who wish to give him what he *needs* (or what is "good" for him).

Newer Guidelines to Weeding

1. *That weeding should increase circulation.* It has become an increasingly recognized fact that proper weeding should increase circulation. Winsche and Molesworth report that "a well weeded collection is more heavily used."[7] McKee produced a statistical verification of this concept and reports that a strong positive relationship exists between a "declining book stock and increasing circulation."[8]

2. *That collections should be weeded so that the speed of access is increased, and so that the accuracy in retrieval is improved.* For many years it has been observed that smaller and more compact collections of materials reduce the time needed for retrieval.[9] In libraries where speed is essential, this is often a prime consideration. For instance, in newspaper libraries (morgues), where deadlines must be met, the growth of collections and cumulation of irrelevant materials can block reasonable usage.

3. *That those books least likely to be used in the future be removed.* In contrast with the goals of maintaining collections at a given size, this approach attempts to keep a collection that will satisfy a predetermined amount of future use. It tries to identify core collections that will satisfy 95 or 99 percent of the present demands made upon the collection, and to do this with the smallest identifiable core collection. A very large part of the serious research in weeding has used this approach. Trueswell started to popularize this approach in his many studies. Turner has summarized this technique.

> Trueswell's technique relies upon the comparison of two curves that are constructed by calculating the time elapsed since the last due-date of books in circulation and for books in the stacks. We can use curves to determine the proportion of books in the stacks that are responsible for any given proportion of the number of future circulations of books from the *current* set of books in the stacks. . . . For example, (in an example given) 96 percent of the books currently circulating . . . represent only 65 percent of the books available for circulation.[10]

One characteristic of these studies is the implication that weeded books be removed to secondary storage in less accessible areas. Another recurring theme relates to the endless growth of the size of collections and the constant pressure for new buildings. The studies often attempt to determine long-range solutions and frequently try to make predictions of the percentages of the collection that can be removed at various levels of retained usage. They accept, as a basic premise, that usage is a valid criterion for keeping volumes on open stacks, or in main library buildings. Furthermore, they aim to find objective criteria for weeding. This present volume has accepted these assumptions as basic to its theme.

Additional Methods

While all of the above reflect some current goals of weeding, other methods of reaching these same goals have been suggested. It is obvious, for instance, that the space needed to store materials can be reduced substantially through the use of microreproduction. Microfilm, microfiche, and microprint can be found in many libraries. While many people feel that such reduction in size makes the materials harder to use, the whole question of size reduction is an important but unresolved one.

In addition, libraries have attacked the problems through limiting the subject areas of their collections or assigning different specializations to other libraries in a cooperative fashion. The Library of Congress has agreed with the National Library of Medicine and the Department of Agriculture Library not to overlap their specialized collections unnecessarily. The Farmington Plan, now defunct, was another attempt to assign areas of subject or language specialization.

Many other attempts have been made. Union catalogs, interlibrary loans, computer databases, deposit collections, and library systems have all contributed in some way toward fulfilling the above goals.

Notes

1. W. D. Nelson, "Library Board Maintains Freedom to Weed," *Wilson Library Bulletin* 55 (May 1981): 681.

2. Sharon Bonk and Sara Williams, "Stock Revision, Retention and Relegation in US Academic Libraries," in *Collection Management in Academic Libraries* (Brookfield, VT: Gower, 1991), 232.

3. Carol Truett, "Weeding and Evaluating the Reference Collection: A Study of Policies and Practices in Academic and Public Libraries," *The Reference Librarian* 29 (1990): 61-63.

4. Lawrence L. Reed, "Weeding: A Quantitative and Qualitative Approach," *Library Acquisitions: Practice and Theory* 17 (Summer 1993): 179.

5. Lenore Clark, ed., *Guide to Review of Library Collections: Preservation, Storage, and Withdrawal* (Chicago: American Library Association, 1991), 2.

6. Fremont Rider, *The Scholar and the Future of the Research Library* (New York: Hadham Press, 1944), 44-46.

7. E. Winsche and B. Molesworth, "Collection Weeding—York Regional Library," *APLA Bulletin* 44, no. 4 (January 1981): 38.

8. Penelope McKee, "Weeding the Forest Hill Branch of Toronto Public Library by the Slote Method: A Test Case," *Library Research* 3 (1981): 298.

9. Stanley J. Slote, "An Approach to Weeding Criteria for Newspaper Libraries," *American Documentation* 19 (April 1968): 168.

10. Stephen J. Turner, "Trueswell's Weeding Techniques: The Facts," *College & Research Libraries 41 (March 1980): 134.*

3

Library Standards
Relating to Weeding

A study of the various standards will show that weeding is either recommended or completely disregarded; it is never suggested that no weeding be done. If recommended, however, the force with which weeding is emphasized varies. These standards have been classified as follows:

1. Standards not mentioning weeding.

2. Standards recommending weeding in principle.

3. Standards establishing some criteria.

4. Standards employing past usage as a criterion for weeding.

The following are just a sample of the existing standards and no attempt has been made to be all-inclusive.

Standards Not Mentioning Weeding

There are very few standards today that do not mention weeding. An exception is the 1992 "Guidelines for Libraries Serving Persons with a Hearing Impairment," which makes no mention of weeding at all.[1] However, in these standards the emphasis is on the special services and special problems involved when serving the hearing impaired.

Standards That Recommend Weeding

Most existing standards mention weeding without explaining how to do it or when to do it. They limit their statements to a sort of general agreement that weeding is beneficial and ought to be done. They range from a perfunctory mention of weeding to an attempt to emphasize its importance by recommending the creation of written policies or programs. In "Library Standards for Adult Correctional Institutions 1992," the recommendation is made for the development of ". . . procedures for weeding outdated and unnecessary materials from the collection." "The collection shall be weeded . . . continuously and systematically."[2]

Several standards recommend the creation of written weeding policies without offering further details about how to proceed. "Standards for Appellate Court and County Law Libraries," in discussing acquisitions, says:

> Written policies for collection development, including criteria for
> . . . discarding of materials . . . should be formulated . . .[3]

> All superseded material . . . should be retained only if it continues
> to serve as a useful source of information . . .[4]

> A written collection development policy, including criteria for . . .
> weeding materials . . . is recommended."

> The authority to weed . . . should be at the discretion of the . . .
> librarian.[6]

Stronger statements encouraging weeding can be found in "Service to Iowa:
Public Library Measures of Quality, Second Edition." Weeding is mentioned in two
different contexts: as a necessary policy of the library and as a standard for
evaluating the library. It examines a library to see that:

> The library has a collection development policy that includes . . . weeding
> of the collection.[7]

> The library maintains a current, thoroughly weeded collection of
> books appropriate to the role(s) the library has chosen.[8]

The standards then list recommended minimum holdings for different population groups and, to meet this standard, it must be a "CURRENT, THOROUGHLY
WEEDED COLLECTION."[9]

The Iowa standards go one step further and mention the frequency and depth
of weeding.

> Every item in the library's collection is evaluated for retention,
> replacement, or withdrawal at least every three years to determine its
> usefulness according to the library's collection development policy.
> Three percent or more of the collection is withdrawn each year.[10]

The "Tennessee Minimum Standards for Non-Metropolitan Public Libraries"
divides their libraries into six levels, depending upon the population being served.
In each level the same statement appears, recommending that at least 5 percent of
the collection be weeded out yearly.

> Selects for and weeds the collection in accordance with a written
> collection development policy which has been endorsed by the
> library board. Discards at least 5 percent of the collection each year
> through a regular program of collection evaluation and weeding.[11]

Iowa suggests 3 percent of the collection be weeded out yearly, Tennessee 5 percent. It is not an uncommon experience to find such differing opinions relating to all aspects of library weeding.

Standards Establishing Some Criteria

Some standards producing institutions have come out in favor of qualitative standards, avoiding numerical or quantitative ones.[12] They suggest that weeding should improve the quality of a library and list specific criteria to be considered. These give valuable but rather generalized advice on what and what not to weed. The "Standards for College Libraries, 1995," quoted in part earlier in this book, sets as criteria "usefulness, clear purpose, and enrichment." It states:

> The library collection should be continually evaluated against standard bibliographies and evolving institutional requirements for purposes of both adding new titles and identifying for withdrawal those titles which have outlived their usefulness. No title should be retained for which a clear purpose is not evident in terms of academic programs or extra-curricular enrichment.[13]

These standards then recommend using subject lists for colleges, and general bibliographies, such as *Books for College Libraries*, for identifying important titles.

Several standards suggest weeding books in poor repair or obsolete. For example, "Standards for Church and Synagogue Libraries" repeatedly recommends weeding and states:

> The collection is continually reevaluated. . . . This process . . . leads to . . . the discarding of materials no longer useful and the replacement of materials in poor repair.[14]

An even stronger statement can be found in the 1994 "Standards for Community, Junior, and Technical College Learning Resources Programs":

> Obsolete, worn-out and inappropriate materials should be removed based upon a policy statement. . . . De-selection or withdrawal on a regular basis is indispensable to a useful collection and should be done systematically. . . . From three to five percent of the collection should be replaced annually.[15]

The age of materials is dealt with in the "New York State Public Library Service: Minimum Standards."

> Any collection should be dynamic, vital and continually changing. . . . Items no longer useful should be regularly withdrawn from the collection and discarded . . . at least 25 percent of the collection should consist of materials published or produced in the last five years.[16]

More detailed advice on weeding in the standards can be found in *Information Power: Guidelines for School Library Media Programs*. This publication suggests the need for a detailed plan with criteria for removing items and specifically focuses on outdated and inaccurate materials as well as physical deterioration, obsolescence, and appropriateness:

> Data from inventory counts are useful in the process of removing obsolete items from the collection. Having outdated or inaccurate materials in a collection discourages use, gives a false impression of the adequacy of the collection, wastes the time of the staff, and obstructs the users in their search for useful materials. . . . Criteria for removing items are identified in the schools' collection development plan and provide guidelines for evaluating physical deterioration, obsolescence, and appropriateness for the current needs of the school community. Duplicate copies, out-of-date materials, materials no longer used or of slight utility, almanacs, yearbooks and encyclopedias that have been superseded by newer editions should be covered in the criteria for removal from the collection. Materials in which any significant portion of the information is outdated are withdrawn.[17]

Standards Establishing Use as a Criterion

It is very difficult to find standards employing past use as a criterion for weeding, even though such a criterion has been used successfully in many libraries and reported with some frequency in the literature (see bibliography). *Information Power: Guidelines for School Library Media Programs* provides a hint of such a criterion: "Modern automated circulation systems provide fast and accurate ways . . . to provide statistical information useful to collection building and maintenance."[18] The publication recommends a collection development plan for removing, among other things, "materials no longer used."

Recommended Standards

The author recommends the following set of standards for material that normally circulates:

1. The objective of weeding should be to maintain a core collection of books that would satisfy 95 to 99 percent of the present demands made upon the entire present collection, including in-library use.

2. All books weeded should be considered for secondary or centralized storage.

3. One complete weeding of the library should take place in each year.

4. The weeding criteria to be used should be based solely upon the likelihood of a volume's being used in the future.

5. The shelf-time period established for each library should satisfy the above standards and should result in an objective similar to this: "All volumes should be removed that have not been circulated or experienced in-library use since (date). This shelf-time period should take into account the use patterns of no less than one full year."

6. Similar criteria should be established and used, in modified form, for the different *types* of material as follows:

    a) For runs of periodicals, remove all before a specific publication date. This date should be established separately for each run.

    b) For reference books, weeding should be performed as for circulating works, attempting to keep a core representing 99 to 99.5 percent of the present usage.

    c) For archives and special works (such as works of local authors) no weeding should be done.

The basis for such standards will be developed in later chapters of this work.

Notes

1. New York Library Association, Roundtable for Libraries Serving Special Populations, "Guideline for Libraries Serving Persons with a Hearing Impairment," *Library Trends* 41, no. 1 (Summer 1992): 164-72.

2. American Library Association, The Association of Specialized and Cooperative Library Agencies, *Library Standards for Adult Correctional Institutions 1992* (Chicago: American Library Association, 1992), 23.

3. American Association of Law Libraries, State, Court and County Law Libraries Special Interest Section, "Standards for Appellate and County Law Libraries," *Law Library Journal* 81, no. 2 (Spring 1989): S8.

4. Ibid.

5. Ibid., S14.

6. Ibid.

7. (Iowa) State Library Standards Committee, *In Service to Iowa: Public Library Measures of Quality*, 2d ed. (Des Moines, IA: 1989), 13.

8. Ibid.

9. Ibid., 37.

10. Ibid., 14.

11. Tennessee Public Library Standards Committee, "Tennessee Minimum Standards for Non-Metropolitan Public Libraries," *Tennessee Librarian* 43, no. 4 (Fall 1991): 26.

12. "New Public Library Standards for North Carolina," *North Carolina Libraries* 45, no. 2 (Summer 1987): 106.

13. American Library Association, Association of College and Research Libraries, College Library Standards Committee, "Standards for College Libraries, 1995," *College and Research Libraries News* (April 1995): 247.

14. Church and Synagogue Library Association, *Standards for Church and Synagogue Libraries; Guidelines for Measuring Effectiveness and Progress*, 2d ed. (Portland, OR: 1993), 20.

15. Association for Educational Communications and Technology and ACRL. "Standards for Community, Junior, and Technical College Learning Resource Programs," *College and Research Libraries News* 55, no. 9 (October 1994): 581.

16. Committee on Minimum Public Standards for New York State. *New York State Public Library Service: Minimum Standards* (August 1988): 12.

17. American Library Association, American Association of School Librarians, *Information Power: Guidelines for School Library Media Programs* (Chicago: American Library Association, 1988), 79-80.

18. Ibid.

4

Present Weeding Criteria Based on Judgment

Difficulties Encountered in Subjective Weeding

The mass of material. In the face of rather indecisive standards or goals for the weeding of libraries, there exists a wide range of specific advice on *what* to weed. Much of this advice assumes that librarians have the ability to make "good" weeding judgments based upon their knowledge of the community, of the users, of books in their own collections, and of society's needs.

It is the contention of this writer that the above assumptions lack the validity usually assigned to them. For example, librarians are supposed to *know* books—to know what exists, what is worth acquiring, what the library holds, and what the library should hold. Can anyone really *know* about books? It is doubtful. The very mass of the accumulation seems to make it improbable. It is likely that there are between 55 and 60 million different titles or works in the world.[1] The holdings of just a few of the major libraries seem to point to the validity of the estimate, although no definitive study has been made of the titles now in existence. Nevertheless, the British Library contains over 14 million volumes of which 75 percent are not among the 16.5 million titles held by the Library of Congress. The Bibliotheque Nationale, with a strong emphasis on French works, contains 12 million titles and the National Library of Russia over 10 million. To this quantity, one also must consider the 600,000 to 750,000 new titles added internationally each year. In addition, several hundred thousand government documents (restricted and unrestricted) published each year are not included in the 600,000 to 750,000 figure. To make the problem more complex, one might want to include the 1 million serial titles, current and retrospective, and hundreds of thousands of other nonbook items such as newspapers, tapes, compact discs, video cassettes, microfilm, pamphlets, and other forms collected by some libraries. The size of the stockpile creates an awesome problem for the librarian.

One of the ways librarians obtain information about books is through critical reviews. Unfortunately, only a small fraction of books published are reviewed. And even the reviews that do exist are a massive body of literature.

Another way to *know* books is to read them. A reasonably fast reader, with enough time (our average librarian?), might read one book a day. This would amount to 365 books per year or 1/2000th of the current output and perhaps 1/150,000th of the total of all works that exist. This does not even begin to deal with other serious problems that block this approach, such as one reader's inability to handle the diversity of languages or the lack of availability of these volumes to librarians.

Can a librarian really *know* books? It is hard to believe that such knowledge can be anything but extremely perfunctory. It is hard even to *know* the literature in one restricted field like librarianship. There are at least 700 periodicals of librarianship. Counting regional periodicals, irregular ones, and newsletter types, the number must exceed 1,000. How many of these does the average librarian get to read? It is difficult to find anyone, even in the academic world, who is confident about keeping up with the literature of librarianship.

Knowledge of the community. Other assumptions upon which subjective weeding is based also have serious flaws. For example, librarians are charged with "knowing their communities" and thereby "catering to their needs." Is this possible? How many people even know their own needs and can cater to them? Or the needs and wants of their children? Their students? What unique characteristics, training, and experience do librarians have that equip them for such a commitment? If it is true that they understand and know how to serve their communities, why have they not done so?

Every survey of use shows that libraries get relatively little use. It has been reported that only 10 percent of the adult population really use the public library, that 42 percent use it less than once a year, and that a large percentage of college students use it rarely or not at all.[2] Librarians have trouble satisfying the needs of their patrons, much less the community.

Consider the frequent failures that occur when the library tries to serve minority groups. No matter how exhaustive the study of a community, there exists no agreed upon, specific, or valid response to that study. To date, libraries have identified large groups of non-users but have not identified the techniques required to attract such non-users in any significant way.

Therefore, the author tends to reject the purely professional and subjective approach to weeding. The assumption that librarians really *know* which books to retain to satisfy the patron is invalid, unless it is based upon *use studies* within a library. Furthermore, attempting to keep what is best for some vague nonuser seems a waste, considering the difficulties encountered in trying to completely satisfy present users. Why look for new challenges before responding to the older, closer, and more immediate challenge of running present libraries better?

In reading the following weeding criteria one must be suspicious of the basis of the judgments that created them. Nonetheless, these criteria do create a starting point for current weeding practice.

Specific Weeding Criteria

The following weeding criteria have been culled from the sources in the additional reading section at the end of this chapter. Essentially this information has been published in the how-to literature of librarianship, usually for specific types of libraries. However, where the overlap is great, no attempt has been made to identify the type of library involved. It is the purpose of this chapter to demonstrate the range of criteria available.

Weeding based upon appearance or condition. The most universally accepted criterion for weeding is based upon the *appearance or condition* of the item. Often, however, this criterion calls for caution—to avoid discarding rare books—and for judgment—to determine whether or not the volume should be replaced. Some of the specific advice is to weed:

1. Books of antiquated appearance that might discourage use.

2. Badly bound volumes with soft pulpy paper or shoddy binding.

3. Badly printed works, including those with small print, dull or faded print, cramped margins, poor illustrations, or paper that is translucent so that the print shows through.

4. Worn-out volumes whose pages are dirty, brittle, or yellow, with missing pages, frayed binding, broken backs, or dingy or dirty covers.

5. Audio cassettes with poor sound.

6. Dog-eared volumes.

7. Material that looks unappealing.

8. Tatty materials.

9. Books with cracked spines.

10. Filmstrips with scratches or torn sprockets.

11. Compact discs with chips, cracks, deep scratches, or warps.

12. Video cassettes damaged or worn beyond repair.

13. Computer software with floppy disks that do not work.

14. Art reproductions that are faded, scratched, warped or otherwise shabby; frames that are worn, damaged or separating; or mats soiled or water damaged.

Weeding of superfluous or duplicate volumes. It is easier for most librarians to agree upon the criterion of weeding duplicate volumes than upon any other criterion, since this approach retains one copy of the title in the collection. Books similar to other books fall easily into this category. Some examples to weed are:

1. Unneeded duplicate titles.

2. Duplicates except for date, place, or reprint.

3. Inexpensive reprints.

4. Older editions.

5. Editions in languages other than English when the English version is held by the library.

6. Highly specialized books when the library holds more extensive or more up-to-date volumes on the same subject.

7. Superfluous books on subjects of little interest to the local community.

8. Older editions of computer software when new editions or versions have been purchased.

Weeding based upon poor content. Weed:

1. When information is dated.

2. When the book is poorly written.

3. When information is incorrect.

4. When improved editions exist.

5. Earlier titles in repetitious fiction series.

6. Books that are harmful or useless.

7. Sexist materials.

8. Old conservative books.

9. Sports rules that have been changed.

10. Etiquette books where patterns of etiquette have changed.

11. Books on textiles, shop, and crafts where changes have occurred.

12. Social sciences when they manifest outdated theories and practices.

13. Materials not related to pupils' needs.

14. Uninteresting material.

15. Books with cultural bias.

16. Books with condescending attitude toward one or another group.

Weeding based upon language. Weed:

1. When the language is not called for in your library.

2. Editions in uncommon or foreign languages when an edition in the native language is also held by the library.

3. All but the most popular language.

4. Classical music when it is not in major European languages.

Specific classes of materials that particularly lend themselves to weeding.
Weed:

1. Books that should not have been bought in the first place.

2. History books with inaccurate or unfair interpretations.

3. History books poorly illustrated.

4. History books inefficient at getting their information across.

5. Grammars that are old.

6. Geography books not reflecting changes in areas or countries.

7. Fiction not in modern and well-presented editions.

8. Ordinary school dictionaries.

9. Almanacs and yearbooks that have been superseded.

10. Religion and philosophy texts when superseded; old theology; old commentaries on the Bible; sectarian literature; sermons; books on the conduct of life; popular self-help psychology.

11. Books that no longer relate to the academic curriculum or extracurricular enrichment.

12. Dated software.

13. In university collections:

    a) Inspirational literature, juvenile literature, elementary and secondary textbooks, noncontemporary minor authors, crank literature, biographies of obscure people.

    b) Personal war experiences.

    c) Student course outlines.

    d) Correspondence school material.

    e) Accession lists of general libraries.

    f) Press releases.

    g) Publications of colleges and universities, for example, newspapers, newsletters, press releases, humor magazines, or literature magazines edited by students; files of programs; noncurrent books of views or alumni publications.

    h) Programs of meetings.

    i) Speeches of officers of corporations published for purposes of advertising.

    j) Speeches of government officials.

    k) Dissertations.

    l) Subjects of little interest to a specific university because of its curriculum.

    m) Reprints.

    n) Mysteries.

Weeding based upon age alone. Frequently this advice is hedged by exception. Weed:

1. Books held 30 years.

2. Books over 20 years old.

3. Books not in a standard list and over 10 years old.

4. Fiction best sellers of ephemeral value after 10 years.

5. Out-of-date books and pamphlets.

6. Books over 5 years old.

7. Early volumes of serials.

8. Books in which the last copyright date is more than 8 years old.

Specific classes of works with specific age for weeding. Weed:

1. All ordinary textbooks after 10 years.

2. Books on medicine, inventions, radio, television, gardening, and business between 5 and 10 years old.

3. Travel books after 10 years.

4. Economics, science, and useful arts books in teachers' colleges when the books are more than 10 years old.

5. Fiction best sellers of ephemeral value after 10 years.

6. Senior encyclopedias from 5 to 10 years old.

7. Encyclopedias at least every 10 years.

8. Encyclopedias at least every 5 years, preferably every year.

9. Junior encyclopedias from 3 to 5 years.

10. Almanacs, yearbooks, and manuals—get the latest editions, and keep older editions at least 5, preferably 10 years.

11. Almanacs and yearbooks after 2 years, but keep older editions for at least 5 years.

12. Directories when a new one arrives, but retain old ones for 3 to 4 years.

13. Directories after 5 to 10 years, but get the latest edition.

14. Inexpensive geographic sources—5 to 10 years. Expensive ones—never.

15. Social science, topical material, after 10 or 15 years.

16. Geography books over 5 to 7 years old.

17. Books on occupations after 5 years.

18. Computer books after 5 years.

19. Materials on ecology, pollution, and conservation after 5 years.

20. Books on society and the role of families, men, and women after 10 years.

21. Materials on natural resources and industry after 5 years.

22. Science after 5 years, except natural history and botany after 10 years.

23. Medical, health, nutrition, drugs after 5 years.

24. Technology, applied science after 5 years.

25. Photography books after 5 years.

26. Novels after 1 to 5 years.

27. Civil service exam books after 5 years.

28. Annuals, keep current edition and last two previous editions.

29. Buying guides after 2 years.

30. Logic and math books after 10 years.

31. Bibliographies after 10 years.

32. Library science after 10 years.

33. Philosophy after 10 years.

34. Psychology after 3 to 5 years; texts after 5 years.

35. Religion after 10 years.

36. Sociology after 5 years.

37. Politics after 5 years.

38. Economics after 5 years.

39. Personal finance after 5 years.

40. Real estate after 2 years.

41. History of law after 5 years.

42. Uniform building codes, last two editions.

43. Education after 5 years.

44. Radio after 5 years.

45. Farming after 5 years.

Weeding criteria for periodicals and serials. Weed:

1. Periodicals not indexed.

2. Serials that have ceased publication and have no cumulative index.

3. Incomplete sets.

4. Early volumes of serials, especially longer runs of 50 or 60 volumes.

5. Journals in English petroleum libraries after 13 years.

6. In school libraries, keep periodicals 3 to 5 years; 1 year if not indexed.

Weeding criteria based upon use patterns. While this entire book relates to weeding criteria based upon previous use patterns, the suggested patterns are to be developed by carefully controlled statistical data. The use patterns below were developed, as were the other criteria in this chapter, by the judgment of experts. This is what accounts for the wide divergence of opinions. Weed:

1. Books not circulated in 3 years.

2. Books unused for 5 years that do not appear on a standard book list.

3. Books that have not circulated for 3 to 5 years, that have not been used for reference, and that are not standard titles.

4. Books 5 years old and not circulated in the last year.

5. Books that have not been read in years.

6. Books not called for in a university library in 20 years.

7. Books that have not circulated since 1950.

8. Books not enjoying a "density of use."

Divergent opinion. It must be emphasized that there is a body of divergent opinion in the area of use patterns. The fact that the volumes are not used in one, two, or five years is not proof that they are not needed. Also, the fact that a book has not circulated during the past few years should not be held to its discredit to an appreciable degree, since potential circulation value may still exist.

Keeping criteria. A word might be added about "keeping" criteria, which are the other side of the coin of weeding criteria. If we know what to keep, we save ourselves the trouble of having to consider that material for weeding. Here are some examples gleaned from the literature:

1. Keep if listed in one of the standard catalogs.

2. Keep if charged out within the past five years.

3. If a title has been frequently used during the past few years, it should probably be retained.

4. If it circulates, keep it.

5. New books.

6. Unabridged dictionaries.

7. City directories.

8. Biographical dictionaries.

9. Subject dictionaries, handbooks, and other reference works in the humanities.

Other Criteria Used for Weeding

The following are factors mentioned in the literature that might be considered when making weeding judgments:

1. Book reviews.

2. Special unique features in a book.

3. Permissibility—limitations imposed by taxing agencies, special grants, or donations.

4. Book available elsewhere.

5. Level of treatment.

6. MUSTY: *m*isleading, *u*gly, *s*uperseded, *t*rivial or no longer needed in *y*our collection.

Summary of Weeding Criteria

Several characteristics of the above criteria might be noted. In many cases, considerable work is needed to apply the criteria. The decision date may be impossible to reconstruct. For example, if the transaction card system is used, how does one tell when or how many times a volume has circulated? Or in another case, the checking of works against a standard catalog is a rather tedious job. In many cases, the judgments to be made are based on vague, difficult interpretations. What are an "older edition," "small print," "superfluous books on a subject," etc.? There are many contradictions among the criteria. There is, nevertheless, some rationale to much of what is proposed. Many of these criteria seem to satisfy the needs for weeding criteria and might relate closely to more objective criteria produced by careful study.

Notes

1. These figures represent an estimation by the author derived from information obtained from the Library of Congress.

2. Mary Jo Lynch, *Libraries in an Information Society: A Statistical Summary* (Chicago: American Library Association, 1987), 10.

Additional Reading

Boyarski, Jennie S., and Kate Hickey. *Collection Management in the Electronic Age: A Manual for Creating Community College Collection Development Policy Statements* (Chicago: American Library Association, 1994).

Brown, Chris. "Selection for Rejection," *School Librarian* 40, no. 4 (November 1992): 135-36.

Butt, Carolyn R., and Richard Spenner. "Weeding: A Job for the Strong at Heart," *Indiana Media Journal* 11 (Summer 1989): 30-32.

Clark, Lenore. *Guide to Review of Library Collections: Preservation, Storage, and Withdrawal* (Chicago: American Library Association, 1991).

Hennepin County Library, Material Selection Section, Collection and Special Services Division. *Collection Maintenance Manual* (April 1988): 12-40.

(Iowa) State Library Standards Committee. *In Service to Iowa: Public Library*, 2d ed. (Des Moines, IA: State Library Standards Committee, 1989).

Johnson, Douglas A. "Weeding a Neglected Collection," *School Library Journal* 36, no. 11 (November 1990): 48.

Roy, Loriene. "Weeding," *Encyclopedia of Library and Information Science*, Allen Kent, ed., vol. 54, sup. 17 (1994): 378-86.

Slote, Stanley J. *Weeding Library Collections: Library Weeding Methods*, 3d ed. (Littleton, CO: Libraries Unlimited, 1989).

Wallace, Danny P., et al. *Age Analysis of Public Library Collections: Final Report* (Baton Rouge: Louisiana State University, School of Library and Information Science, 1990).

5

Recommended
Weeding Objectives

Introduction

It seems evident that the objectives of weeding should help fulfill the basic objectives of the library. Libraries claim to have specific, clear-cut goals, but in practice they are likely to have vague, generalized objectives. These objectives, while rarely stated clearly or considered in day-to-day decision making, still seem to be in the minds of library administrators.

Depending upon the library, these objectives might include supporting school, college, or university curricula; supporting research efforts in university or special libraries; supplying recreational, informational, and educational services and materials in public libraries; supporting the aims of some larger institutions, as in the case of special libraries; or serving as centers or repositories of civilization's heritage, as with national and major regional libraries. In no case does weeding reduce the ability to fulfill these objectives. On the contrary, weeding seems to increase accessibility, improve efficiency, reduce costs, and in many other ways improve collections and services to the average user. Even though libraries have goals that vary considerably, they all might gain by using the same general weeding objectives, which could be varied quantitatively depending upon the needs of the clientele.

Goals Relating to Weeding

The goals relating to weeding discussed below should be considered by libraries:

The primary collection areas should consist of a core collection of books (and other materials) most likely to be used by the clients. ("Primary collection areas" refers to the open stacks, areas accessible to users, or the other library areas housing the readily available collections.)

The remainder of the books, those least likely to be used (the noncore collection), should to be located in secondary storage areas, moved to other libraries, or discarded, depending upon the major objectives of the library and the potential value of the noncore collection. ("Secondary storage areas" refers to compact storage, depository storage, or areas that are less accessible than the primary areas and that represent less expensive storage space.)

The core collection should retain _____ *percent of the likely future use of the present collection.* (The percentage is to be filled in individually for each library, depending upon its objectives and the possible unfavorable impact of lost usage upon the clients.) If conditions warrant, the core collection may be broken down into subcollections by types of material, location, department, service, or in any other convenient way. For example:

1. Reference is to retain _____ percent of its anticipated future use.

2. The fiction collection is to retain _____ percent.

3. Adult nonfiction is to retain _____ percent.

4. Art is to retain _____ percent.

5. The Dewey 900s are to retain _____ percent.

6. Microfilm is to retain _____ percent.

7. Periodicals are to retain _____ percent.

8. Branch libraries are to retain _____ percent.

Problems Relating to These Objectives

In order to implement the objectives mentioned above, two immediate problems must be solved. First, how are the percentages of anticipated future use of a collection to be determined? That question will be answered rather precisely in future chapters. At this point it should be assumed that these percentages *can be determined* both accurately and practically.

The second problem cannot be dealt with so easily. What percentage of the future usage of a collection should one hope to retain with the core collection? This question entails both personal judgment and practical considerations. Conservative judgments are called for. An arbitrary figure must be selected. A small public library does not risk much if it retains 95 percent of the anticipated future circulation of the present fiction collection, in fact, even 90 percent might be reasonable.

However, as the data develop, certain practical considerations may assist in making such decisions. Table 5.1 shows that 96 percent of the anticipated future use of the Briarcliff fiction can be retained with 56 percent of the present fiction collection. Ninety-nine percent of the future use can be retained with 84 percent of the present collection. If the library is pressed for space, and if the additional gain of shelf space is more important than the possible 3 percent loss in usage of this material, then perhaps 96 percent would be a reasonable retention figure. However, if weeding out 16 percent of the collection will solve the current space problem, perhaps it would be better judgment to retain 99 percent of the future use.

Table 5.1.
Shelf-Time Periods of the Circulation and Collection Samples Compared (Percent)
Source: Stanley J. Slote, "Five Libraries Study."

Cumulative Shelf-Time Period (Mos.)	Briarcliff Circulation	Briarcliff Collection	Tarrytown Circulation	Tarrytown Collection	Morristown Circulation	Morristown Collection	Trenton Circulation	Trenton Collection	Newark Circulation	Newark Collection
0	72	22	69	24	87	41	55	12	49	14
1	79	30	77	34	93	52	65	16	62	19
2	85	37	83	42	97	56	70	20	70	22
3	86	41	85	47	–	60	76	22	75	26
4	90	47	88	51	98	63	79	24	78	29
5	94	52	89	55	–	65	80	27	81	32
6	96	56	91	58	–	68	82	29	83	34
7	97	64	93	61	99	71	85	31	84	36
8	–	68	–	62	–	72	86	33	–	39
9	98	70	–	65	–	74	–	35	87	41
10	–	72	94	67	100	75	88	37	88	42
20	99	84	97	82	–	84	93	53	95	60
30	100	92	98	89	–	90	–	61	97	70
40	–	96	–	94	–	93	97	67	99	74
50	–	99	99	96	–	96	–	72	–	78
60	–	–	–	97	–	–	98	74	–	83
100	–	100	100	99	–	97	99	80	100	92
200	–	–	–	–	–	–	–	92	–	98
300	–	–	–	100	–	100	100	97	–	–
400	–	–	–	–	–	–	–	99	–	100
600	–	–	–	–	–	–	–	100	–	–

Subobjectives Relating to the
Mechanics of Measuring
Meaningful Shelf-Time Periods

In order to assist the entire weeding process, a series of subobjectives has been recommended. The additional objectives aim to build in practical safeguards against discarding needed materials, to create meaningful data, and to develop reports about weeding experience that would be useful to others. In this book, the basic criterion involved in making decisions for keeping or weeding is called "shelf-time period." This period estimates or measures the length of time a book remains on the shelf between successive uses. The author has found, as a result of his studies, that this criterion is the best predictor of use of a book.

The following objectives should be used selectively by individual libraries, depending upon their individual needs, wants, resources, and long- or short-term goals.

That records or controls be established, so that shelf-time periods can be identified. This may be done by any method that would indicate and record circulation and in-library use of library materials. It can be done mechanically by using and keeping intact the circulation records developed when using the book card method of circulation control; by the use of coded circulation-indicating dots on the back of the book card when using the transaction system for circulation; or by circulation date printouts from computer circulation systems. Most computer library operating systems store the needed data and require only minor reprogramming to become efficient weeding machines.

There are several other methods that may be used. The use of the transaction card system of circulation control, often with no easily available indication of an individual book's circulation activity, needs to be modified or augmented so that such information becomes available. Records for in-library use of both circulating and noncirculating materials must be kept if such materials are to be weeded using shelf-time period. This often requires new techniques, records, or procedures.

That procedures and techniques be established that would simplify the compilation of shelf-time period data for individual volumes or materials. For example, when book cards are filled up and there is no space to indicate a new date due, they are frequently removed and replaced with new cards. This destroys valuable data. Such old cards should be left in the book, or the last date of use should be transcribed from the old card onto the new card. A second example would be the application of a coded mark on the spine showing use. Then use data could be observed without removing a book from the shelves.

That shelf-reading be done on a regular basis so that all volumes in the entire collection will be in correct classified order. To the user, a misshelved book is equivalent to a lost book. If no use occurs because a book is improperly shelved (and thus not accessible to the user), such a title is likely to be weeded under the shelf-time period criterion. Whether this weakens the collection appreciably needs to be examined more closely.

That use data be recorded and preserved as carefully as is reasonably possible. This means that circulation desk personnel must be careful and accurate when charging books in and out. This objective has been included for two reasons. First, it is obvious that careless compilation of data will cause the weeding of volumes or materials that should not be weeded and the keeping of other materials that should have been weeded. Careless data control can destroy the validity of this whole procedure. Second, in a field study of circulation control made by the author, a check of the quality of the work being done uncovered hundreds of errors. Unless people realize the importance of careful work, and unless they are trained and supervised, the level of performance is likely to be poor.

That books from locked and inaccessible collections, which are to be weeded, be placed upon the open shelves or in primary storage areas before a decision is made on their removal from the collection. It was found, as might be expected, that such materials are not able to compete for user attention with the rest of the collection. If weeding is contemplated, the books should be tested in the marketplace of normal use. This author made an in-depth study of books located in restricted storage areas. It showed that usage was one-fourth of that experienced by similar titles located on open shelves. Perhaps the restricted books should be returned to open stacks since such restrictions reduce their value. The purpose of relocating books is defensive, to prevent the discarding of books that would have been identified as being part of the core if they had been stored differently.

The reshelving period should not be less than a shelf-time that would be represented by a circulation shelf-time period to include 95 percent of the future use, or whatever other percentage might have been predetermined for the keeping level.

That libraries establish written objectives yearly that relate to the purposes of weeding. Weeding can be done for many reasons, and the exact reasons become important in the decision-making processes involved in the weeding procedures. When the library's greater goals are clearly defined, levels of weeding or nonweeding become easier to determine.

That libraries should annually establish the exact level of future use to be retained by the present collection. This can be determined for the library as a whole or for individual parts of the collection (see page 211). The decision should be made in advance.

That the library's catalog be kept up-to-date, so that it more nearly reflects the library's holdings. Many libraries are still operating with card catalogs, which (along with shelf-lists and other records) must be weeded when the collection is weeded. Computer generated catalogs are easier to weed but should be updated regularly and carefully. Implicit in the need for up-dating the catalog is the necessity for periodic book inventories. Computer readable identification numbers should make this task easier.

That inventory be taken at least once a year and unintentional gaps in the collection be filled in. Since the suggested criterion for weeding is past due, the absence of books from the collection due to theft or loss will result in distorted shelf-time data for remaining works, and the core collection concept will be distorted. The distortion of data works in two ways.

First, a missing volume affects use of other works. If a user seeks information in a volume that is missing (the preferred work), he may look for the information in another book. That book, which ordinarily might not have had a recorded use, will now show a use at the expense of the preferred volume. Second, it is impossible to know if a lost book should be identified as part of the core collection. Therefore, it must be recognized that, since data can be collected only for books in the existing collection, it is necessary for the library to attempt to replace missing books meant to be in the collection.

If volume 2 of the *World Book Encyclopedia* were lost, it would be recognized that the entire set was an integral part of the collection and the missing volume would be replaced. Subjective judgment is called for in determining which books to replace in the collection in the absence of shelf-time data, but it is the same judgment used in the initial ordering of new books, which is a normal part of the book selection process.

That libraries keep records on characteristics of the collection or the library that directly affect the use of materials, thereby altering the composition of the core collection. It is apparent that while use is the best predictor of core collections, many things affect usage.

Use is affected by accessibility, location in the library, height of the shelves, seasonal variations, appearance of the volumes, form of the materials, special shelving, librarians' recommendations, special promotion, bibliographies, dust covers, loan periods, reserved collections, etc. As an objective, it is suggested that each library keep records for one year on some variable and quantify its effect upon usage. Such variables that affect usage, were they known, could help to maximize circulation, to change the composition of the core collection (perhaps by making it smaller), and to produce a knowledge base replacing the intuitive base now used by librarians for many decisions. For example, if books at eye-level are used more than books on top and bottom shelves, the core collections, if kept in their present locations, will still satisfy the predicted future use; however, the core collection and the library will not have maximized the usage of the total collection. One solution might be that no books should be stored on shelves where the location adversely affects book use.

A special set of problems besets university libraries. The impact of reserve collections, restricted collections, multiple library locations (departmental and undergraduate libraries, for instance), changes in curriculum, special assignments, and long-term loan periods to faculty all might affect the core collection concept. In Yale University the library collection can be found in at least 64 different places, and the University of Oxford, England, uses 72 separate locations for its volumes.

Special Objectives Relating to Computer Installations

We are living in the age of the computer, and the entire weeding process can be made easier, faster, and less expensive with the installation and proper utilization of computers and the relevant computer programming. The objectives discussed below may be long- or short-range depending upon whether a library is computerized or using some other kind of library control system. From the point of view of weeding, if the funds are available, a primary objective for libraries not currently computerized might be that mentioned below.

That the library convert to an automated system, and from a card catalog to a computer catalog. Because of the complexities involved in both the concept and mechanics of weeding, a computer controlled circulation system programmed for weeding would produce an almost ideal solution to the weeding problem. With the use of a computer catalog, the removal of records of missing or weeded volumes from the catalog becomes much easier.

For those libraries with computer installations already in place, consider the objectives discussed below:

That the system be programmed for the "Slote Method" of weeding. This involves having the computer perform all of the functions required, including recording and summarizing the shelf-time periods at the circulation stations, recording the date of the in-library use of each volume, recording and summarizing the shelf-time periods experienced by the books not currently in circulation, predetermining cut-points, and identifying weeding candidates.

That machine-readable identification numbers be installed on the spines of all volumes in the collection. Numbers on the spine of each volume that can be read by a computer are a great labor saving device. It means that books do not have to be removed from the shelves and opened in order to take inventory or to weed the collection.

That appropriately programmed portable computers be acquired that could be used in the stacks to read the book numbers. Such computers can be used to identify the books and book-use information, for inventory purposes, to reshelve books that are misshelved, and to indicate the weeding candidates. The advantage of portable computers is that the books do not have to be removed from the shelves to get their identification numbers into the computer system. When such a tool is not available the weeding process is slowed down appreciably. The larger the number of portable computers available, the more weeders or shelf-readers who can work simultaneously, and the quicker the process will be completed.

That shelf-reading be done by portable computer at least once per year. Because of the ease of computer assisted shelf-reading, the process becomes rapid and inexpensive. As a subobjective, *the portable computer should be programmed to identify any item on the shelf that is misshelved.*

That weeding be done whenever the computer reports that _____ percent (say 10 percent) of the collection could be weeded at this time. A program must be created to estimate the number of volumes likely to be weeded at any time. The computer will report when that number is large enough to make the weeding necessary.

That the computer be programmed so that the books weeded or missing will be automatically removed from the computer-produced catalog. If properly programmed, the computer can simplify the process of taking the inventory and amending the public catalog and shelf list to reflect the existing collection.

Summary

The purpose of these objectives is to clarify exactly what a library wishes to do about weeding and to make weeding easier and more valid. The objectives for weeding listed above should be chosen to coincide with each library's goals. The subobjectives offer a method for meaningful weeding.

6

Weeding Methods
Used in Libraries

Approaches to Weeding

A number of different general approaches to weeding have been given serious attention. Several of these are discussed below:

Subjective weeding. This method involves a series of rules, principles, or guides that require subjective judgment on the part of the weeder. This is the most common form of weeding found in libraries today.

Age. With this method of weeding, books are removed from the shelves according to the date of imprint, copyright, or acquisition. Such age data are often used to assist decision making when doing subjective weeding. Future usage patterns can be reliably predicted when age is used as a criterion (see page 38).

Curriculum-related weeding. This method, used by libraries in educational institutions or other places offering formal course work, involves a knowledge of what courses are no longer being offered and are unlikely to be offered in the future. It attempts to remove the volumes related directly to those courses.

Shelf-time period. The length of time a book remains unused on the shelf between circulations is called its shelf-time period. This method is often used intuitively together with subjective criteria.

Mathematical approaches. Several complex formulas or models have been suggested that, in fact, use information covered by the methods listed above. To date, these have been theoretical suggestions of questionable validity.

Combined criteria. The use of shelf-time period and imprint date, or any other combination of criteria, has been investigated and utilized in weeding. Such combinations have not been found to improve the quality of weeding.

Problems Encountered
Using These Approaches

Each of these approaches presents serious difficulties. Following is an attempt to outline the problems:

Subjective weeding. When using subjective criteria the weeder has selected criteria satisfactory to that individual but unsubstantiated by objective evidence. If two experienced weeders are given the same collection to weed, widely different collections of weedable volumes are likely to be identified. In addition, the procedure is a lengthy one. Since weeding is considered to be a professional task, it is left (in small libraries especially) to a professional who already has many other responsibilities. It is not uncommon that the weeding procedure may take two or three years in a public library. It is also not uncommon, under these circumstances, that a weeding program has been started and left unfinished when enthusiasm has flagged. The methodology in subjective weeding is to make up rules that *seem* rational and apply them in a way that *seems* reasonable.

Age. When using age as a criterion for weeding, several decisions must be made before weeding can start. It must be decided what date is to be used. The following are some of the dates that can be employed.

1. *Copyright date.* The date used can be the earliest, the most recent, or an average of these two dates. It can be a date reflecting a major reworking of a title, a revised edition, or a new edition.

2. *Imprint date.* Here again the date used may be the first or last imprint date of a volume. Sometimes no copyright of a work exists and the only date available is the imprint date.

3. *Purchase or acquisition date.* If the "newness" of a volume is to be judged by some date, the purchase date or acquisition date could give more accurate information than copyright or imprint dates for the collection in question. An even more reasonable date would be the date the book was shelved. It has been suggested that when using the book card system of circulation control, the original shelving date should be the first date entered on the card. Such dating would simplify subsequent data interpretation.

4. *Date originally written or published.* This date reflects the age of a work but not the age of a volume. If more newly created works are the ones that are used most, such a date may be significant. However, newer editions of classics tend to be used more than older, especially as typeface and size improves.

5. *Some other date.* A date that a volume is rebound, for example, might be of significance.

Once the desired date is selected, two serious questions remain. What date is to be used if a title is to have all of its volumes considered together? Where does one find the date desired, and is it a practical source? The problem of multiple volumes for one title is not serious if these are different editions and are treated as separate works. Generally, a new edition of a classic will be preferred to an older edition. Therefore, it is advisable to consider volumes independently rather than as a group.

However, if all similar titles are to be considered together, the decision of which date to use becomes a major problem, since a weeding decision might be hard to apply. There does not appear to be a satisfactory solution to this difficulty.

The difficulty in determining what date to use manifests itself in other ways. If titles are to be considered as a group, all of the copies of the same title held by the library must be uncovered. The card catalog or shelf list will be the authority but will not indicate that a cataloged volume has been stolen or otherwise removed from its normal place. In addition to reading the shelves, all date-due records will have to be checked. If the volume itself lacks dates, a bibliographic search to determine when it was written, printed, or published will be required.

Curriculum-related weeding. This type of weeding is a rational and rather simple approach. It is particularly valuable when duplicate copies of a book have been acquired to support a specific course. The major shortcoming is that, in this age of interdisciplinary studies, books that relate only to one specific course are becoming rarer. For this reason, weeding methods employing the shelf-time period measurements will remove irrelevant single-focus books. If books still have some remaining use, they will not become weeding candidates.

Shelf-time period. There are three major methods of developing shelf-time period (discussed in detail in part 2), and each of these has its problems both in the development of the criterion and in its application. What follows is a selective summary:

1. *Shelf-time periods developed from book cards.* The book card system of circulation control presents a number of problems. When book cards are lost or used up and discarded, information is lacking. When information is given only for circulating volumes, it is difficult and time-consuming to create comparable data for in-library use of books that are part of the circulating collection.

2. *Shelf-time periods developed by marking spines.* When using this method, confidence in the data is weakened by the difficulties of controlling the accuracy of the spine-marking. The physical markings can be removed, obscured, or overlooked. Careless or uninterested personnel at the circulation desk can fail to make the proper marks. The spine-marking system is valuable, however, in that books can be weeded without opening them up or inspecting them in any other way. The spine-marking system is applicable to in-library use where all volumes used within the library could be spine-marked and reshelved by library personnel.

3. *Computer methods.* Computer weeding is being undertaken today using printouts showing the number of circulations a volume has experienced and the date of the last circulation (see chapter 13). Computer assisted weeding will be improved when librarians and library computer programmers accept three things: the belief that shelf-time period is the best predictor of future use of a book; the advantages in using a computed cut-point, to preserve a predictable amount of future use; and the need to record the dates of in-library use of books and to use these dates in creating cut-off dates for weeding. Then when all books have computer readable identification numbers on the spine and computers are programmed as suggested, a handheld computer in the stacks could instantly

identify each weeding candidate, and weeding would become rapid, inexpensive, and valid.

Mathematical approaches. The mathematical approach involves quantifying certain variables and computing them in a specified formula or equation. The method is difficult to understand and to apply, and the data are difficult to uncover; complex mathematics is misused in this situation. Further, in the use of mathematical models, the accepted assumptions are quantified to give percentages, costs, or other specific units upon which to make decisions. From a practical point of view, these mathematical results tend to be far from reality, since, in general, a whole series of assumptions (themselves unproved and often untested) is quantified. The combining of a series of *assumptions* to give precise mathematical results is considered to be an invalid approach.

For example, certain formulas assume that, on the average, obsolescence increases with age. While this may be true, *on the average*, assuming a steady rate of obsolescence and using it in a decision-making formula compounds the error. Individual volumes differ from "average behavior." A formula produced in this manner will lend an unjustified confidence to decision making.

7

Core Collections
for Specific Types of Libraries

Introduction

The following are some ideas that might prove helpful in creating the core collection percentage figures for different kinds of libraries and different types of materials. What percentage of present use should one aim to keep? It must be emphasized that the higher the use-percentage kept, the smaller the amount of weeded material. Nevertheless, even at the level of keeping 100 percent of the future use of a collection, weeding will still be indicated.

It is not easy to establish "keeping" percentages. The basic difficulty is that all of these percentages are based in part upon subjective judgment and are likely to change with experience.

Small Public Libraries

Small public libraries are those libraries that are not meant to be permanent storage centers for the world's heritage. They frequently have limited reference collections and minimal reference services. Typically they are the hundreds of big city branch libraries and the libraries in many cities of under 20,000 population. Their services are basically threefold: they supply recreational and informational materials to their clients, they serve as a supplement to the public school educational program, and they supply a limited number of reference works. Their reference services tend toward ready reference and answering simpler rather than more complex questions. All of their services relate to the limitations imposed upon them by their budgets.

The core collection can be subdivided into rather broad areas without exposing society to great inconvenience. Limited experience in several such libraries indicates that weeding with five separate collection divisions is adequate. These consist of:

1. Fiction, including mysteries, short stories, science fiction, and westerns.

2. Nonfiction, all the Dewey classifications combined as one class. Biographies are also included here.

3. Reference materials, including periodicals, newspapers, pamphlets, photographs, and other miscellaneous materials.

4. Archives, anything in the permanent collection.

5.   Nonbook material, including videotapes, records, films, audiotapes, etc.

Each of these areas tends to have a shelf-time period differing significantly from the others, yet within each group a certain reasonable consistency exists.

One might start by trying to retain 95 percent of the present usage for fiction, 97 percent for nonfiction, and 99 percent for reference; archives would not be weeded at all, except as the objectives for this collection might change; nonbook material might be kept at the 95 percent level.

A small project was undertaken by the author to observe the effect of combining fiction and nonfiction into one collection for weeding purposes, even though the weeding was not actually performed. It was decided to keep 97 percent of the anticipated future circulation. The impact on the separate classes was not unexpected. In the library studied, over 99 percent of the fiction used and about 93 percent of the nonfiction used would have been retained.

Furthermore, nonfiction would have had to be weeded more extensively than fiction. This result was not as disturbing as might at first appear. Fiction is likely to have a much longer useful life and be more valid as it gets older. Nonfiction (textbooks, for example) tends to be full of errors a few years after publication. In an average small public library, there are hundreds of classics in fiction but only a handful of useful classics in nonfiction.

Another aspect of small library weeding is that such weeding is unlikely to do much harm. The sale, donation, relocation, or destruction of the weeded collection has few dangers. However, it is suggested that special regional libraries be given an opportunity to add these weeded volumes to their permanent collections. An occasional volume may fill a gap in a larger collection. It is also suggested that regional libraries make their collections more widely available to the average reader.

Major Public Library Research Collections

Much of what has been said about smaller public libraries also relates to those massive and outstanding research libraries that have developed in major urban areas. These include libraries such as the John Crear in Chicago, Enoch Pratt in Baltimore, the Newark Public Library, and many other large libraries located in the bigger cities. They are frequently trying to perform two distinct functions.

One function is to serve as the popular public library, satisfying a number of recreational, educational, and ready reference functions. In these areas, weeding may follow the general pattern of the small public library. In the "Five Libraries Study," it was found that an outstanding collection, such as that of Newark, had lower circulation figures in fiction than the smaller collection in the Morristown (New Jersey) Public Library, which contained one-quarter the number of fiction volumes. Insofar as it operates as a local circulator of popular materials, weeding can keep 95 to 99 percent of the anticipated future use without denying patrons what they want.

The second important function, that of a regional resource and reference center, calls for the use of higher keeping levels for the core collection or perhaps a different approach to weeding. For example, in a regional resource center it is likely that none of the books should be discarded unless they are either duplicates or are being replaced with the same or similar material. Furthermore, much of the material being weeded might well be retained in secondary storage areas. It is good practice to determine in advance the number of duplicates that are to be retained. Some libraries protect their collections by retaining two copies of a title.

Reference and information collections may have even greater limitations put upon them. Depending upon the level of the reference services the library is called upon to perform, no weeding should be done except for replacing certain works with newer editions or more definitive works. Even here, out-of-date editions often become important resources.

However, with massive research and reference collections it is frequently the case that one part of the collection is more accessible than other parts. Often a closed stack area exists. The weeding procedure may then identify reference works that are likely candidates to be removed from the open stacks and reestablished in the closed stack area. Certainly for important, large, heavily used reference collections, the core collection should satisfy at least 99.5 to 100 percent of the anticipated use.

Medium-Sized Public Libraries

Little information needs to be added for those libraries that fall between the above two groups. Many medium-sized centralized libraries are characterized by the dual role of the major library; often the branches are the popular circulation libraries and the downtown central branch is a resource and reference center. The degree to which these libraries are used should determine the characteristics of the core collections. As with major resource centers, the library might be more interested in replacing lost and stolen books than in weeding out current holdings. The usage, objectives, and client expectancy should help determine weeding levels.

Where public libraries of any size have divided subject responsibility for collections or have specialized collections of value, it is obvious that weeding must be considered in the light of the library's goals.

School Library Media Centers

It is the basic objective of the school library media center to support the curriculum of the school as well as perform related services for the staff, administrators, and parents. Media centers emphasize the intellectual and physical access to materials in all formats, print and nonprint. This involves specialized instruction in the use of the materials, familiarity with specialized equipment, the learning of research techniques, etc. The center is charged with synthesizing the newer approaches with the older. As courses and syllabi change, as new subjects appear and old disappear, as students' interests and awareness broaden, and as new technologies are developed and made available, great challenges are presented to media centers.

It has been observed that most students using the school library media center find it beneficial to augment such use with the public library. This fact means that school media centers can be weeded with greater confidence since they are sharing a part of the educational responsibility with another institution. In addition, they do not have any responsibility to preserve the national heritage, to be the definitive research resource center, or to be complete or comprehensive in any area.

In weeding the print materials, as far as the recreational collections are concerned, it is suggested that school libraries try to retain 90 percent of anticipated future use and buy heavily to build up greater usage, since what is newest is what tends to be most in demand. In the area of the reference collection, 95 percent is adequate, since supplemental collections are to be used anyway. Even the most perfunctory look at school libraries reinforces the opinion that deep weeding would improve collections. When dealing with the nonprint materials, weeding is just as important as with the print materials. While the growing variety of such materials— videotapes, films, filmstrips, slides, audiotapes, computer games, computer programs— complicates the weeding process, nonuse is just as valid a criterion for weeding these items as it is for print materials. It is suggested that the 96 percent level be applied for identifying weeding candidates.

One of the advantages of a school library media center is that one year's use patterns are generally adequate for prediction unless new courses have been added to the curriculum. Conversely, lack of use in one year is often the first indication to the librarian that a course has been dropped. The one-year natural cycle means that the weeding criteria can almost always be developed within one year without worrying about long-range cyclical influences. This is a characteristic not found in other types of libraries, with the possible exception of undergraduate college libraries.

Junior College Libraries

Everything said about the school library might be considered valid to some degree for the junior college library. Since some of these libraries are newer than university or school libraries, less weeding may be called for. In addition, weeding seems to present less risk than in other libraries for two reasons. In the first place, a large number of courses generate relatively little use of library material. This may be a result of the more practical nature of the terminal courses. These libraries have only a very small influence on a large segment of their students. Second, the yearly cycle helps to accelerate decision making and adds confidence in identifying materials not likely to be used again. Thus, a reasonable standard for core collections would be one that would satisfy between 90 and 95 percent of the anticipated future use.

College and University Libraries

The focus of most weeding research has been upon college and university libraries, since this is where many of the most serious problems exist. Many such libraries have had critical space shortages because they lack the financial resources necessary for expansion. Rapid growth of the major universities (and their libraries), financial pressures due to increased costs and decreased donations, an increase in the number of advanced degrees awarded, and recent cutbacks of government support have forced these libraries to seek relief.

For years university libraries have projected an image of collectors and preservers of knowledge. It is not true, however, that these libraries are solely repositories of the great national and human heritage. Collections of old textbooks, workbooks, out-of-date and useless non-fiction, low quality gift books, and books that have never been used, abound in most of these collections. Therefore, it is suggested that in nonresearch collections, such as fiction, textbooks, etc., weeding be done as it is elsewhere, keeping in the core collection those works likely to retain 95 percent of their future usage.

In the remainder of the collection, weeding can be applied at any reasonable level, because transfer from primary to secondary storage should be the basic form of disposition of noncore works. Where no other factors are involved, the 97 percent future use level is recommended.

One other kind of weeding of main collections is possible. When departments have independent or geographically decentralized collections, it is possible to remove a complete section of the main library to such separated libraries in the system. Of course, such action must be based upon clear-cut objectives relating to the ease of access desired and the resources of money, space, and personnel available. Duplication of collections in the main branch and its departmental libraries is expensive, but it improves access dramatically.

The overlapping nature of modern disciplines and the interdisciplinary character of many courses complicate the solution to easy access. Departmental libraries increase accessibility to some and reduce it to others, unless considerable duplication of materials exists.

Even in monolithic libraries, where no departmental libraries exist, materials are scattered rather widely. This occurs because of types of format (books, oversized books, pamphlets, microfilm, periodicals, audiovisual materials), age of material (different runs for older materials), new book displays, archival collections, condition or state of processing (new books, periodicals being bound, books partially cataloged, temporarily lost volumes, etc.), special needs (reserve collections, circulating and noncirculating collections, government documents), and divisions within one library. One can logically locate similar subjects in dozens of different places in a large library—a fact that reduces easy access. When duplication is used to facilitate access, the space problem worsens.

Since "easy accessibility" does not seem to be a major objective in many of the massive libraries, secondary storage may have little serious effect on the overall level of service. Use of secondary storage might well increase accessibility to the primary collection to such a degree that overall service is improved.

While generally a 97 percent core collection keeping level is called for, weeding in much greater depth is not completely out of the question. The weeding level for these libraries may be determined by other practical considerations. It may be that the number of volumes currently held in primary storage completely fills up the library, so that no additional space is available. Instead of predetermining the keeping level on the basis of usage, one can determine the number of volumes to be retained in the primary storage area stacks and accept whatever level of future use this will produce. The size of the core collection may also be decided by determining the most economic mix of primary and secondary storage, considering all the costs involved for book removal, library maintenance, cost of services, etc.

As large libraries grow, these more practical considerations can be taken into account and careful research should be undertaken to help in the decision-making processes.

Special Libraries

Librarianship in general has been hurt by attempting to group a large miscellaneous, dissimilar group of libraries into one class and calling them "special libraries." At best, there is a very tenuous similarity between the various types of special libraries. How do large legal libraries relate to small stock photography libraries? How do hospital, music, and newspaper libraries interrelate? Their materials, staff, size, objectives, and services frequently bear no visible relationships.

It is suggested that the various types of libraries might create their own concepts of core collections. Even within individual types, subtypes would be required. Clearly, then, each library must be considered in terms of its objectives—those relating both to its materials and services, and to the alternatives available. For example, some newspaper libraries not only clip and file their own newspaper but also index it. Obviously, older clippings can be weeded with much less exposure when an index exists.

Criteria can be developed. National news, well indexed and reported elsewhere, can be weeded in-depth without exposure. The general technique advocated here, that of anticipated use, can still be valuable and is perhaps the best approach to creating weeding criteria for special libraries. Most special libraries lend themselves to weeding in-depth, even though generalized keeping levels are hard to recommend for special libraries as a group.

As with archives, the objectives often prevent weeding of special materials on the basis of shelf-time period. One example was found by the author in a music publisher's library where all copyrighted songs, sheet music, records, original manuscripts, etc., were retained. This was the stock in trade of the main business, and legal or financial matters could arise from any music holding, no matter how long its shelf-time period.

Library Systems

Ideally, public library systems have the advantage that certain centralized services can make weeding in-depth less threatening to the integrity of the combined collections. Centralized or regional resource centers could be responsible for holding unique but little-used volumes.

Perhaps the best tool to encourage weeding is a union catalog. The easy accessibility of works at a neighbor's library reduces the need to hold many questionable volumes. When electronic union catalogs permit interlibrary loans with either conventional pickup and delivery services, or through computer networks, e-mail, fax machines and computer printouts, members of systems often take on some of the characteristics of branches, and they can weed at the 90 to 95 percent use level.

Summary

The purpose of this chapter is to give some guidelines for determining the acceptable level of use retained by core collections. It can be seen that librarians must use considerable judgment, experience, and professionalism in achieving this. Under the proposed methods, these judgments are limited to judgments of objectives, goals, and services to be given, rather than individual titles to be saved or weeded. At the worst, it gives us two groups of books: the core collection, from which *no* volumes will be weeded, and the noncore collection, from which *all* the weeded volumes will be selected.

Real judgment is also essential in disposing of the weeded volumes, in evaluating secondary storage, and in following up on the success of a weeding program. This total approach does not lower the professionalism of librarianship, but raises it. It replaces the primitive technique of selecting titles or volumes for weeding with a quantified criterion, created through objective observation.

8

Analysis and Review
of the Literature of Weeding

Purposes for a
Study of the Literature

There has been a massive quantity of material published on the subject of library weeding. Almost 1,500 use studies can be identified, if one adds the more current works to Jain's list of 631 works.[1] Within this mass are selected reports that add substance to the specific approaches used in this book. These selected reports represent the background for the present work, which has attempted to take another step forward.

The purpose or motivation behind the production of a book or article often becomes rather clear upon reading it. Its purpose affects its tone and content. There are many reasons for studying or adding to the literature of a subject:

To compare what one is doing with what is being done elsewhere in the field.

To look for hard facts—real evidence that would cause one to reinforce or discard certain accepted techniques.

To uncover limitations of the knowledge in a field in order to undertake research, starting from the present knowledge base.

To examine the suggestions of thinkers in the field, in order to give direction to further thought and study.

To read of the experience of others as a guide to identifying pitfalls to be avoided.

To find out specifically how to perform certain operations.

To keep current with the literature.

To create new knowledge in the field.

Criticism of Library Literature

Two characteristics of the literature in librarianship (and weeding in particular) are that there is little cumulation of knowledge, and that there is no consistency in the objectives of the overall literature in the field. Current articles frequently show no knowledge of the history and past thought of the subject. It is a serious criticism of the literature of librarianship, including the more than 700 periodicals in the field, that articles currently appearing could have been written 15 to 75 years ago. Editors accept such articles without limitation or discrimination.

What is needed is not only the publication of the first stirrings of new knowledge, hard facts, tendencies and information gained from experiment, and careful observation, but also a willingness on the part of readers to accept what is known.[2] It has been known for at least 20 years that shelf-time period is the best criterion for identifying core collections. Yet, many articles and books published in the past 20 years do not accept this finding, which apparently has been one of the best-kept secrets in librarianship.

The most serious criticism of the literature of librarianship concerning weeding, core collections, and shelf-time period is that the literature has had little impact on the practitioners, teachers, and leaders in the field. It is possible that the very mass of publications has blocked the view of what is significant.

What is *needed* are facts, data, or ideas that will stimulate serious students or practitioners to better their performance and enlarge their knowledge in the field. The following section makes an attempt to classify some of the literature. What has been said about the literature of weeding might well be repeated for almost any topic in librarianship.

Characteristics of the Literature

In much of the literature of weeding and library usage, there is a similarity in the type of works published year after year. In general, these types of works can be characterized in the following discussion.

Repetitive. Repetition can be one of three kinds—either the actual reprint of an article that has been published before; summaries or analysis of previous works; or a fresh presentation of what has been said before, with little credit given to the originator. While a certain amount of repetition might be helpful for the learning process, librarians have been bombarded with repetitions of the same old, and perhaps invalid, ideas for 100 years.

"How-to" literature. How-to articles are generally authoritative but give little evidence, few facts, and no sources. A better way to do something is claimed, even though it is frequently a method that has been alternately recommended or rejected throughout the decades. The ultimate authority is personal judgment, often not even supported by a simple literature search or by the most basic attempts to compare two different techniques. One interesting characteristic of this kind of work is the conflict and disagreement that it creates among the authorities.

Scholarly historical summary. Such work is generally a carefully documented study of the past literature of the subject, usually selective, in order to emphasize the development of the field and the best practices. This kind of article has form, meaning, and usually a good point. It is a short-cut for a new student in the field, and might be considered a guide to the best literature of a subject.

Broad philosophy. This is an attempt to synthesize past knowledge and to reinforce newer valid concepts. It always has some strong base for the concepts contained, often the most recent research reports or new technologies (computers and advanced math, for example). This approach tends to make its points in an organized way, as contrasted to the authoritative approaches.

Controlled study. A controlled study is a carefully planned, scholarly attempt to uncover new knowledge. It is a scientific, experimental approach with enough of the data, background, methodology, and techniques reported so that the experiment can be replicated. It uses the "scientific method," with an attempt to observe one variable at a time. The conclusions follow directly from the data, and the range of their reliability is clearly defined. Where variables are not being manipulated by the researcher, an attempt is made to be unobtrusive and avoid having the observation affect the results. Usually the claims made for the findings are modest.

Problems in the Application of the Literature

The literature of weeding is characterized by a number of other general problems:

1. There is a great variety in the quality, style, and value of the articles. This mix, even within the confines of one publication, must make one wary about the quality of the editing of even the best of the scholarly journals.

2. In general, there has been a lack of cumulative study in the field. Strangely, there is a certain amount of repetition and replication of each of the new techniques that have been reported, as if no one ever starts where the last researcher left off. Nor have the researchers themselves seemed to develop knowledge banks of increased information.

3. Access to the literature through bibliographies and indexes is difficult, inefficient, and incomplete.

4. Very few reports are complete. Fragmentation is common. Articles omitting data, techniques, background, or meanings are the norm. The reader is unable to tell whether what has been omitted was invalid, was left undone, or was omitted through carelessness.

5. There is much opinion and little hard knowledge in the literature. Many periodicals avoid articles with data, research, statistics, and methodology as being "too academic."

Summary of the
Literature of Weeding

Criteria used. In general, the studies that follow have used two principal weeding criteria: 1) the age of a volume, and 2) the length of time a volume remains in the library between successive uses or the number of uses in a given period of time (shelf-time period). Various dates have been used to represent the age of a volume: the publication date, the year of accession, and the copyright date. In addition, the language of the publication and its country of origin have been used as variables. These variables have also been used in combinations. However, shelf-time period has the most serious support, with respect to both the number of supporters and the validity of the research evidence.

Methods of recreating use patterns. There has been some discussion in the literature concerning how to uncover the past patterns of book use in a library. Most of the studies relied upon book cards for their information; several reconstructed the information needed during the study, with no reference to past records; often, a combination of these methods was used. Two major approaches have been suggested for reconstructing circulation patterns as described by shelf-time periods.

1. The "historical reconstruction" approach is an attempt to record, in terms of the chosen variable, the entire use pattern of a volume since its acquisition in a library. When this method has been used, however, most researchers have limited their study to the last several years of use. The weakness of this method is that much of the important data may be missing. Cards from well-used books are often filled up and discarded, books are lost or stolen along with their book cards, charging systems are changed, and cards are replaced. In general, the information available might be very unreliable.

2. The "current circulation" method looks at a very recent period of circulation (usually the most recent few days or weeks) and assumes that the present pattern of use at circulation is a valid sample of the total use pattern. Several such samples of circulation may be taken over a period of time and compared for consistency. The weaknesses here are that seasonal patterns might not show up and that there are other factors that might make a short-term sample unrepresentative of the whole pattern. School assignments can change, different days of the week may have different use patterns, and the relative use (the percentage of the whole class represented by the sample) is disregarded. However, as techniques are developed to overcome these weaknesses, the "current circulation" method has increasingly become the preferred method of recent researchers.

Aims of the studies. The scope of the studies was often restricted by the aim of the work, especially in the area of validating findings relating to weeding. Attempts were often made to find weeding criteria useful in identifying core collections.

However, studies were also made in order to justify automated circulation methods, to compute and compare the cost of various kinds of primary and secondary storage, to evaluate collections, to test mathematical formulas, and to limit the growth of active collections stored in the primary collection area. Therefore, the studies vary tremendously in their emphasis or lack of emphasis on weeding and its usefulness.

Findings of the studies. There has been a wide range of findings, and certain conflicting results have been reported as follows:

1. In general, shelf-time period was found to be the most acceptable variable for identifying core collections. The methodologies and assumptions were often validated with strong evidence for the superiority of the shelf-time period variable in predicting future use. Most studies agreed that this is the most valuable variable revealed.

2. The age of the volume was found to be somewhat predictive of future use, but generally of little practical value. Basically, the rejection of a small number of older volumes—the classics, which circulate with patterns similar to those of newer books—causes the age of volumes to be an inferior predictor of future use.

3. Several explanations were found as to why shelf-time period produced a smaller core collection than the age of a volume.

4. Techniques for uncovering the information needed to produce weeding criteria have been simplified and improved.

5. Objective weeding was frequently recommended as a replacement for the subjective weeding most commonly used. Wherever controlled testing has been undertaken, the objective criteria have proven to be as valid as, or more valid than, subjective weeding.

6. Few examples could be found where weeding was based solely on objective criteria, in most cases some subjective criteria were added, often as an afterthought. Apparently it was emotionally difficult to weed using only objective criteria.

7. The problems of the growth of collections and the need for weeding were highlighted in almost every study. Weeding always appeared to be the solution, yet few reported that it had solved long-term shelf space needs. Nor have any libraries reported a consistent long-term weeding effort.

The Literature Reviewed

The following reports have been divided into two groups—those based on judgment, which, in retrospect, proved to be valid judgment; and those based on research. The first group of studies has identified the problems that encourage weeding and has recommended approaches that have been later validated.

Studies Identifying the Problems

Charles W. Eliot. Charles William Eliot, then president of Harvard, in discussing the rapid growth of libraries, stated in 1902:

> Under these conditions the great need of means of discriminating between books which may fairly be said to be in use and books which may fairly be said to be not in use has been forced on me, . . . I admit at once that the means of just discrimination between books in use and books not in use are not easy to discern or to apply.[3]

He hinted at the idea of using objective weeding criteria: ". . . it might naturally be suspected that a book which had not been called for in a university library for twenty years possessed but a faint vitality."[4]

Samuel Ranck. Samuel Ranck, in a use study at the Grand Rapids Public Library, found that 20 percent of the books had not circulated at all during the previous two years and 10 percent had not circulated in the previous five years.[5] His findings are strikingly similar to those of more recent studies elsewhere (see table 8.1).

Lee Ash. Ash's report is a summary of extensive and detailed studies made at Yale during a three-year period[6] to establish practical guidelines for "the selective retirement program." The studies combined objective weeding criteria with judgment and library expertise, and concluded: "If a book has been charged out on an average of once a year or more for the past five years, it should be considered 'heavily used' material and should not be transferred."[7]

This criterion of *repetitive* use to identify core collections is not commonplace in the literature of weeding. Most of the studies have shown that a use once in five years (rather than once a year for five years) is a valid signal not to weed.

The report stresses one of the most troublesome problems faced by weeders— the need to overcome the emotional response to what should be an objective procedure.

In considering the impact of storage on the overall use of the collection, Ash reported that in two years only $3\frac{1}{3}$ percent of the library usage came from the stored collection. Yale has a "Compact Storage Plan," and Ash included detailed cost data on its advantages.

For the more conventional weeders, Ash offered strong support:

> In the actual process of selection for a book retirement program, we have found very little that can be reduced to a formula or routine. . . . The execution of selective book retirement becomes increasingly a matter of knowledge, judgment and wisdom. . . . [Weeding] cannot be determined solely on the basis of use.[8]

Table 8.1.
Comparison of Data: Ranck 1911 vs. Slote 1969 Collection Characteristics
Source: Stanley J. Slote, "Five Libraries Study."

	Ranck	Briarcliff	Tarrytown	Morristown	Trenton	Newark
% of *fiction* not circulating in last two years	15.1	12.1	15.0	12.6	44.2	37.1

% Previously Charged Out

Fiction Only

Shelf-Time Period	Total Collection	Briarcliff	Tarrytown	Morristown	Trenton	Newark
24 months	79.2*	87.9	85.0	87.4	55.8	62.9
60 months	90.4	99.7	96.8	96.5	73.5	82.7
120 months	95.8	100.0	98.9	97.7	82.8	92.9
204 months	98.6	-	99.8	100.0	92.2	98.0
300 months	99.0	-	100.0	-	97.2	99.8
312 months and over	100.0	-	-	-	100.0	100.0

*Figure for fiction was 84.9%.

Elizabeth Mueller. Mueller found that the age of a volume was a poor predictor of future use and that certain older titles had circulation characteristics very similar to those of the new titles.[9]

Mueller also reported on fiction circulation rates of 4.4 to 7.3 circulations per volume per year, comparable to 2.8 to 6.2 volumes in this author's "Five Libraries Study."

M. K. Buckland. Buckland attempted to create computer-compatible mathematical codes to determine "for how long should the documents, so painstakingly added to stock, be retained?"[10]

One of the assumptions of his formula—that the cost of discarding material is "trivial"—is a subject that needs considerably more study, as it has rarely been tested in a careful manner. "[In] practice this might not be true, and the situation could arise where it is cheaper *not* to discard even if a document is totally unused."[11] Then, turning to the subject of core collections, Buckland reported what is a rather well-known characteristic of libraries—that "20 percent of the . . . stock generates 80 percent of borrowing."[12]

In this report, Buckland recognized the weakness of subjective weeding: "It has been established that records of past use are the simplest and best available predictors of future use (considerably better than the unaided subjective judgment of either teachers or librarians)."[13]

Philip Morse. In his book, Morse evaluated and reported on some of the findings of various studies made at M.I.T.[14] The whole thesis of Morse's approach to weeding is the predictability of future usage. Morse wanted to discover the "pattern" of book use; but since the data necessary for such information is expensive to obtain, it had not been done. He noted that computer use would make it easier to gather such data.[15]

Morse argued that with a weeding system based on sufficiently reliable predictability, "the fraction of disadvantaged borrowers might be small enough to be endurable."[16]

Morse pointed out that it would be advantageous to discover what data are needed for decision making in weeding. He reported on a study of book retirement based upon the criteria of age and noncirculation. By noncirculation, he meant volumes with relatively long shelf-time periods. Using age as a criterion caused 5,200 inconveniences, while using noncirculation as a criterion caused only 3,600 inconveniences.[17]

Stanley J. Slote. This author has conducted a use study involving nonbook material.[18] In most newspapers, metal "cuts" were used to produce the photographs that appear in print. These cuts were filed for reuse in case a person or event became newsworthy again. A systematic sample was taken from the entire collection. The conclusion was that no cut should be reused after the eighth year from its first use, provided that it had not been reused before. This meant that a shelf-time period of eight years would describe a core collection including all the cuts likely to be used in the future, provided that these cuts had been previously used only once.

It was also found that no cut had been used after its fourteenth year in the file, even if reused in the interim period. Ninety-two percent of the cuts had never been reused, an indication that better keeping criteria and procedures might have been called for. Thus, the age of the cut and the time between uses (shelf-time period) were combined to create the weeding criteria. Employing these criteria, 85 percent of the collection was weeded out.

This basic study alerted the author to the value of determining the "time between uses" (later called "shelf-time period"), which became the backbone of further research. This study was an example of the practical use of objective data for weeding.[19]

Elmer Grieder. Grieder was one of the first to point out the value of being able to *predict* the impact of secondary storage on service to the client.[20] He sought to find out how many volumes might be stored without "serious detriment to service." He made some statistical counts similar to those suggested in this volume, first recording the "date of last circulation" of books at the circulation desk. He tabulated these data from the charge slips representing volumes in circulation, then sampled the books on the shelves for the same variable.[21] This information was then tabulated, as shown in table 8.2.

Table 8.2.
Grieder Study*, 1949

Date of Last Circulation	Cumulative Shelf-Time Period	
	Collection	Circulation
1949	22%	63%
1948	32	79
1947	39	85
1946	44	87
1945	47	88
1940-1944	61	93
1935-1939	71	96
1930-1934	78	98
1925-1929	83	99
1920-1924	88	
1915-1919	92	
1910-1914	95	
1905-1909	98	
1900-1904	99	
Before 1899	100	100

*Figures revised and simplified.

Grieder's conclusion was that 39.2 percent of the books had not circulated in the previous 15 years and thus 76,656 volumes could have been stored in secondary areas "with no serious disruption of service." He stated that he could predict the amount of future use of volumes to be stored.

To validate this belief, Grieder made a two-week study of the books circulating, to determine the date of last circulation. He reported that if these 15-year noncirculators had been stored, only 4.01 percent of the circulating volumes would have had to come from storage. If the 56,375 volumes that had not circulated in 20 years had been stored, only 2 percent would have had to come from storage. This study is important in that it anticipated the conclusions made by later studies and uncovered the best techniques for the prediction of future demand.

Marianne Cooper. Cooper reported on the application of Trueswell's approach (see page 61) to the collection at the Chemistry Library at Columbia University in 1965.

The purpose of the study was to find a way to reduce the number of volumes on the accessible shelves in the library. The methodology was to observe 135 charge-out cards, and to tabulate the use patterns. The data presented were as follows:

> 99 percent had been borrowed at least once in the past eight years.
> 97 percent had been borrowed at least once in the past five years.
> 95 percent had been borrowed at least once in the past three years.
> 71 percent had been borrowed at least once in the past year.[22]

It was decided to keep in the active collection those volumes borrowed at least once in the last five years and to transfer or store the rest. The faculty rechecked weeded volumes and returned to the active collection a number of the volumes selected. Thus, shelf-time period was not the sole criterion used for weeding, such criteria as reference value were also considered. This refusal to accept completely the objective criterion for weeding is not unusual.

Research Studies

The following reports are all serious research efforts that relate directly to weeding criteria and that deal with the variables of age of the volume, shelf-time period, or both. Purposes, methodology, data, and findings are reported in detail. In most cases, they are doctoral dissertations, funded research projects, or shorter reports on such projects. They are considered to be most significant.

Winston Lister. Lister's dissertation focuses on uncovering the real costs involved in compact storage. Accepting the findings that the two best predictors of future usage are the age of the materials and the book usage rate, he studied the economic impact that results when these two criteria are used to select books for compact storage.

Lister concluded that such storing is of value to the patrons, because they are then "able to locate the bulk of their desired materials more easily and more quickly."[23] He also considered ways of determining the optimal number of books that should be separated into storage.[24]

The Lister study, at three Purdue University branch libraries, consisted of taking a 20 percent sample of the titles from the shelf list and tabulating use and age data by computer. Judgments were made concerning the costs of the various aspects of use and storage. These included building and equipment costs, maintenance and operating costs, circulation costs, and relocation costs. Formulas were developed to measure the total cost of using both criteria for decision making. Since cost was the principal focus, weeding criteria were relegated to a rather junior position in this study.

The following conclusions are important:

> The author sincerely believes that selection of an item for storage should be based entirely upon its current (or immediate past) rate of usage. . . . As has been repeatedly pointed out in the literature, other measures of usage are not nearly so reliable as past history. In this research the age criterion, which is apparently the next best predictor of usage, was found to be far inferior to the usage rate criterion for scientific monographs. . . . There is evidence which illustrates extreme variability in the current usage rates of books of a common age, demonstrating the infeasibility of a single age-related obsolescence function.[25]

In addition, Lister affirmed two other points: "It is possible to establish simple decision rules regarding the selection of library material for storage."[26] Intellectual weeding policies, which require judgment and are based upon somewhat intangible variables, usually turn out to be time consuming, expensive, and qualitative attempts to predict future usage.[27]

Concluding that some mechanical techniques could be very helpful, Lister maintained that computerized circulation systems would make the whole weeding process much easier, from the point of view of both selecting the volumes to be removed and altering the catalogs to reflect such moves. As an alternative, he suggested that "it might become advantageous to mark, in some way, the outside covers of the books to provide usage rate indicators."[28]

Edward A. Silver. Silver's approach was to investigate the effects of various decision criteria on the weeding of library collections.[29] His objective was to find a cut-off point (a specific last date on a book card) that would enable the librarian to keep the number of books on the shelves at the same level, whenever it is applied. For example, if he wanted to keep 5,000 volumes on the shelves, he would find the cut-off point that would give him this result.

Approximately 100 samples were chosen from eight different subject areas in the science library at M.I.T. The related variable was the "shelf-time since last circulation."

Among the conclusions were:

1. that the exclusive weeding policy should be based upon shelf-time since last use;

2. "that a criterion of this nature eliminates the need of technical aid in the weeding operation";[30]

3. that there are substantial variations among the different subject groups, in relationship to the selected variable;

4. that there is also a substantial variation from the mean within each group; and

5. that books that never circulate or that contain no circulation data are a serious problem to the researcher in use studies of this kind.

Silver concluded that a weeding policy ought to be based upon the need for shelf space.

Aridaman K. Jain. Jain has produced two works that relate to book usage. The first is based upon pilot studies and the second, a much more complete study, follows the leads uncovered in the pilot.[31] In his pilot study, an interesting question was asked: what data can a librarian use to reconstruct usage patterns when historical records are not available? Jain was trying to identify criteria useful in selecting books for storage.

His methodology was to take a systematic sample of parts of the collection, using the shelf list for selecting the sample. All the titles in current use during a five-week period, both at home and in the library, were recorded. An attempt was made to use the following as variables: language, country of publication, year of publication, and the year of accession. The method of evaluating the data was called "relative usage." It relates the number of titles being used in any category to the total number of volumes in the collection in the same category.

No firm conclusions were reported, except that the findings could be used to make decisions for storing books. This exploratory study was an attempt to test a proposed methodology and a special approach.

In his more complete work, Jain studied criteria that might be useful in determining titles to be stored in secondary locations.

He emphasized the importance of use studies and listed 631 works relating to book usage, discussing the more thorough and outstanding works.[32] His approach consisted of reviewing the previous work done, stating the weaknesses of these studies, and, through mathematical computation, developing a study without the same weaknesses. He covered 61 pages with mathematical proofs and argued for the "relative usage" approach found in his first study. Based upon this new approach, he concluded:

> In spite of the recent tendencies to overemphasize usage histories, this study shows that age is a significant variable in studying usage of monographs. As pointed out in this study, there are several problems associated with the usage histories of monographs and it is hard to say how much reliance can be placed on the usage histories under the current methods of record keeping. Also, while usage rates of individual monographs have considerable variation even over a short period of time, the usage rates of various age groups do not show any significant differences over time.[33]

The phrase "overemphasize usage histories" was found in Jain's conclusions with no evidence found in his report that usage history was, in fact, studied by him and found wanting. This is the only study of significance that preferred to use age rather than usage as the criterion for weeding decisions.

Herman H. Fussler and Julian L. Simon. Perhaps the most thorough research done in the area of use patterns has been by Fussler and Simon.[34] In order to select books for compact storage, this study endeavored to find a characteristic or variable that would predict which books were most likely and which least likely to be used.

The basic technique of the Fussler and Simon study was a modification (cross-sectional approach) of the historical approach to the past use of individual books.[35] The data came from the entire collection, as compared to the "current circulation method," in which the data came from the circulation desk only. The historical method ideally consists of recording the complete history of the past uses of the volumes, and ranking all of the volumes in accordance with the number of such uses per year. Since not all data were available, the authors modified this and used the "cross-sectional approach," recording all uses during previously determined periods of time, 5 years and 20 years. They assumed that future usage would continue at the same rate as in the past (though slightly reduced). They then related this use-ranking to the variables to be considered, such as age of the volume or date of last use. How "good" the function was, was judged in relationship to a book storage program. The "best function" is the one that identifies the fewest books in a core collection, which would maintain a predetermined level of use. In other words, the "best function" permits the storing of the most books at a given use level.

The major findings that related to shelf-time period or to the age of a volume are as follows:

> Employing *years since last use* as the only variable, gives strikingly good results. . . . Characteristics such as the age of a book and its language are less satisfactory in predicting future use than in past use. It is doubtful that any other variable will suddenly appear on the research scene and greatly increase predictive accuracy. . . . *Past use, where sufficient data are available, was found to be the best single predictor of the future use of a book. . . .*[36]

Using the historical method, Fussler and Simon did get better results when a longer use history was projected. They implied that differences in libraries necessitate individual study for each collection,[37] and they attempted to combine variables to see if a better criterion would result: "Even if we consider the best of the rules that do not employ past use . . . the results are not very satisfactory."[38]

Fussler and Simon also approached the question of whether there are better ways to select books for storage. They compared their criteria with the results obtained from the consensus of a group of scholars in a subject field. Without rejecting the validity of scholars' judgments, they concluded:

> The various parts of the investigation convince us that with our rules we may predict the future use of books at least as well as any other method known to us. The objective system seems to agree with the consensus of a group of scholars.[39]

In one sense, Fussler and Simon's entire study was a validation. A prediction was made based on the use patterns prior to 1954, and the period of 1954 to 1958 was then checked to validate the prediction.

Richard William Trueswell. Trueswell has published five works that are significant. In his dissertation, he approached the weeding problem from the point of view of its applicability to data processing and computer techniques.[40] The study consisted basically of a number of questionnaires used to determine the "behavioral patterns and requirements of users of a large university library system."[41] As a reinforcing effort, "samples of current circulation were made to determine circulation rates, charge date distributions, and book age distributions."[42] It was this offshoot of the main research that is of most interest.

The basic purpose of this part of the study was to identify a core collection. It was an assumption of Trueswell, gathered from the literature, that "only a very small portion of the library's holdings are in circulation very frequently."[43] He described this subset of volumes as the "core" and defined "core collection" as a percentage of the collection that should satisfy a given level of the user circulation requirements.[44]

He examined the books currently circulating in two libraries in terms of book age and of the previous time that the book had been in circulation.[45] Concerning the present circulation, he maintained that it is reasonable to assume that the "frequency distribution of the circulation is representative of future circulation."[46]

His methodology attempted also to create core collections at a level that would satisfy 99 percent of circulation need. His major findings were that "approximately one-fourth of the current holdings in the Technical Institute Library should satisfy over 99 percent of the requirements for circulation," and that at Deering: "20 percent of the present holding could be expected to satisfy over 99 percent of the circulation requirements."[47]

In addition:

> The core collection concept can be extended further for use as a
> tool to thin out the current holdings of the library. Analysis of
> circulation patterns reveals that over 99% of the current circulation
> activity is from a population of books each of which has been
> loaned at least once during the past 18 years for the Deering Library
> and the past 8 years for the Tech Library.[48]

In his second work, Trueswell dealt with a strategy for weeding employing
user needs as a criterion.[49] Again he used "last circulation date" as a circulation
predictor. He began by stating that he did not advocate "the arbitrary thinning and
discarding of books from a library" and that the decision to do so is a policy decision
that must be made by the administration of the library. Nevertheless, a major problem
of libraries is how to cope with the increasing size of their holdings. Because
periodicals are not very likely targets for thinning, the focus was on monographs.

Trueswell concluded that age of a volume was not a useful determination factor
for thinning, but urged, "Remove all books that have not circulated during the
previous eight year period."[50]

In Trueswell's next significant contribution, he combined most of the information and opinion found in his two previous works, using the article to restate and
reaffirm his findings.[51]

In another article by Trueswell, he studied two libraries not previously reported
upon. These were the Mount Holyoke College Library and the Goodell Library,
University of Massachusetts. The data from these libraries were compared with the
Deering Library data. His conclusions were that "the experience of these three
libraries proved to be surprisingly similar."[52] He also had suggested that this
technique should have application in "circulation-oriented public libraries."[53]

His approach toward identifying a core collection might have some practical
use for libraries without adequate circulation records.

> We, therefore, go back x years and starting at that point in time, we
> adopt in our model the procedure of placing a red X on the cover
> of each book borrowed. As time progresses, more and more of the
> books borrowed will have a red X on the cover. After several years,
> we will reach a point where ninety-nine percent of the books
> brought to the desk for circulation will already have red X's.[54]

At this point, the core collection would consist of all having the red X.

Trueswell recommended the employment of "the last circulation date" as a
statistic to help describe library user circulation requirements.[55] This would determine what to hold and what to weed and could help decide which titles should be
acquired in multiple copies. While no clear-cut decision rule was given, it was
suggested that volumes having the most recent circulation dates be considered first
when ordering duplicate copies.

Stanley J. Slote. This author conducted three serious research studies: the "Five Libraries Study" in 1969; the Harrison Public Library Study in 1973;[56] and the Larchmont Public Library Study in 1980.[57] The "Five Libraries Study" dealt only with adult fiction collections. The Harrison Study involved weeding the adult fiction and biography collections and gathering data on the entire library collection. The Larchmont Study included the entire adult collection.

The three objectives of the "Five Libraries Study" were:

1. To determine if certain variables could be used to create meaningful weeding criteria. In each of five public libraries, two such variables were studied in-depth and evaluated. These variables were the "shelf-time period," the time a book remains on the shelf between successive uses, and the age of a book as indicated by the most recent date printed on the title page or its verso, called "imprint age."

2. To compare the two criteria to determine which was a "better" criterion, that is, which would yield a smaller core collection that would satisfy a given level of predicted future use.

3. To determine if the pattern of use of the volumes currently in circulation (books actually out of the library at the time of the study) was as valid a predictor of future use as are historical reconstructions of usage over much longer periods of time.

The basic findings of this study were:

1. Past use patterns, as described by shelf-time period, are highly predictive of the future use, and can be used to create meaningful weeding criteria.[58]

2. The imprint age is a weaker predictor of future use than shelf-time period.

3. The shelf-time period is a predictor of a "better" core collection than the most recent imprint date because it describes a smaller core collection for the same level of predicted future use. From a practical point of view, the difference was so significant that the imprint date should not be considered as a useful weeding criterion.[59]

4. That each library tends to have its own unique patterns of circulation, and each needs to be studied individually.[60] No method was found to apply the information developed in one library as a weeding criterion for another library.

5. That the "current circulation" method creates shelf-time period patterns that are as valid for predicting future use as is the method of historical reconstruction.[61]

6. That shelf-time period patterns predict future use patterns.[62] A return to Tarrytown seven weeks after predicting the use to be made of the core collection showed such a prediction to have been accurate.

The study of the Harrison Public Library was an attempt to put into practice the theoretical findings of the earlier study, in which no actual weeding had taken place. The adult fiction and biography collections were weeded, using the spine-marking method (see chapter 11). The goals of this study were:

1. To validate the theory of weeding by use of the shelf-time period criterion. A prediction was made about the impact weeding would have on future circulation, and such prediction was checked periodically after the weeding had been completed.

2. To discover if in one library different classes of books varied in their shelf-time period patterns.

3. To validate the spine-marking method of weeding. This is the first time a library was weeded exclusively by this method, and a study was made of its value as a practical weeding technique.

The major findings were:

1. When shelf-time period was used as the weeding criterion, the amount of circulation was not reduced by the removal of a substantial number of volumes from the collection.[63] This was the most unexpected result of the study. Although it had been predicted that only 96 percent of the former fiction circulation would be retained, in fact, circulation increased. Six months after removing approximately 20 percent of the volumes from the collection, the circulation increased to 106.2 percent of previous circulation; and 20 months later it increased to 121.2 percent.[64] This was in a library where the rest of the collection enjoyed no increase in circulation. In the biography collection, with almost 50 percent of the volumes removed from the shelves, circulation remained constant. Weeding the collections seemed to increase usage, not reduce it, as predicted.

2. The library's holdings in the various classes were not in proportion to the use being made of those classes.[65] Table 8.3 illustrates this characteristic. For example, although 25 percent of the Harrison adult holdings were fiction, 48 percent of the adult usage was fiction. It was hypothesized that an idealized collection, optimizing book investment, should hold classes of books in proportion to their usage. A "better collection" would have 48 percent of the collection experiencing 48 percent of the use.

Table 8.3.
Percentage of Use vs. Percentage of Holdings, Harrison, Adult Collection

Adult Collection

Class	Percentage of Circulation Represented by This Class	Percentage of the Library's Holdings Represented by This Class
Fiction	48.2	25.8
Paperbacks	6.5	3.0
Biography	3.4	5.5
Non-Fiction-Other	41.9	65.7
Total	100.0%	100.0%

Children's Collection

Fiction	45.5	40.1
Picture Books	25.8	11.9
Biography	2.6	5.2
Non-Fiction-Other	26.1	42.8
Total	100.0%	100.0%

3. There were substantial differences in shelf-time periods among the various classes of books.[66] Tables 8.4 and 8.5 reflect these differences, in a number of arbitrarily selected classes.

4. Substantial monthly pulsations of circulation patterns called for caution in making the final weeding decision too rapidly or with too few samples.[67] Table 8.4 shows these fluctuations. The fiction sample, which had at least 200 cases each month, had the least fluctuation. The other classes had relatively few samples per month, sometimes as few as five. It is recommended that for any class being weeded, the weeding decision be made from a sample of at least 400 cases.

5. Noncore volumes, retained because of professional judgment, should have been weeded.[68]

6. The spine-marking method of weeding is a valid and useful method, but needs to be applied with care.[69]

The Larchmont Library Study was made to compare the "current circulation method" of creating shelf-time periods, from a sample of the most recent week's usage, with the "historical reconstruction method," which creates shelf-time periods from a sample of 10 years' usage. This study showed that at levels likely to be used for weeding, no significant differences could be detected (see page 113). It confirmed again the likelihood that usage patterns do not change over extended periods of time.

Table 8.4.
Shelf-Time Periods of the Circulation and Collection Samples Compared (Percent), Harrison, Adult Section

Cumulative Shelf-Time Period	Fiction Circulation	Fiction Collection	Paperbacks Circulation	Paperbacks Collection	Biography Circulation	Biography Collection	Non-Fiction 000-999+ Circulation	Non-Fiction 000-999+ Collection	Total Circulation	Total Collection
0	49	29	–	29	–	8	47	13	50	17
1	78	42	68	26	67	14	60	21	70	26
2	97	51	77	35	100	17	72	26	83	32
3	84	57	64	45	62	20	69	29	75	36
4	86	63	73	54	75	23	66	35	76	42
5	76	75	88	63	86	30	77	43	78	52
6	96	78	90	63	100	27	83	47	90	54
7	95	80	63	69	79	36	74	51	83	59
8	96	84	85	73	75	43	82	53	87	61
9	95	85	90	64	88	42	84	57	90	63
10	99*	93	77	68	81	44	77	59	86	69
11	99	93	87	71	92	46	93	61	96	73
12	98	93	84	69	90	42	89	60	94	72
13	99	95	91	74	91	61	92	69	96	80
14	98	–	80	–	91	–	90	–	93	–
15	99	–	91	–	91	–	90	–	94	–

*Collection weeded.

Table 8.5.
Shelf-Time Periods of the Circulation and Collection Samples Compared (Percent), Harrison, Children's Section

Cumulative Shelf-Time Period	Fiction		Picture Books		Biography		Non-Fiction		Total	
	Circulation	Collection	Circulation	Collection	Circulation	Collection	Circulation	Collection	Circulation	Collection
0	62	33	61	61	43	8	39	17	58	28
1	81	37	63	78	–	12	68	23	75	23
2	84	46	71	78	–	14	80	27	76	29
3	81	51	87	83	14	17	58	29	75	33
4	77	54	71	86	100	20	59	35	70	37
5	90	56	89	90	63	22	49	37	73	40
6	85	58	94	95	100	26	73	47	86	48
7	88	60	95	95	52	30	75	48	84	49
8	91	61	95	89	50	39	79	49	88	49
9	90	68	100	89	71	42	91	55	91	53
10	85	70	90	89	43	48	86	57	84	55
11	90	69	92	81	–	49	81	59	88	55
12	90	75	90	88	60	49	88	59	88	57
13	92	77	86	–	83	54	90	65	90	61
14	97	–	100	–	62	–	89	–	96	–
15	100	–	100	–	71	–	91	–	96	–

W. M. Shaw. This study was restricted to bound journal volumes in the Case Western Reserve University Libraries: The Freiberger Library, with 59,000 volumes of 2,700 titles, and the Sears Library with 24,000 volumes and 1,600 titles.[70] Users were requested not to reshelve the volumes they had used, and before reshelving the *first* time, a pressure sensitive dot was applied to the spine of the volume. The volumes dealt with the humanities, social sciences, and behavioral sciences at the Freiberger Library and science, engineering, management, and economics at the Sears Library. After 32 months, "The most striking feature of the analysis . . . is the small fraction of volumes and titles that have been used in the two libraries. At the Sears library 35 percent of the volumes and about 77 percent of the titles generated use. At the Freiberger Library about 22 percent of the volumes and about 58 percent of the titles generated use. These results indicate that over 61,000 volumes and 1,500 titles have generated no use during the course of this study."[71]

Allen Kent and others. The University of Pittsburgh Study took place over a period exceeding seven years.[72] It recorded the acquisitions made from October 1968 through 1975 and observed the use made of these acquisitions as time passed. According to this report, materials should be "both useful and used." A goal of the research was to develop measures for determining the extent to which library materials are used and when materials should be purged from the collections.

Among the findings were that:

1. A minority of titles account for a majority of uses.

2. Books and journals are subject to rapid rates of aging and obsolescence.

3. Of the books acquired in 1969, 39.8 percent never circulated during the first six years on the library's shelves.

4. There is no objective way to make acquisition decisions with certain knowledge that what is acquired will be used.

5. External circulation data can be utilized with a high level of confidence to measure total book use.

6. Random samples of loan records representing as few as three days produced correlations as high as .95 with total population in regard to present circulation use. (One does not need long-term data to predict future use.)

7. Of the total collection, 48.37 percent did not circulate in seven years.

8. A definite aging pattern emerges. As books get older, first-time use is reduced. For example, for 36,869 books acquired in 1969:

Year #	First Circulated
1969	9,708
1970	6,424
1971	2,449
1972	1,452
1973	915
1974	644
1975	580

9. Each year's acquisitions behave much like any other year.

10. Only objective techniques of weeding should be used.

11. Past use is the best indicator of the future use of material.[73]

Weeding Studies Using Noncirculation as a Criterion

Gary L. Ferguson. The Louisiana State Library wanted to weed at least 20 percent of the collection, or 30,000 volumes, to make room for new acquisitions, arriving at the rate of 10,000 per year. Samples of the collection, for each Dewey 100 classification, were made to see what cut-date would produce this result. It was concluded that books not circulated in the last 10 years were candidates for weeding, even though the cut-dates produced by the samples ranged from 8 to 12 years.[74]

Self-adhering dots were applied to the spines of all volumes that had not circulated in 10 years and 18.5 percent of the volumes were so dotted.[75] A holding section was prepared and groups of weeding candidates moved to this areas. Twenty-five subject areas were selected and a librarian assigned to each area, depending upon expertise and interests. Weeders were given written guidelines including many of the conventional criteria (age, condition, vanity publications, etc.). Some 40,000 volumes were removed, and only 5 percent of the weeding candidates, or 2,000 volumes, were returned to the active collection.[76]

The amount of time needed for this project is reported in detail and included 3,400 hours for removing cards from the catalog, 2,000 hours for rearranging the collection, and 775 hours of actual weeding time.[77]

Eugene A. Engeldinger. In a unique study of reference usage, the Eau Claire Library at the University of Wisconsin kept records of usage of its reference collections over a period of five years, 1981-1986.[78] All items requiring reshelving were counted as having been used. A stick-on dot was placed inside the back cover of every reference book being reshelved. A limit of five dots per title prevented the whole inside cover being filled with dots. The number of uses, by class, is shown on page 70.[79]

Table 8.6.
Eau Claire Library Reference Collection Usage

	0 Uses		1 Use		2 Uses		3 Uses		4 Uses		5 Uses		1-5 Uses		Total Vols. in Classification
A	90	50%	25	14%	12	7%	11	6%	8	4%	33	18%	89	50%	179
B-BF	47	34%	15	11%	6	4%	7	5%	12	9%	51	37%	91	66%	138
BH-BZ	45	16%	53	18%	39	14%	25	9%	30	10%	95	33%	242	84%	287
C	51	26%	42	21%	35	18%	16	8%	10	5%	46	23%	149	75%	200
D	176	32%	89	16%	72	13%	46	8%	35	6%	136	25%	378	68%	554
E	158	46%	64	18%	37	11%	26	7%	12	3%	50	14%	189	54%	347
F	42	25%	17	10%	13	8%	12	7%	10	6%	75	44%	127	75%	169
G	48	12%	35	9%	34	9%	38	10%	34	9%	198	51%	339	88%	387
H-HF	58	12%	61	13%	40	8%	48	10%	37	8%	244	50%	430	88%	488
HG-HZ	373	41%	153	17%	87	10%	58	6%	39	4%	190	21%	527	59%	900
J	112	32%	54	15%	42	12%	28	8%	22	6%	95	27%	241	68%	353
K	491	52%	175	19%	90	10%	64	7%	50	5%	74	8%	453	48%	944
L	60	16%	35	9%	31	8%	22	6%	31	8%	194	52%	313	84%	373
M	132	31%	72	17%	52	12%	24	6%	24	6%	122	29%	294	69%	426
N	65	30%	37	17%	27	12%	20	9%	22	10%	47	22%	153	70%	218
P-PN	270	24%	154	14%	104	9%	85	8%	92	8%	402	36%	837	76%	1107
PQ-PZ	138	41%	61	18%	47	14%	23	7%	18	5%	51	15%	200	59%	338
Q	152	29%	85	16%	57	11%	50	10%	38	7%	137	26%	367	71%	519
R	41	25%	29	18%	14	9%	10	6%	13	8%	57	35%	123	75%	164
S	17	24%	14	19%	8	11%	2	3%	7	10%	24	33%	55	76%	72
T	105	27%	74	19%	38	10%	28	7%	26	7%	125	32%	291	73%	396
UV	3	9%	8	25%	7	22%	3	9%	2	6%	9	28%	29	91%	32
Z	1072	49%	438	20%	219	10%	125	6%	89	4%	233	11%	1104	51%	2176
Totals	3746	34.8%	1790	16.6%	1111	10.3%	771	7.1%	661	6.1%	2688	24.9%	7021	65.2%	10767

It was found that if they "accepted a use level for an item to remain in reference at one use in five years," 34.8 percent of the books could be removed from the collection. If two or more uses in five years was the keeping criterion, 51.4 percent of the volumes could have been removed.[80] "Logic would dictate that if an item turns out to receive little or no use, it should lose its reference status" because reference collections are an inconvenience to users wishing to withdraw a book from the library.[81]

Loriene Roy. Roy reports on a research project in four rural public libraries which aimed at removing 10 percent of their collections by identifying books with low circulation rates.[82] Shelf-time period and subjective opinion were used as weeding criteria. This was a test to see whether weeding would result in increasing the rate of annual circulation in these libraries. In an attempt to use a simple objective criterion, shelf-time period was chosen. In order to gain library cooperation, subjective opinions were solicited and certain books were retained on that basis. The actual weeding of about 1,200 books from each collection (or about 11 percent) took between 4½ and 6 hours.

The book cards, showing the date of last use, of one hundred volumes were inspected and the books not used in the past two years were turned onto their front edges and identified as candidates for weeding. If more than 10 percent of the volumes in the collection were identified, the date was extended. In two libraries a two year date was used; in the other two, a five year date was used. Where book cards lacked adequate information, accession dates were used. If any doubt remained about a book having been circulated or not, it was not weeded.

The results of the study produced these conclusions:

1. The weeded libraries showed no significant increase in stock turnover rate.[83] It should be noted, however, that a 9 percent increase in turnover rate did occur, but this was not "statistically significant."[84] In addition, "The researcher felt that weeding has the potential to significantly increase stock turnover rate but only if the weeding is substantial, i.e. above 10 percent . . ."[85]

2. ". . . Weeding probably did not result in an appreciable loss of circulation."[86] Fewer than 1 percent of the weeded volumes were requested after the weeding was completed.

3. ". . . weeding criteria used were effective in identifying books that were not likely to be in demand."[87]

4. "Shelf-time period is a convenient and practical criterion that accurately identified books the public is no longer interested in reading."[88]

Jeff Selth, Nancy Koller, and Peter Briscoe. A seven year study was undertaken in the library of the Riverside Campus of the University of California to determine whether or not in-library use of books mirrors their circulation.[89] At least three major studies during the last 30 years had concluded that in-library use mirrored circulation use: Fussler and Simon (see page 60), Trueswell (see page 61) and Kent (see page 68).

The Riverside Campus library has over 1.1 million circulating volumes, and a random sample of 13,029 was studied. For seven years "every book left lying on a table, ledge, shelf, etc. or beside a photocopying machine"[90] was stamped so that in-library use could be identified. At the end of seven years, the use data were fed into computers, and the following information was extracted from the data:

1. 11.2 percent of the monographs and 13 percent of the serials did not circulate but had some in-library use; 19.5 percent of the monographs and 12.8 percent of the serial volumes had not recorded in-library use but circulated. Consequently, a total of 30.7 percent of the monographs and 25.8 percent of the serial volumes had one kind of use but not the other.[91]

2. 112,000 volumes, which had been used in a seven year period, would have been weeded because of a lack of circulation. "The true figure must be much higher than that, since our method captured only a fraction of the number of times in-library use actually took place," because many users reshelve the volumes themselves.[92]

3. In some cases, the number of recorded in-library uses was quite high, even when there was little or no external use. Volumes with no circulation had as many as 10 recorded uses within the library; those with only one circulation, up to 13.[93]

The method of counting books left on the tables is flawed. Using the research of others, the authors estimate that the in-library use is much greater than reported, possibly many times greater. They discuss the possibility of putting slips in the books that would be disturbed if the book were used and thus identify a use.[94]

They conclude: ". . . the key component of our findings is that of the books with no circulation but some in-library use. They are after all the potential victims of any weeding procedure based on circulation alone."[95]

Lawrence L. Reed and Rodney Erickson. Two sections of the Moorhead State University Library were weeded using three criteria.[96]

1. All books that had not circulated in 15 years were removed from the stacks.

2. Of the books removed, those listed in any one of three bibliographies were returned to the shelves. The three were *Books for College Libraries*, *Essays and General Literature Index*, and *Reader's Advisor*. This was done in an attempt to compensate for the effort of "using noncirculation as the sole criterion for weeding. . . ."[97]

3. Additional books were returned to the shelves upon the advice of librarians and faculty members.

Of the 36,308 books in the collections, 5,048 books were removed based upon the criterion of noncirculation. Slightly more than half of these, ultimately, were

Of the 36,308 books in the collections, 5,048 books were removed based upon the criterion of noncirculation. Slightly more than half of these, ultimately, were returned to the shelves based upon the bibliographies and expert advice, leaving 2,531 weeded volumes.

The researchers concluded that the method was "workable and productive."[98] They noted that "faculty participation was disappointing," that "librarians tended to find little time for the task" of weeding, and that "motivation for working on the project was difficult to maintain."[99]

Studies Using the "Slote Method"

The remaining reports all refer to the use of the "Slote Method" to weed libraries. The procedures employed are described in detail; findings are tabulated and analyzed. In all cases operating collections were actually weeded. The methods used were those described in the previous editions of this book.

E. Winsche and B. Molesworth. This is a preliminary report on the weeding of three libraries in the York Regional Area, Nova Scotia, testing the "Slote Method."[100] It is unique in that two different techniques for determining shelf-time period were employed. Weeding criteria for one library were developed by the book card method, in which the book cards reflect dates indicating previous circulations (see chapter 10); and for the other library by the spine-marking method, in which a visible dot is applied to the spine of each volume going into circulation (see chapter 11).

The Nashwaaksis Public School Library, in a junior high school serving 900 students, was weeded rapidly because the book card method was used. Adult and children's collections were treated as separate collections. It was found that:

1. Ninety-eight percent of the books circulating had circulated previously within the last three years. Ninety-nine percent had circulated within the last four years. "It made no appreciable difference if the book was fiction or nonfiction, adult or juvenile."

2. Between 15 and 25 percent of the books on the shelves were not part of the core collection (the part of the collection likely to be used).

3. "It is an established fact that a well-weeded collection is more heavily used." A study of book use showed that "the patrons want the new books and the tried and true books."

4. The tables indicating the use patterns of the adult and juvenile collections taken from data at different times show a consistency and a reliability that characterize a valid method.[101]

Concerning the use of the spine-marking method underway in the Oromocto and Fredericton libraries, it was reported that:

1. This method "is establishing . . . a coherent view of the reading patterns of our patrons." It highlights the high use sections of the library.

2. "Bright coloured dots (used in this system) on the spine of a book increase its interest to the next patron and can be seen to also increase its circulation."

3. After three months of dotting the spines of books as they circulate "extrapolating from already achieved results, . . . the vast majority of our books will have dots on them by the end of the year, somewhat along the lines of the almost astonishing results at Nashwaaksis."[102]

Penelope McKee. The purpose of this study was to discover a "simple, cheap and effective method of weeding" the Forest Hill Branch of the Toronto Public Library.[103] McKee decided to test the findings and methodology reported in the first edition of *Weeding Library Collections* and to use the "Slote Method" of weeding. With a focus on reader satisfaction, the study weeded the collection based upon past use as a predictor of future use. It also examined the effect that weeding had on subsequent circulation. The author had the staff double dot the spines of all books being returned to the shelves and segregated those volumes that had not circulated by the time 95 percent of the circulation was made up of dotted volumes. These candidates for weeding were displayed prominently to give them a chance to circulate. The volumes that still did not circulate were weeded from the collection. Prior to weeding, an inventory was taken to determine how many volumes had been stolen from the library. This number was compared with the number of volumes actually weeded from the collection. McKee reported:

1. That there is some likely validity to the concept that "the true core collection (the part of the collection most likely to be used if it were present) has been stolen."

2. That the spine-marking method (see chapter 11) involved savings in time and money over the conventional methods, and that it involved the handling of only 8 percent of the collection. The actual amount of time necessary to weed out 1,675 volumes was 10 hours.

3. That statistical evidence was produced to indicate that this method of weeding does increase circulation.

4. That the findings were similar to those of the Harrison Library Study as reported in *Weeding Library Collections*. The method was "highly visible, quick, cost effective and reliable."

5. That "past use is the best predictor of future use."[104]

Roy Williams. Williams produced a report on the weeding of the Inglemire Avenue Site Library of Humberside College, an English academic library containing 90,000 volumes, of which 20,000 were removed using the "Slote Method."[105] As with many other libraries, Inglemire was running out of space and found itself with books in "corridors, offices and cupboards" and with no new space in the offing. A study of the literature and previous experience with the "Slote Method" convinced the library that using the concepts of shelf-time period and core collection offered a reasonable and feasible approach to weeding. It was decided that the method used had to satisfy the political climate in the university, consider service to the user, and be accomplished in one college year.

This library used the book card method (see chapter 10) as found in the second edition of *Weeding Library Collections.* Five hundred book cards from 500 consecutive circulations were collected in a two-week period and analyzed. The data were tabulated and by sample checking, the 96 percent keeping-level was used except in the education stock, and this was later reduced from 99 percent to 96 percent. The faculty board and key teaching staff and members of the library staff were involved and given the opportunity to replace any book weeded by this method. Only the author catalog was amended to reflect the weeded volumes. Weeded volumes were donated to other libraries, or when in poor condition, destroyed.

Williams reported that:

1. "Our experience leads us to recommend Slote's method to any academic library . . . where lending is the prime function."

2. Circulation increased 13 percent in the year after weeding as compared with 2 percent the year before.

3. The subsequent year circulation increased another 16 percent although other changes were made that also might have influenced circulation.

4. Concerning the actual experience of weeding:

   a. Weeding went rapidly.

   b. Relatively few books were returned to the shelves either by the faculty or staff librarians.

   c. Amending the catalog to reflect the weeded volumes is very arduous, unreliable work.

   d. Different subject areas experienced different patterns of circulation usage.

   e. Hardly any comment was received criticizing the library for removing 20,000 volumes.[106]

Notes

1. Aridaman K. Jain et al., "A Statistical Study of Book Use Supplemented with a Bibliography of Library Use Studies" (Ph.D. diss., Purdue University, 1967).

2. Charles H. Busha and Royal Purcell, "A Textural Approach for Promoting Rigorous Research in Librarianship," *Journal of Education for Librarianship* 14 (Summer 1973): 3.

3. Charles William Eliot, "The Division of a Library into Books in Use, and Books Not in Use, with Different Storage Methods for the Two Classes of Books," *Library Journal* 27 (July 1902): 52.

4. Ibid.

5. Samuel H. Ranck, "The Problem of the Unused Book," *Library Journal* 36 (August 1911): 428.

6. Lee Ash, *Yale's Selective Book Retirement Program* (Hamden, CT: Archon Books, 1963).

7. Ibid., 81.

8. Ibid., 66-67.

9. Elizabeth Mueller, "Are New Books Read More Than Old Ones?" *Library Quarterly* 35 (July 1965): 166-72.

10. M. K. Buckland et al., *Systems Analysis of a University Library*, Occasional Papers no. 4 (Lancaster, England: University of Lancaster Library, 1970), 8.

11. Ibid., 12.

12. Ibid., 52.

13. Ibid., 53.

14. Philip M. Morse, *Library Effectiveness: A Systems Approach* (Cambridge, MA: M.I.T. Press, 1968).

15. Ibid., 5.

16. Ibid., 83-84.

17. Ibid., 167-68.

18. Stanley J. Slote, "An Approach to Weeding Criteria for Newspaper Libraries," *American Documentation* 19 (April 1968): 168-72.

19. In the "Five Libraries Study," much material was excluded from the sample because no data were available on the book card. It was felt that often this was because the material had never been used. Such observation led to the suggestion that all book cards be *dated* when placed into books.

20. Elmer M. Grieder, "The Effect of Book Storage on Circulation Service," *College & Research Libraries* 11 (October 1950): 374-76.

21. This technique may have the weakness that books in the hands of the clients at any one moment may not represent the true circulation pattern. Certain types of books may be returned more rapidly than others, and then recirculated. For instance, if 1,000 fiction and 1,000 nonfiction volumes were in circulation at one time, and fiction was kept out for 10 days on an average while nonfiction was retained for 20 days, fiction would be underrepresented by 50 percent in the sample.

22. Marianne Cooper, "Criteria for Weeding of Collections," *Library Resources and Technical Services* 12 (Summer 1968): 349.

23. Winston Charles Lister, "Least Cost Decision Rules for the Selection of Library Materials for Compact Storage" (Ph.D. diss., Purdue University, 1967): 12.

24. Ibid., 6.

25. Ibid., 223, 226.

26. Ibid., 224.

27. Ibid., 223.

28. Ibid., 115-16.

29. Edward A. Silver, "A Quantitative Appraisal of the M.I.T. Science Library Mezzanine with an Application to the Problem of Limited Shelf Space" (term paper for M.I.T. graduate course 8:75, Operations Research, 1962).

30. Ibid., 50.

31. A. K. Jain, "Sampling and Short-Period Usage in the Purdue Library," *College & Research Libraries* 27 (May 1966): 211-18; Jain et al., "Statistical Study of Book Use Supplemented with a Bibliography of Library Use Studies" (Ph.D. diss., Purdue University, 1967).

32. Jain et al., "Statistical Study of Book Use," 128-220.

33. Ibid., 125.

34. Herman H. Fussler and Julian L. Simon, *Patterns in the Use of Books in Large Research Libraries* (Chicago: University of Chicago Press, 1969).

35. Ibid., 7.

36. Ibid., 45-52, 30, 31, 15, 144 (pages listed in order statements appear).

37. Ibid., 66-67.

38. Ibid., 143.

39. Ibid., 147.

40. Richard William Trueswell, "User Behavioral Patterns and Requirements and Their Effect on the Possible Applications of Data Processing and Computer Techniques in a University Library" (Ph.D. diss., Northwestern University, 1964).

41. Ibid., iv.

42. Ibid.

43. Ibid., 35.

44. Ibid., 109-16.

45. Ibid., 44.

46. Ibid., 105.

47. Ibid., 113.

48. Ibid., 180.

49. Richard W. Trueswell, "A Quantitative Measure of User Circulation Requirements and Its Possible Effect on Stack Thinning and Multiple Copy Determination," *American Documentation* 16 (January 1965): 20-25.

50. Ibid., 22.

51. Richard W. Trueswell, "Determining the Optimal Number of Volumes for a Library's Core Collection," *Libri* 16 (1966): 49-60.

52. Richard W. Trueswell, "User Circulation Satisfaction vs. Size of Holdings at Three Academic Libraries," *College and Research Libraries* 30 (May 1969): 204.

53. Trueswell, "Determining the Optimal Number of Volumes," 49.

54. Ibid., 52.

55. Richard W. Trueswell, *Analysis of Library User Circulation Requirements* (Amherst, MA: University of Massachusetts, 1968), abstract.

56. Stanley J. Slote, *Weeding Library Collections* (Littleton, CO: Libraries Unlimited, 1975).

57. Stanley J. Slote (unpublished study).

58. See Slote, *Weeding Library Collections*, 81.

59. Ibid., 82.

60. Ibid.

61. Ibid.

62. Ibid., 81-82.

63. Ibid., 86.

64. M. Poller, "Weeding Monographs in the Harrison Public Library," *The De-acquisitions Librarian* 1 (Spring 1976): 7.

65. Slote, *Weeding Library Collections*, 93.

66. Ibid., 81, 87-88.

67. Ibid., 86.

68. Ibid., 93.

69. Ibid., 86.

70. W. M. Shaw Jr., "A Practical Journal Usage Technique," *College and Research Libraries* 39 (November 1978): 479-84.

71. Ibid., 482.

72. Allen Kent et al., *Use of Library Materials: The University of Pittsburgh Study* (New York: Marcel Dekker, 1979).

73. Ibid., 2, 9, 2, 10, 13, 14, 19, 48, 49 (pages listed in order statements appear).

74. Gary L. Ferguson, "A Deselection Project at the Louisiana State Library," *Louisiana Library Association Bulletin* 45, no. 2 (Fall 1982): 73.

75. Ibid., 74.

76. Ibid., 73-77.

77. Ibid., 77.

78. Eugene A. Engeldinger, " 'Use' as a Criterion for the Weeding of Reference Collections," *The Reference Librarian* 29 (1990): 123.

79. Ibid., 125.

80. Ibid.

81. Ibid., 120.

82. Loriene Roy, "Weeding Without Tears: Objective and Subjective Criteria Used in Identifying Books to Be Weeded in Public Library Collections," *Collection Management* 12(1/2) (1990): 83-92.

83. Ibid., 90.

84. Loriene Roy, "Does Weeding Increase Circulation? A Review of the Related Literature," *Collection Management* 10(1/2) (1988): 153.

85. Roy, "Weeding Without Tears . . . ," 90-91.

86. Ibid., 91.

87. Ibid.

88. Ibid., 92.

89. Jeff Selth, Nancy Koller, and Peter Briscoe, "The Use of Books Within the Library," *College and Research Libraries* 52, no. 3 (May 1992): 197-205.

90. Ibid., 199.

91. Ibid.

92. Ibid.

93. Ibid., 200.

94. Ibid.

95. Ibid., 202-203.

96. Lawrence L. Reed and Rodney Erickson, "Weeding, A Quantitative and Qualitative Approach," *Library Acquisitions: Practice and Theory* 17 (1993): 175.

97. Ibid., 177.

98. Ibid., 179.

99. Ibid.

100. E. Winsche and B. Molesworth, "Collection Weeding—York Regional Library," *APLA Bulletin* 44 (January 1981): 39.

101. Ibid.

102. Ibid.

103. Penelope McKee, "Weeding the Forest Hill Branch of Toronto Public Library by the Slote Method: A Test Case," *Library Research* 3 (1981): 283-301.

104. Ibid., 292, 295, 296, 298, 299 (pages listed in order statements appear).

105. Roy Williams, "Weeding an Academic Lending Library Using the Slote Method," *British Journal of Academic Librarianship* 1, no. 2 (1986): 147-59.

106. Ibid., 157, 156, 154, 155, 153, 156 (pages listed in order statements appear).

Part 2
THE WEEDING PROCESS
FOR
CIRCULATING COLLECTIONS

9

The New Concept
in Weeding

Background

For hundreds of years library weeding has been accomplished by the subjective application of vague rules, concepts, or feelings—difficult to describe accurately, difficult to apply consistently, and difficult to evaluate. This book discourages the use of this approach, an approach that lacks the ability to predict which volumes are likely to enjoy future usage and which are not. The result is that many useful works are discarded and many useless ones are retained. To replace this method, the author searched for, found, and studied a simple variable that could predict future usage with certainty. This variable was based upon past or current usage patterns observed in the library. During the last 30 years, other possible variables have been studied and rejected as lacking practical, efficient predictive strength. These discarded variables have included the age of the volumes, the language used, the subject matter, and the type of work.

A Weeding Variable

The nature of the desired variable can best be understood by reducing the concept to absurdity. Suppose, for instance, it was discovered in a specific library that only volumes with green bindings were used. No book (regardless of subject, title, author, age, or location) was used if it did not have a green binding. If the library then removed all volumes that lacked green bindings, theoretically, the usage of that library would remain unaffected. There would now be left in the library a subset of volumes that could be described or defined by the simple variable: "green bindings." This subset or "core collection" would satisfy 100 percent of all future demands made upon this library.

In this example, one could say that a variable has been identified that predicts with confidence the subset of volumes that experience 100 percent of all the usage. (This assumes that no short-term event or condition has caused exclusive use of green bound volumes.) Library usage would not be reduced by the removal of the nongreen volumes. A variable has been identified that predicts the future usage of the library. Of course, this example is foolish, as no such situation was ever encountered, nor is likely to be encountered. However, it highlights the concept involved in searching for a variable that could describe the current library usage.

Shelf-Time Period as a Variable

As this book has stated, a variable has been uncovered, studied, applied, and found to be of value in solving the weeding problem. This strong, valid, positive, predictive, meaningful variable is called *shelf-time period.* Shelf-time period is the length of time a book remains on the shelf between uses. For practical purposes, it also may be considered an open-ended period, reflecting the time that has passed between the previous usage of a book and the day weeding is being done. In this case, the open-end shelf-time period measures a period still ongoing, and therefore it measures a period of time *no less* than the next true shelf-time period would have been if the volume had been given the opportunity to be used again.

To better understand the concept and use of the shelf-time period, replace the variable "green bindings" with the variable "one year shelf-time period." Suppose that every volume that was used during the entire history of a library had remained on the shelf less than one year since its previous use or its acquisition. This means that 100 percent of the usage had a shelf-time period of under one year. If one then removes from the library shelves all the volumes that have remained on the shelves unused for one year or more, one would have removed books that will not be used in the future. The result would be a core collection that would likely retain 100 percent of the future use of the library.

Theoretically, past use is not an absolute predictor of future use. But practically, in library after library where the assumption of predictability has been tested, it has been shown that past use has been a reliable, valid predictor of future use. Furthermore, in every case where shelf-time period has been used for weeding, contrary to expectations, usage was found to increase (see page 64). Thus, this variable as a predictor of future use can be applied without fear of reducing the value of the collection.

Intuitively, most librarians can accept the principles being advanced above. For example, if advised to remove all volumes that have experienced no usage in 20 years, few would resist this advice. If a book hasn't been used in the last 20 years it seems unlikely that it will be used in the next 20 years. However, as the time span is reduced, resistance to weeding is increased. A few librarians would resist if asked to remove volumes not used for 10 years; and even more would resist five years. Under the methods to be described shortly, the cut-off point is frequently two or three years; and sometimes it is as little as one year. And here massive resistance is likely unless librarians understand the underlying concepts.

Once librarians agree to the principle, it is necessary to measure the shelf-time periods of volumes in use and try to predict what will happen when books are removed from the shelves based upon such measurements. The following four chapters deal in detail with the processes used to weed a library without fear of depriving the clients or harming the collection.

The Core Collection

Another concept is integral to understanding this approach to weeding. Through our studies it has been found that *every library consists of two distinguishable collections, the collection that is used and the collection that remains in the library unused.* These two collections are not apparent to the naked eye, even to the experienced eye of a well-trained librarian. The collections look alike. Each subset consists of newer volumes and older ones, of all the subjects, and frequently one author has volumes in both collections. These subsets are called the *core collection* and the *noncore collection.* The core collection is the subset of holdings that should be retained by the library for its clients' use, and the noncore collection is the subset representing little or no usage that should be considered for weeding. The problem to be dealt with is how to identify these two subcollections with confidence and certainty.

Once these two collections are identified, the following rule should be followed: *No volume in the core collection should be considered for weeding.* And, as a corollary of the above rule: *All books in the noncore collection are candidates for weeding and probably should be weeded.*

It has been observed that librarians studying the noncore collection frequently identify volumes they are reluctant to remove from the primary holding areas. The reasons are many: these volumes may have been gifts from trustees or local authors, they may be related to local history, or they may be by famous authors. Such volumes and others that librarians identify for keeping may be retained, although they will not experience much use. They become permanent shelf-sitters and will show up again during the next weeding effort as belonging to the noncore collection. So keep whatever your judgment dictates. If done in moderation, retaining noncore volumes in the core collection will not subvert the beneficial effects of weeding.

Patterns of Use

Almost all of the recent studies in book use have reinforced the needs and pressures for weeding. Some even question present techniques of book acquisition. Perhaps no study is more important than that at the University of Pittsburgh, which found that 40 percent of all books purchased by the university library are never used (see page 68). This means that newly purchased books frequently enter the noncore collection immediately and never serve any practical purpose as far as the library client is concerned. The removal of these volumes would have no known negative effect. This present work does not address the problem of preventing such terrible waste. Unfortunately, weeding attacks the problem after the fact. It would be extremely valuable if a predictor could be discovered to identify, in advance, volumes that will never be used, but to date no such predictor has been uncovered or reported in the literature. By using the methods that follow, such volumes will be weeded from the collection after the user has cast a vote on their value by permitting them to remain unused on the library shelves.

It would be unfair to conclude that all kinds of libraries suffer from the same problem. The purchase of useless books is mainly a problem for research, university, college, and special libraries; it has not been a problem in most public libraries or in school library media centers. A major finding of our studies is that in middle-sized and smaller public libraries, practically all new books enjoy use while they are relatively new. In studying the fiction collections of seven public libraries, this author found *no case of a new book remaining on the shelf unused during the first two years after its acquisition and shelving.* To put it another way, in these libraries all fiction volumes, when first acquired, became part of the core collection.

The Core Collection Changes

The above pattern of book use in a public library is well known to working librarians. New books, especially bestsellers, are in tremendous demand while they remain in the public eye. The library is able to satisfy only a small part of the demand. Then usage generally tapers off a little, and in a year or two circulation either stops altogether or becomes sporadic. Some volumes taper off more slowly and may receive substantial use for 5, 10, or even 20 years. Ultimately, all but a handful of books (which from the point of view of use might be considered "the classics") move into the noncore collection and get little or no use. It is for this reason that weeding is a never-ending process.

As can be seen, the core and noncore collections in active libraries are in a constant state of flux, with all but a tiny amount of the movement being from the core to the noncore collection. A new book is received and shelved. It receives rather heavy usage for a time, and then the rate of usage is reduced rather steadily. Finally, unless it is a classic, all or most usage stops. On the other hand, a counter trend also exists. Authors and titles occasionally are revived. This is particularly true if a movie or television presentation generates new interest in a work. And so, on rare occasions, volumes move from the noncore back to the core collection. This means that at any time there is some usage of the noncore collection and some nonusage of the core collection. *Under any method of weeding, it is likely that some books that are removed might have been used if they had not been weeded.*

Effects of Weeding

In using the methods recommended in this book, weeding is frequently done at the *96 percent keeping level.* That is to say that theoretically the core collection retained after weeding will retain 96 percent of the collection's former use. The noncore collection, now weeded, therefore represented 4 percent of the usage. In the field it was observed that, generally, between 10 and 50 percent of the collection could be weeded out at this keeping level; and that 50 to 90 percent of the collection (the remainder) represented 96 percent of the use. This is only theoretical, for *in every case where libraries were weeded the book use (as reflected by the circulation count) increased.* Thus, while some books that would have been used have been removed, the general appearance, quality, and tone of the remaining books seem to encourage more, rather than less, use. In reality, at no substantial cost, the library has been enlarged by making room for more new books, and active usage of the existing collection has been increased. This is the best of both worlds, for now fewer books create more usage.

Procedures Which Reduce the Core Collection Unintentionally

Book-use studies have uncovered two library procedures which reduce the use that new volumes would normally experience. Such procedures make rational weeding procedures less effective.

First, as mentioned above, as new books start to age they tend to lose their client appeal. It was observed that some libraries catalog new acquisitions so slowly that on an average they take between one year and 18 months to reach the stacks. The quickest and most satisfying way to increase library usage is to get new books on the shelves immediately upon their receipt, even if complete cataloging must be deferred. The presence of a volume on the shelf is vastly more important to its future use than the precision of its cataloging. The slowdown in processing frequently destroys any reader interest that might have existed earlier. Books become automatic members of the noncore collection and candidates for weeding through this delay. No library practice could be more destructive to normal use patterns.

Second, and perhaps less forgivable, is the practice of librarians storing new books in their own offices or homes for future reading before these books have been made available to the clients. In one small library, it was observed that over 150 new or practically new volumes were being kept in the head librarian's office waiting to be read before being shelved. The tendency to put off the actual reading (sometimes permanently) often causes a core book to be moved to the noncore collection. To prevent this destructive practice, all librarians should be subject to the same circulation rules as their patrons.

Retaining the Core Collection

All of the recommended methods of weeding work the same way. They analyze the book use in terms of shelf-time period. Having analyzed the use pattern, the data are quantified. This tabulation then creates a *cut-off point* so that the entire collection can be altered in such a fashion that only the core collection is retained in the primary storage areas (the stacks).

The methods are based upon the realization that all volumes currently circulating (or enjoying in-library use) are part of the core collection. By measuring the shelf-time periods of the volumes being used, the methods create a specific date to be used as a cut-off point. It might be concluded, for example, that all volumes not used since December 4, 1987 are to be weeded and that the core collection consists of all volumes used at least once since that date. Where a date is not stated as such in the result (as in the spine-marking method), it, in fact, still exists.

Sampling to Determine
the Cut-Off Point

All the methods about to be described call for no fewer than 400 useful samples. This number has a solid statistical basis. For practical purposes, it is wise to collect 500 samples so that useless samples can be discarded and at least 400 meaningful uses are available for the tabulations.

In-Library Use

The weeding methods recommended by this author focus on measuring the shelf-time period of books that either are used within the library or are charged out. This represents a major change from earlier editions of this book, which utilized only books which circulated. There now is strong evidence that in-library use does *not* mirror the circulation use.[1]

Therefore, libraries that experience in-library use must establish a procedure to identify such usage, so that books recently used are not weeded. This means additional work and ingenuity on the part of almost all libraries, and it calls for additional expense and effort. Every book used in-library must be identified. A number of the following problems can arise.

1. All serious research has shown that it is extremely difficult to prevent the clients of a library from reshelving books they use in the library. Broadus points out that no one has really solved the problem.[2] It is not sufficient to put up a few signs requesting that the books be left on tables or desks. A serious campaign must be undertaken to prevent users from reshelving books. A large number of signs explaining the reasons for not reshelving should help, especially if accompanied by a serious publicity campaign. Above all, more desks, tables, and special collection areas must be established in the library to make it more convenient to leave a book unshelved. There is a need for further research, and successful techniques should be broadcast more widely.

2. These books, before being reshelved by pages or clerks, must have their use recorded in some fashion: a date-stamp on a book card or book cover, a self-adhering colored dot applied to the spine or inside cover, an entry made in the computer system, etc. This is an entirely new procedure for most libraries, where in-library use is rarely recorded in any fashion. Obviously, such a procedure will involve more labor and additional costs, but it is absolutely necessary if collections are to be weeded with confidence.

3. Even if measurement of in-library use is not a regular procedure in a library, such a procedure should be established several years before a library is to be weeded.

4. There are likely to be substantial differences in the impact of not considering in-library use for different types of libraries. Perhaps the libraries that would be most damaged would be academic libraries where serious research and study use is made of the materials. Libraries could try to identify whether they are high-risk or low-risk candidates. But all libraries experiencing in-library use must consider that use in establishing cut-dates and when identifying weeding candidates.

This also means that all sampling must now be done of both the books that circulate and the books that are used within the library. It means that when establishing a cut-date for weeding, before the books used in-library are reshelved, the date of last use of these volumes must be recorded on the forms provided during the sampling period. The impact of this major change is dramatic: cut-points will now be of a shorter duration. Perhaps if the cut-point formerly was three years, it will now be reduced to two years. This will occur because cut-points are directly related to the number of times per year the average book in the library is used—the greater number of times per year, the shorter the cut-point.

One of the advantages of our new approach is that librarians can weed with more confidence. Librarians have always been advised to look over weeding candidates to determine if some of the volumes should be returned to the circulating collection. Using the new system, it is likely the time consumed by this job can be reduced and many fewer volumes will be returned.

When In-Library Use Is Not *Recorded*

While the author has stressed the importance of controlling in-library use in the same fashion as circulating use, few libraries have incorporated in-library control techniques. Nevertheless, all of the recommended methods of weeding can be used without considering in-library usage, to establish the cut-points and to identify *candidates for weeding.* If further study of a volume seems to indicate that it might be used within the library, even though it has not circulated since the cut-date, the volume should be retained.

The ideal method of weeding would have libraries record both in-library use and circulating use, and then weeding could be done more or less mechanically without much further study of the weeding candidates. But if libraries are recording only circulating use, they should not hesitate to use these recommended methods, modified to disregard the fact that in-library use has not been recorded. Follow the procedures, disregarding the instructions concerning in-library use. The methods still will assist and simplify the weeding process. However:

1. The recommended methods, modified to omit consideration of in-library use, still identify only a small portion of the volumes on the shelves as valid weeding candidates, and therefore the weeding process is simplified. *Do*

not consider any book for weeding unless it has been identified as being a weeding candidate.

2. While all the methods in this edition include in-library use in the data, in the past these same methods, without consideration of in-library use, always resulted *in increased library circulation.*

3. The librarian's judgment of which books might be experiencing only in-library use becomes important. It is essential to study the weeding candidates and return to the shelves volumes that might have been used in the library and not circulated.

Recommended Weeding Methods

There are four valid methods for developing the kind of weeding criteria recommended in this book. The practical choice depends upon the information that is readily available or can be made available conveniently. These are

1. The book card method (chapter 10), or the substitute book card method (chapter 10).

2. The spine-marking method (chapter 11).

3. The historical reconstruction method (chapter 12).

4. The computer assisted method (chapter 13).

How to Select
the Best Weeding Method

The best method for weeding a circulating library depends upon the system of circulation control being used. Four major systems of circulation control are in general use. However, in each method, the completeness of the data available and the ability to use such data are of prime importance in determining the weeding method. From the point of view of circulation control systems, following is a guide for the selection of the proper weeding method.

The Book Card System of Circulation Control

In this system, a book card remains in the book when on the shelves, is removed at the circulation station when the book is circulated, and is stamped with a due date. The book card is then filed at the circulation desk, usually by due date, and is reslipped into the book when the book is returned to the library and discharged.

If the book card contains the complete due date, including the year, use the book card method of weeding. If the rate of book use is so slow that it would take too long (months or years) to accumulate 400 samples, combining both circulation and in-library use, apply the historical reconstruction method. This method is particularly effective when only one small class of books is being weeded. *If the date due indication lacks the year, use the spine-marking method. If the book cards of books currently being used, either in circulation or in-library, are not available to the weeder, use the historical reconstruction method.* Such a case would be a central library that supplies branches with books but experiences no book use of its own.

The Transaction Card System
of Circulation Control

Most photographic systems fall under this heading. The book cards remain permanently in the book and are not marked with a due date. The book information is recorded on a transaction card and on the user identification card. The due date is shown on the transaction card, which is slipped into the book pocket when the book is charged out. When the book is returned, the transaction card is removed and its transaction number tabulated. If any successive number in a run is missing, it is looked up on the permanent records (photo or computer) in order to reconstruct the book and client information necessary to undertake the overdue procedures.

If the transaction card system controls the circulation, use the spine-marking method for weeding.

The Charge Slip System
of Circulation Control

This system has the client filling out a preprinted form that records all the information needed: the user, the book information, and the date. These slips are frequently filed by classification number and are used to locate a specific book that has been requested and not found on the shelves. Multiple copies of the form permit other filing runs, such as due date, if deemed useful. This is an older system used mostly in research and university libraries, and its usage is decreasing.

If charge slips control circulation, use the spine-marking method of weeding.

Computer Circulation Control

Here the information relating to due date, borrower, and the book is machine-readable and is recorded by a computer. The book information is captured when the computer readable identification number is fed into the computer. The book is discharged by the computer reading the identification number. This enables it to print out lists of overdues and send overdue notices, among other things.

If circulation is controlled by computers, use the computer assisted method of weeding (chapter 13).

Other Circulation Techniques
Permitting Weeding

All of the following accidental or intentional coding of books at the circulation station permits the use of a standard weeding method. If this coding exists, the time lag normally required in some weeding methods can be dramatically reduced and weeding can be accelerated.

1. *Machine charge method with dotting (case I).* Certain charging machines are supplied with a little pen tip which can be color-coded. As each book card is machine charged, in addition to its other functions, the machine applies a small dot on the rear of the book card. *If the color-coded dot has been changed yearly, use the substitute book card method of weeding* (see page 108).

2. *Color-coded due date method.* If the book card method of circulation control is being used, and the year was omitted from the due date stamp but the color of the ink used for the stamp has been changed yearly, use the substitute book card method of weeding, "a special case" (see page 108).

Notes

1. Jeff Selth, Nancy Koller, and Peter Briscoe, "The Use of Books Within the Library," *College and Research Libraries* 53 (May 1992): 197.

2. Robert N. Broadus, "The Measurement of Periodicals Use," *Serials Review* (Summer 1985): 58-59.

10

Method 1:
The Book Card Method

When to Use It

This method can be used only if the following conditions prevail:

1. *The book card method of circulation control has been used.* It is essential that all the circulating volumes in the library that have been charged out have been date-stamped each time they were circulated. This date might appear either on the book card, the book pocket, or a special form permanently attached to the volume.

   Ideally, all books experiencing in-library use should be date-stamped by library personnel before reshelving. While this would improve the validity of the method, the method can be employed even if in-library use data is not available.

2. *All of the dates stamped contain at least the month and the year.* The absence of the *year* makes this method unusable; the absence of the *month* might make it unusable.

Advantages of the Method

The book card method of weeding is an easy, fast, and reliable method of weeding circulating collections. The cut-off date usually can be developed within one hour. In addition, weeding candidates can be selected by nonlibrarians since the only expertise required is the ability to read dates.

Finally, the library can be weeded rapidly. In the field, it has been observed that a motivated worker can examine between 200 to 500 volumes per hour, and select the weeding candidates. However, with no in-library use data, librarians must examine each of the weeding candidates and attempt to determine which volumes might have been used in-library since the cut-date.

Steps to Be Taken Before Weeding

Step 1: Appoint a weeding manager. Since this entire operation should take only a few days, a senior staff member should be permitted to spend full time organizing and supervising the operation.

Step 2: Organize the entire operation. A complete plan should be created, in writing, covering the following tasks:

1. Establish the date or dates that the actual weeding will take place.

2. Schedule the staff or volunteers who will do the work. A group of 10 assistants is sufficient for most medium-sized libraries.

3. Acquire an adequate number of storage boxes to hold the volumes removed from the stacks. Try to estimate the number needed, figuring that between 10 and 30 percent of the volumes are likely to be removed.

4. Acquire tape or string to secure the packed boxes and marking pencils to note their content.

5. If possible, get one book truck for each worker so that there is a convenient place to put the books as they are removed from the shelves.

6. Schedule a person to physically move the books or boxes from the stack area to storage areas. Maintenance personnel can be used for this purpose.

7. Locate and prepare adequate storage space to hold the books removed from the shelves.

8. Have a half-hour training session with all involved personnel before the weeding starts. (See "Instructions for Weeding," page 95.)

9. Announce and publicize the fact that the library will be closed during the weeding period.

10. Schedule a day before the actual weeding for data collection and cut-off point determination.

11. Get 3 x 5-inch cards, two for each shelf involved in the weeding.

12. Get foot stools, tall stools, and short stools so weeders can work sitting down.

Step 3: Test out the system in a trial run. At least one week before the actual weeding, the weeding manager should make a trial run both to create the cut-off point and to identify candidates for weeding. This should work out any kinks or doubts in advance.

Training the Weeding Staff

As advised above, a training session should be set up in advance of the actual weeding. It is good practice to have this session immediately prior to the start of weeding. Following is an example of some weeding instructions the author has used several times:

Instructions for Weeding

1. Weed in a fixed order, from top to bottom and from left to right.

2. Place a 3 x 5-inch card in the middle of a weeded shelf, between two books, clearly visible, to identify that shelf as having been weeded. This is done so that no shelf is unweeded or weeded more than once.

3. The cut-off date is _____. (Insert the cut-off date determined for your library.) Keep all volumes on the shelf that have been used in the following years: _____. (For example, if the weeding takes place in 1997, suppose the cut-off date is 1994. "1994" would appear in the first blank above; the years "1995, 1996, 1997" would appear in the second.) Place on the book truck all volumes *last used* in the year of the cut-off date or earlier.

4. Many cards have the due dates appearing out of chronological order. Search out the date reflecting the most recent use as the criterion for either leaving a book on the shelf or putting it on the book truck. If a Gaylord charging machine is being used, look at all four possible positions to find the most recent date.

5. If a quick glance at a card indicates *any date* listed in 3, above, (1995, 1996, 1997, in the example), the book is to remain on the shelf. It is not necessary to search out the most recent date on the book card.

6. If there is any doubt about whether a book should be retained or removed, keep that volume on the shelf.

7. If a book has no due date appearing on the book card, keep that volume if it seems to be a relatively new book or a book that has been given a new book card in the last five years. Remove undated books from the shelf if dusty, yellowed with age, or containing old-style book cards.

8. Treat duplicate titles as separate works. This means that one might be retained and another weeded out.

9. Keep local authors, gift books, or special books of local subjects if you happen to recognize them. Do not worry about discarding valuable works, since the weeding manager will look at each book before it is discarded.

10. Do not make a subjective judgment about keeping a book because you think the author, subject, or title is important.

11. If you have any serious questions, ask the weeding supervisor.

12. Work as comfortably as possible. The use of different size stools will cut fatigue and increase productivity.

13. Your early selections will be double-checked by the weeding manager, who will give you any additional training you may need.

14. If for any reason you are interrupted in the middle of a shelf, turn the last book observed on its spine so that you can start from where you left off.

The Method Summarized

The book card method ideally consists of taking a sample of 500 books, combining books circulating and books experiencing in-library use, representing the last 500 consecutive uses. If in-library use records are not available, the sample should consist of the last 500 consecutive charge-outs. Then the most recent shelf-time periods are tabulated on the form shown on page 98, one entry for each book. These shelf-time periods are described in terms of "the year of previous use."

A percentage is computed for each year and cumulated, and a table results (see figure 10.1). A reasonable, arbitrary keeping level, say 96 percent, is established and a cut-off point created.

The Method Illustrated

Step 1: Collect 500 book cards representing 500 consecutive uses. Ideally, in those libraries which record the dates of in-library use on the book card, this should be a combination of volumes circulating and those experiencing in-library use.

If in-library use has not been recorded, collect the 500 book cards at the circulation station. Care must be taken to ensure that no book has been reslipped and returned to the shelf before its card was used in the sample. The safest procedure is to remove from the circulation station, each day, all the book cards collected, until the 500 cards have been accumulated.

Step 2: Tabulate all the required data and return the book cards to the circulation desk or reslip the cards into the books from the in-library use sample. The *second most recent year date* appearing on each book card is entered on the form in figure 10.2. Each book card generates only one entry, in the form of a small straight mark in the proper row, under the column entitled "Volumes With This Previous Date Due." The year to be entered is the *second most recent year* shown on the book card. All the book cards have had the current or a future date stamped on them to indicate current in-library use or the date the book is due. Disregard this last date. Take the next most recent date (see figure 10.3 a-c).

(Text continues on page 100.)

Fig. 10.1. Form: summary. Actual size 8½ by 11 inches

BOOK CARD METHOD
(Form for Computing Cut-Date)

Summary of Method (see page 96 for complete details):

1. Collect 500 book cards representing 500 consecutive uses, combining both books being circulated and books having in-library use.
2. Tabulate, below, the second most recent year date on each card.
3. In the column "TOTAL#" enter the total number of cases in each row.
4. Add up the "TOTAL#" column and enter the total at the bottom of the page.
5. Compute the percentage of usage represented by each year. Enter in column headed "TOTAL%."
6. Compute and enter under "CUM.%" the cumulative percentage, starting from the top of the form.
7. Determine the keeping percentage to be used for weeding.
8. Determine the cut-off date to be used for weeding.
9. Remove all books with book cards *not* having dates more recent than the cut-off date.

Date	Volumes With This Previous Date Due	TOTAL		CUM
		#	%	%
1997				
1996	⊞⊞⊞⊞⊞⊞⊞⊞⊞⊞ ⊞⊞⊞⊞⊞⊞⊞⊞⊞⊞ ⊞⊞⊞⊞⊞⊞⊞⊞⊞⊞ ⊞⊞⊞⊞⊞⊞⊞⊞⊞⊞ ⊞⊞⊞⊞⊞⊞⊞⊞⊞⊞ ⊞⊞⊞⊞⊞⊞⊞⊞⊞⊞⊞⊞ ‖‖‖	299	73.5	73.5
1995	⊞⊞⊞⊞⊞⊞⊞⊞⊞⊞⊞ ⊞ ‖‖‖	59	14.5	88
1994	⊞⊞⊞ ‖	16	4	92
1993	⊞⊞⊞ ‖	17	4	96
1992	‖‖‖	4	1	97
1991	‖‖‖	4	1	98
1990	‖	2	.5	98.5
1989	⊞	5	1	99.5
1988	‖	1	.5	100
1987				
Pre 1986				
	Total	407		

Fig. 10.2. Form: blank

BOOK CARD METHOD
(Form for Computing Cut-Date)

Summary of Method (see page 96 for complete details):

1. Collect 500 book cards representing 500 consecutive uses, combining both books being circulated and books having in-library use.
2. Tabulate, below, the second most recent year date on each card.
3. In the column "TOTAL#" enter the total number of cases in each row.
4. Add up the "TOTAL#" column and enter the total at the bottom of the page.
5. Compute the percentage of usage represented by each year. Enter in column headed "TOTAL%."
6. Compute and enter under "CUM.%" the cumulative percentage, starting from the top of the form.
7. Determine the keeping percentage to be used for weeding.
8. Determine the cut-off date to be used for weeding.
9. Remove all books with book cards *not* having dates more recent than the cut-off date.

Date	Volumes With This Previous Date Due	TOTAL		CUM
		#	%	%
1997				
1996				
1995				
1994				
1993				
1992				
1991				
1990				
1989				
1988				
1987				
Pre 1986				
	Total			

*Note: The current year should appear in the top row and earlier years in each successive row.

Fig. 10.3a. Book card.

636.6864/HART

Hart, E.

Budgerigar Handbook

DATE	ISSUED TO
SEP 30 1981	
DEC 29 1987	
AUG 4 1990	
JUN 12 1992	
NOV 29 1996	

CAT. No. 23-115   PRINTED IN U. S. A.

Fig. 10.3b. Book card.

629.45/ALL

Allen, Joseph P.

Entering Space

DATE	ISSUED TO
OCT 8 1992	
JUN 4 1993	
JUL 21 1993	
DEC 3 1994	
FEB 5 1995	
AUG 1 1995	
NOV 29 1996	

CAT. No. 23-115   PRINTED IN U. S. A.

Fig. 10.3c. Book card.

629,47/PEL

Pelligrino, Charles R.

Chariots for Apollo: The

Making of the Lunar Module

DATE	ISSUED TO
SEP 15 1994	
NOV 29 1996	

CAT. No. 23-115   PRINTED IN U. S. A.

In the examples given in figures 10.3 a-c, these cards were removed from the circulation desk on November 1, 1996, and represent books charged out on that day. The library had a four-week loan period. Note that each book card was stamped "Nov 29 1996," showing the current due date for a book now in circulation. This date is to be disregarded, as it measures the end of a shelf-time period, and the next most recent date, which indicates the beginning of that shelf-time period, is entered. The proper tabulation of these book cards is shown in figure 10.4.

If in-library use has been recorded, such books would have been stamped "Nov 1 1996," and again this date should be disregarded and the next most recent date recorded.

Fig. 10.4. Form: step 2.

BOOK CARD METHOD
(Form for Computing Cut-Date)

Summary of Method (see page 96 for complete details):

1. Collect 500 book cards representing 500 consecutive uses, combining both books being circulated and books having in-library use.
2. Tabulate, below, the second most recent year date on each card.
3. In the column "TOTAL#" enter the total number of cases in each row.
4. Add up the "TOTAL#" column and enter the total at the bottom of the page.
5. Compute the percentage of usage represented by each year. Enter in column headed "TOTAL%."
6. Compute and enter under "CUM.%" the cumulative percentage, starting from the top of the form.
7. Determine the keeping percentage to be used for weeding.
8. Determine the cut-off date to be used for weeding.
9. Remove all books with book cards *not* having dates more recent than the cut-off date.

Date	Volumes With This Previous Date Due	TOTAL		CUM
		#	%	%
1997				
1996				
1995	/			
1994	/			
1993				
1992	/			
1991				
1990				
1989				
1988				
1987				
Pre 1986				
	Total			

Note that the first card generates a single mark entered in the line "1992," the second in "1995," and the third in "1994." Continue through the book cards entering all usable data. In this example, taken from an active library, the form now looks like figure 10.5.

Fig. 10.5. Form: step 2A.

BOOK CARD METHOD
(Form for Computing Cut-Date)

Summary of Method (see page 96 for complete details):

1. Collect 500 book cards representing 500 consecutive uses, combining both books being circulated and books having in-library use.
2. Tabulate, below, the second most recent year date on each card.
3. In the column "TOTAL#" enter the total number of cases in each row.
4. Add up the "TOTAL#" column and enter the total at the bottom of the page.
5. Compute the percentage of usage represented by each year. Enter in column headed "TOTAL%."
6. Compute and enter under "CUM.%" the cumulative percentage, starting from the top of the form.
7. Determine the keeping percentage to be used for weeding.
8. Determine the cut-off date to be used for weeding.
9. Remove all books with book cards *not* having dates more recent than the cut-off date.

Date	Volumes With This Previous Date Due	TOTAL #	TOTAL %	CUM %
1997				
1996	ℍℍ ℍℍ ℍℍ ℍℍ ℍℍ ℍℍ ℍℍ ℍℍ ℍℍ ℍℍ (continues for 6 lines of tally marks)			
1995	ℍℍ ℍℍ ℍℍ ℍℍ ℍℍ ℍℍ ℍℍ ℍℍ ℍℍℍℍ ℍℍ ℍℍℍ			
1994	ℍℍ ℍℍ ℍℍ ℍℍ			
1993	ℍℍ ℍℍ ℍℍ ℍℍ			
1992	ℍℍ			
1991	ℍℍ			
1990	ℍℍ			
1989	ℍℍ			
1988	ℍ			
1987				
Pre 1986				
	Total			

Step 3: Total the number of books indicated for each year. Enter each result in the proper row under the column headed "TOTAL #." The form being filled in should now look like figure 10.6. The system using a crossed line for every fifth book makes counting easier. The listing of exactly 50 books in each row serves the same purpose.

In the above example, all volumes last used in 1996, as indicated in the cell headed "Volumes With This Previous Date Due" have been added together, and there were 299 such volumes. The number 299 was entered in the proper column and row. Likewise, the 59 previous uses in 1995 were entered in the same column but the next row. This is continued until all the samples that were recorded in accordance with their shelf-time periods (as expressed in terms of the date of their previous use) have been tallied.

Fig. 10.6. Form: step 3.

BOOK CARD METHOD
(Form for Computing Cut-Date)

Summary of Method (see page 96 for complete details):

1. Collect 500 book cards representing 500 consecutive uses, combining both books being circulated and books having in-library use.
2. Tabulate, below, the second most recent year date on each card.
3. In the column "TOTAL#" enter the total number of cases in each row.
4. Add up the "TOTAL#" column and enter the total at the bottom of the page.
5. Compute the percentage of usage represented by each year. Enter in column headed "TOTAL%."
6. Compute and enter under "CUM.%" the cumulative percentage, starting from the top of the form.
7. Determine the keeping percentage to be used for weeding.
8. Determine the cut-off date to be used for weeding.
9. Remove all books with book cards *not* having dates more recent than the cut-off date.

Date	Volumes With This Previous Date Due	TOTAL #	TOTAL %	CUM %
1997				
1996		299		
1995		59		
1994		16		
1993		17		
1992		4		
1991		4		
1990		2		
1989		5		
1988		1		
1987				
Pre 1986				
Total				

Step 4: Add up the column just tabulated in Step 3. This column represents the total number of books used in the sample. Enter the sum on the bottom line alongside the word "Total." In this case, the number 407 was entered, and the form now looks like figure 10.7.

Fig. 10.7. Form: step 4.

BOOK CARD METHOD
(Form for Computing Cut-Date)

Summary of Method (see page 96 for complete details):

1. Collect 500 book cards representing 500 consecutive uses, combining both books being circulated and books having in-library use.
2. Tabulate, below, the second most recent year date on each card.
3. In the column "TOTAL#" enter the total number of cases in each row.
4. Add up the "TOTAL#" column and enter the total at the bottom of the page.
5. Compute the percentage of usage represented by each year. Enter in column headed "TOTAL%."
6. Compute and enter under "CUM.%" the cumulative percentage, starting from the top of the form.
7. Determine the keeping percentage to be used for weeding.
8. Determine the cut-off date to be used for weeding.
9. Remove all books with book cards *not* having dates more recent than the cut-off date.

Date	Volumes With This Previous Date Due	TOTAL		CUM
		#	%	%
1997				
1996	‖‖ 299		
1995	‖‖ ‖‖ ‖‖ ‖‖ ‖‖ ‖‖ ‖‖ ‖‖ ‖‖ ‖‖ ‖‖ 59	59		
1994	‖‖ ‖‖ ‖‖ / 16	16		
1993	‖‖ ‖‖ ‖‖ // 17	17		
1992	////	4		
1991	////	4		
1990	//	2		
1989	‖‖	5		
1988	/	1		
1987				
Pre 1986				
	Total	407		

Step 5: Compute the percentage of usage represented by each year. This percentage figure should be entered in the column directly to the right of the "TOTAL #" column, and is headed "TOTAL %." To compute the percentage for each year, divide the total number of uses in that year by the total number of books in the entire sample. In figure 10.8, the 299 books for 1996 were divided by the total number of books in the sample, 407. This gave 73.5 percent, figured to the nearest half percent. Repeat the process for each successive year. This produced 14.5 percent for 1995; 4 percent for 1994; etc. Obviously, this computation can be made only for years in which some previous use was recorded on the form.

Fig. 10.8. Form: step 5.

BOOK CARD METHOD
(Form for Computing Cut-Date)

Summary of Method (see page 96 for complete details):

1. Collect 500 book cards representing 500 consecutive uses, combining both books being circulated and books having in-library use.
2. Tabulate, below, the second most recent year date on each card.
3. In the column "TOTAL#" enter the total number of cases in each row.
4. Add up the "TOTAL#" column and enter the total at the bottom of the page.
5. Compute the percentage of usage represented by each year. Enter in column headed "TOTAL%."
6. Compute and enter under "CUM.%" the cumulative percentage, starting from the top of the form.
7. Determine the keeping percentage to be used for weeding.
8. Determine the cut-off date to be used for weeding.
9. Remove all books with book cards *not* having dates more recent than the cut-off date.

Date	Volumes With This Previous Date Due	TOTAL		CUM
		#	%	%
1997				
1996	⫴⫴⫴ ⫴⫴⫴⫴⫴⫴⫴⫴⫴⫴⫴⫴⫴⫴⫴⫴ ⏐⏐⏐	299	73.5	
1995	⫴⫴⫴⫴⫴⫴⫴⫴⫴⫴⫴⫴⫴⫴ ⫴⫴⫴ ⏐⏐⏐⏐	59	14.5	
1994	⫴⫴⫴ ⏐	16	4	
1993	⫴⫴⫴ ⏐⏐	17	4	
1992	⏐⏐⏐⏐	4	1	
1991	⏐⏐⏐⏐	4	1	
1990	⏐⏐	2	.5	
1989	⫴	5	1	
1988	⏐	1	.5	
1987				
Pre 1986				
	Total	407		

Step 6: Compute the cumulative percentage starting from the most recent year. Enter this figure in the column headed "CUM. %." *Cumulative percentage* results from the successive percentages being added together from the top to the bottom of the form. The form now looks like figure 10.9.

Fig. 10.9. Form: step 6.

BOOK CARD METHOD
(Form for Computing Cut-Date)

Summary of Method (see page 96 for complete details):

1. Collect 500 book cards representing 500 consecutive uses, combining both books being circulated and books having in-library use.
2. Tabulate, below, the second most recent year date on each card.
3. In the column "TOTAL#" enter the total number of cases in each row.
4. Add up the "TOTAL#" column and enter the total at the bottom of the page.
5. Compute the percentage of usage represented by each year. Enter in column headed "TOTAL%."
6. Compute and enter under "CUM.%" the cumulative percentage, starting from the top of the form.
7. Determine the keeping percentage to be used for weeding.
8. Determine the cut-off date to be used for weeding.
9. Remove all books with book cards *not* having dates more recent than the cut-off date.

Date	Volumes With This Previous Date Due	TOTAL #	TOTAL %	CUM %
1997				
1996	(tally marks)	299	73.5	73.5
1995	(tally marks)	59	14.5	88
1994	(tally marks)	16	4	92
1993	(tally marks)	17	4	96
1992	(tally marks)	4	1	97
1991	(tally marks)	4	1	98
1990	(tally marks)	2	.5	98.5
1989	(tally marks)	5	1	99.5
1988	(tally marks)	1	.5	100
1987				
Pre 1986				
	Total	407		

In our example, in the row designated "1996," 73.5 percent is carried over from the "TOTAL %" column. Going down one row, the 73.5 percent is added to the 14.5 percent, and 88 percent is written in the "1995" row. For the next year, 4 percent is added to the 88 percent, giving 92 percent, and so forth, until all the percentages have been added together. The total always should equal 100 percent. If, because of rounding, the resultant figure is not 100 percent, cumulate the total number of books, year by year, and recompute the cumulative percentages. Thus, add the 299 books to the 59 books, and divide this new number (358) by the total number of books (407). Enter this percentage in the cumulative percent column. Now add the 16 books in 1994 to the 358 (giving 374) and divide this number by 407. Continue this process until 100 percent of the books have been cumulated and tabulated.

Step 7: Determine the keeping percentage to be used for weeding. This is an arbitrary decision to be made by the librarian, and is discussed at some length in chapter 7. In general, for circulating collections, percentages from 95 to 98 percent have been used successfully by the author. This percentage is the statistically computed percentage of circulation that should be retained after weeding. The higher this percentage, the fewer the number of books that will be weeded. Therefore, it is recommended that the keeping level not exceed 96 percent unless special conditions dictate a higher keeping level. If there is any doubt as to what percentage to select, use 96 percent.

Step 8: Determine the cut-off date to be used for weeding. Run your eye down the "CUM. %" column and draw a line under the box that contains the keeping percentage level just selected in step 7. The form is now in its final condition (see figure 10.10). Now read in the left-hand column the years divided by the line just drawn. This is interpreted as follows: Keep all volumes used last in 1993 or more recently; identify as weeding candidates all volumes used last in 1992 or before. The cut-off point now has been determined—December 31, 1992.

Step 9: In the circulating collection, examine the book card of every book on the shelves and remove all volumes not having dates more recent than the cut-off point date. This is the actual weeding process. One book at a time is removed from the shelf, and the book card is examined carefully. In our example, if the *most recent date* appearing on a book card were 1993 or more recent, the book is replaced on the shelf; if it is 1992 or earlier, the book is removed from the shelf and considered to be a candidate for weeding. It is not necessary to inspect the cards of books in circulation since they *all* have recent dates stamped on their cards. The work of removing the volumes from the shelves can be done by nonlibrarians: clerks, pages, or volunteer workers.

Step 10: Inspect all candidates for weeding and return to the shelves those volumes not to be weeded out. This is a professional job and should be done by the head librarian, or whoever is responsible for building the library collection and maintaining its integrity. Here, judgment is involved. If the in-library use has been recorded, it is axiomatic that the fewer books returned to the shelves the better the collection will be. If in-library use has not been recorded, it is important that librarians attempt to return to the shelves those volumes they judge to have experienced in-library use.

Fig. 10.10. Form: step 8.

BOOK CARD METHOD
(Form for Computing Cut-Date)

Summary of Method (see page 96 for complete details):

1. Collect 500 book cards representing 500 consecutive uses, combining both books being circulated and books having in-library use.
2. Tabulate, below, the second most recent year date on each card.
3. In the column "TOTAL#" enter the total number of cases in each row.
4. Add up the "TOTAL#" column and enter the total at the bottom of the page.
5. Compute the percentage of usage represented by each year. Enter in column headed "TOTAL%."
6. Compute and enter under "CUM.%" the cumulative percentage, starting from the top of the form.
7. Determine the keeping percentage to be used for weeding.
8. Determine the cut-off date to be used for weeding.
9. Remove all books with book cards *not* having dates more recent than the cut-off date.

Date	Volumes With This Previous Date Due	TOTAL		CUM
		#	%	%
1997				
1996	|||| |||| |||| |||| |||| |||| |||| |||| |||| |||| |||| |||| |||| |||| |||| |||| |||| |||| |||| |||| |||| |||| |||| |||| |||| |||| |||| |||| |||| |||| |||| |||| |||| |||| |||| |||| |||| |||| |||| |||| |||| |||| |||| |||| |||| |||| |||| |||| |||| |||| |||| |||| |||| ||||	299	73.5	73.5
1995	|||| |||| |||| |||| |||| |||| |||| |||| |||| |||| |||| ||||	59	14.5	88
1994															16	4	92
1993																17	4	96
1992						4	1	97
1991						4	1	98
1990	||	2	.5	98.5
1989	||||	5	1	99.5
1988			1	.5	100
1987				
Pre 1986				
	Total	407		

The Problem of Book Cards
with No Due Date Indicated

The most serious practical weeding problem relates to the book whose book card has no due date stamped on it. This might involve from 10 to over 50 percent of the book cards. They should be treated as follows:

1. Newly acquired books may not have been given an adequate opportunity to circulate. They should not be weeded if they have been acquired more recently than the cut-off point date. Accession numbers frequently give enough information so that this decision can be made intelligently. Otherwise, a reasonable guess, based upon imprint date, for example, might be in order. If in doubt, do not weed it out, but mark the current date on the book card to prevent a recurrence of the problem on the next weeding.

2. A more serious problem relates to older books with new book cards, usually supplied after rebinding or because the old book card was used up or damaged. Again, some guesswork may be used to judge whether or not the new card was created before or after the cut-off point date. If in doubt, do not weed these volumes out, but date the book cards.

3. Older books with older book cards containing no due dates are easier to handle. This situation normally means that no use was made of the volume since the cut-off date. These books should be considered candidates for weeding. If a real doubt exists, date the book card with the current date and leave it for the next weeding.

Substitute Book Card Method

Certain charging machines apply a small colored dot to the back of the book card when a book is being charged out. If this colored dot has been color-coded so that the year of its application can be decoded, and if the year is missing from the due-date stamp on the book card, the colored dot can be used to create the weeding cut-off point.

Certain extra steps are required for this technique to be of use. The year that any specific color was used must be identified. This often can be done by noting the copyright year of relatively new volumes and noting the successive colors applied to the book card.

Additional Steps

Step 1: Identify the year during which a specific colored dot was being used. A written list should be created showing the results achieved, as follows:

Color Decoding List

Dot Color	Year Represented
Red	1988
Green	1989
Blue	1990
Black	1991
Purple	1992
Yellow	1993
Orange	1994
Pink	1995
Gray	1996

Step 2: Follow weeding steps 1 through 10, just described, using the colored dot as the source of the year of previous circulation. This step makes the entire process more arduous since one must find the most recently applied colored dot on each book card, or the one previous to that. It requires that one refer constantly to the decoding list in order to interpret properly the colored dots. If the colored dots are not in some kind of predetermined order chronologically, this method becomes rather cumbersome.

A Special Case

If the due-date stamp color has been changed yearly but no year was stamped on the book card, use the above method substituting the colored due-date stamp for the colored dot.

The Simplified
Book Card Method of Weeding

The simplified book card method of weeding is recommended to weeders who feel comfortable with mathematical computation. It involves one basic change in the normal book card method of weeding described earlier in this chapter. It replaces tabulating steps 2, 3, 4, 5, and 6 with a mechanical operation. This is the major modification of the regular method.

The method uncovers the cut-off point without the use of the form (see figure 10.2) recommended in the earlier method. Instead it arranges the book cards in chronological order, using the previous due date for this purpose, and selects the one card containing the relevant cut-off date. For instance, if the collection were to be weeded at the 96 percent keeping level, the proper card is located as follows: If there were 400 cards in the sample, the card containing the 384th oldest pervious due date would produce the 96 percent keeping-date (multiply 400 by 96 percent). The 385th card contains the cut-off date.

Step 1: Collect 500 book cards representing 500 consecutive uses, as described in Step 1, page 96.

Step 2: Determine the keeping percentage to be used for weeding, as in Step 7, page 106. For purposes of this example, 96 percent will be used.

Step 3: Convert the keeping percentage into the weeding loss percentage. This is done by subtracting the keeping percentage from 100 percent. In the example, 100 percent minus 96 percent equals 4 percent.

Step 4: Multiply the number of cards in the sample by the weeding loss percentage selected. In the example used earlier in this chapter (see figure 10.11), there were 407 useful samples. Multiply this number by 4 percent and round to the nearest whole number. This gives 16.

Step 5: Sort the book cards into piles by year of previous use (as above), in reverse chronological order: the most current year first, the second most recent year next, etc. In the example used, there would be 299 cards in the first pile representing 1996, 59 for 1995 in the second, 16 for 1994 in the third, etc. (see figure 10.11).

Step 6: Select the pile containing the card showing the cut-off date. In the example, the card containing the sixteenth oldest previous due date should be located. That card is in the pile representing the 1992 uses.

Step 7: Take this pile of cards and put them in reverse chronological order by year of previous use. In the example, those four cards contained the following dates and were put in this order:

Dec 11, 1992

Sept 4, 1992

June 12, 1992

Jan 23, 1992

Step 8: Select the card containing the cut-off date. There were 12 cards with dates older than 1992. Jan 23, 1992 was the thirteenth oldest, June 12, 1992 the fourteenth, etc.

Dates Found	Chronological # from Oldest
Dec 11, 1992	16th
Sept 4, 1992	15th
June 12, 1992	14th
Jan 23, 1992	13th

The cut-off date becomes Dec. 11, 1992

Step 9: Weed the collection keeping any volume used since the cut-off date, and removing all volumes used last on the cut-off date or before. In the example, keep all volumes used Dec 12, 1992 or more recently, and remove from the shelves those last used Dec 11, 1992 or earlier.

Step 10: Inspect all candidates for weeding and return to the shelves those volumes not to be weeded out, as in step 10, page 106.

Fig. 10.11. Form: summary.

BOOK CARD METHOD
(Form for Computing Cut-Date)

Summary of Method (see page 96 for complete details):

1. Collect 500 book cards representing 500 consecutive uses, combining both books being circulated and books having in-library use.
2. Tabulate, below, the second most recent year date on each card.
3. In the column "TOTAL#" enter the total number of cases in each row.
4. Add up the "TOTAL#" column and enter the total at the bottom of the page.
5. Compute the percentage of usage represented by each year. Enter in column headed "TOTAL%."
6. Compute and enter under "CUM.%" the cumulative percentage, starting from the top of the form.
7. Determine the keeping percentage to be used for weeding.
8. Determine the cut-off date to be used for weeding.
9. Remove all books with book cards *not* having dates more recent than the cut-off date.

Date	Volumes With This Previous Date Due	TOTAL #	TOTAL %	CUM %
1997				
1996	(tally marks)	299	73.5	73.5
1995	(tally marks)	59	14.5	88
1994	(tally marks)	16	4	92
1993	(tally marks)	17	4	96
1992	////	4	1	97
1991	////	4	1	98
1990	//	2	.5	98.5
1989	/////	5	1	99.5
1988	/	1	.5	100
1987				
Pre 1986				
Total		407		

Methods to Improve
Future Weeding

Present procedures in the library frequently make use of the book card method of weeding less reliable than it could be. It is suggested that all libraries using the book card method of circulation control augment the present procedures with the following:

1. All new books should have an initial date stamped on the book card when the book is being processed. Ideally this should be the date the book is shelved. This gives a starting date to assist in measuring the shelf-time period, and prevents the weeding of a newer book that hasn't had a chance to circulate.

2. Whenever books are rebound and new book cards are inserted, the date of last use should be brought forward from the old card to the new one.

3. Whenever a book card is replaced because there is no more room on it for new due dates (or for any other reason), the date of last use should be carried forward as the first entry on the new card.

4. When books are returned to the library after being long overdue, the date of reshelving ought to be entered on the book card. This prevents a book that had no chance to circulate from being weeded prematurely.

5. When books have been held in the librarian's office or taken out of normal use by the staff, the date of shelving the book in publicly accessible places should be added to the book card.

6. The book cards of all books experiencing in-library use should be date marked to indicate such usage. Patrons should be prohibited from reshelving books used in the library.

7. Due dates should be stamped on book cards in chronological order instead of in random order so that the most recent activity can be identified easily.

Some Theory:
Current Circulation Patterns
vs. Long-Range Circulation Patterns

The book card method of weeding has been based, in part, upon an assumption some people find difficult to accept—that the patterns of circulation do not change significantly over a long period of time. It further assumes that a sample of the circulation taken for a week, more or less, has the same shelf-time period characteristics as a sample taken over 5 or even 10 years. It assumes that such shelf-time characteristics will remain unchanged in the future.

All of these assumptions have been tested carefully, and there is strong evidence that they are valid. They have been reported upon elsewhere in this volume. A study was made by the author in Larchmont, New York, to test long-term and short-term shelf-time characteristics. Table 10.1 shows the result of this study.

Table 10.1.
Current Shelf-Time Periods vs. Long-Term Shelf-Time Periods

Shelf-Time Period Under	Cumulative % of Use Having This Shelf-Time Period	
	Source: 1 week's current circulation	*Source: Last 10 years of circulation*
2 years	96%	95%
3 years	98%	97%
4 years	99%	99%
5 years	99%	99%
6 years	99%	99%
7 years	99%	100%
8 years	100%	
9 years	100%	
10 years	100%	

The percentage differences reflected in the chart are statistically insignificant. It can be assumed that a sample of circulation in the Larchmont Library, taken over a current one-week period, has the same shelf-time period characteristics as a sample taken over 10 years.

11

Method 2:
The Spine-Marking Method

When to Use It

The spine-marking method should be used only when other methods cannot be used, for it involves a substantial time lag before weeding can be undertaken. It is the method of last resort. The other methods use information already created and recorded. The spine-marking method starts to create the needed data only on the day it is put into effect. In this respect, it must continue to be applied until a *weeding signal* is received—a period of time that could extend from a minimum of one year to a practical maximum of 5 or even 10 years. This method should be used only where no history of book use has been recorded.

Advantages of the Method

This method is applicable to some of the volumes in *every* library. In every library, no matter what systems are in effect, part of the usage tends to go unrecorded, or if recorded, such records are not usable for weeding purposes. At the least, the unrecorded usage normally includes the in-library usage by both the clients and the staff.

There are a number of other advantages to the method:

1. *The spine marking method can be used to assist in weeding at any time,* even before a weeding signal is received. This is due to the fact that a spine-marked volume is automatically a member of the core collection and should never be considered for weeding. This reduces the number of volumes that have to be considered as likely weeding candidates, even if subjective weeding criteria are to be applied.

2. *The actual weeding itself can be done more rapidly than by any other method known.* While the wait for the ultimate weeding signal may be long, once it is received things move very rapidly. One merely removes all volumes lacking a spine mark.

3. *The weeding itself is a low-cost operation.* This work can be done by untrained volunteers or any other form of low-cost labor—a considerable asset in these times of financial belt-tightening.

4. *The spine mark can be a potent tool to assist in the acquisition of books.* As the spine-marking process proceeds, it becomes apparent that in some segments of the collection many volumes are spine-marked, and in other segments very few volumes are. By focusing acquisition efforts in the most heavily marked areas, substantial usage for new acquisitions is assured, and as far as client satisfaction is concerned the library optimizes the money it has spent for books. The spine-marking technique can become a major tool for creating a library where the classes of volumes held are numerically proportionate to the relative use of those classes.

5. *Spine-marking permits an ongoing weeding procedure* that can be built into the normal, long-term routines of the library, and with relatively little thought or effort weeding can be done on a continuing basis. By changing the color of the dots used for spine-marking (dotting over old dots is suggested), one can start setting up a new shelf-time period as soon as the previous weeding operation has been completed. Since books move constantly from the core to the noncore collection, this continuous weeding will keep the collection vital and fresh.

6. *The spine-marking procedure is simple, and of the methods recommended it involves the least amount of mathematical computation or manipulation of the data.*

Steps to Be Taken Before Weeding

Step 1: Appoint a weeding manager. This operation may take from one to perhaps five or more years, so the manager should be a senior staff member likely to be around for that period of time.

Step 2: Organize the entire operation. A complete plan should be created, in writing, covering the following points:

1. Establish the date on which the weeding procedure will be started.

2. Establish reporting forms to assure that all people involved are cooperating. Reports on numbers of books dotted each day might help encourage such cooperation. Those involved are all the people who charge out volumes, process books, and reshelve books, and all library personnel using books in the library. Practically all people working for the library are involved in one way or another.

3. Schedule and hold training sessions with each group of workers, defining their tasks as follows:

   Clerks at circulation stations: Spine-mark all undotted books as they are charged out. Tabulate the number of books dotted and undotted monthly, or as scheduled.

   Clerks discharging books: Spine-mark all books which are undotted and are being returned after circulating.

Shelving clerks: Before reshelving, spine-mark all undotted volumes. These are the books that have just been discharged or have experienced in-library use.

Personnel processing new acquisitions: All new books are to be spine-marked before being shelved for the first time.

All other personnel: Spine-mark all volumes you have used and are reshelving. Reference librarians must tabulate monthly the data relating to volumes dotted or undotted in order to recognize the weeding signal.

4. *Procure all supplies and forms needed.* These include enough Avery self-adhering dots to spine-mark every book in the library twice. One-quarter inch dots, all of one color, have been used successfully. Also, produce 50 to 100 sets of the two forms shown on pages 134 and 136.

5. *Supply dots to all library personnel using them.*

6. *Notify the library's patrons as to what is happening and instruct them not to reshelve volumes used in the library.* Signs and publicity help, but the library staff must be prepared to supervise and enforce this new rule.

7. *Organize the weeding operation when the weeding signal is received.* Follow the suggestions listed in step 2 for the book card method of weeding (pages 96-101).

Step 3: Pretest the various procedures recommended in the step-by-step descriptions. The weeding manager should perform each operation personally, until familiar and comfortable with each step. Make sure no major hitches arise, that all kinks and doubts have been worked out, and that each step is understood.

Training the Personnel Involved

Instructions for Weeding

In order to assist in the training of personnel, the following instructions should be included in the recommended training sessions:

1. For every volume used, apply two small dots to the book's spine, one inch from the bottom edge of the book. (This location should be changed if necessary so that call numbers are not obscured.) If the book has been dotted previously, do not add dots. For all circulating books, the dotting should take place at the charge-out station, at the discharge station, and when the book is being reshelved. This triple procedure is used to make sure that the book does not slip through unmarked.

2. All volumes added to the collection should be spine-marked before they are shelved. This prevents new additions from being weeded before being used.

3. For books that have experienced in-library use:

   a. Clients should not reshelve them. Clerks should spine-mark them before placing them back on the shelves.

   b. Reference works used only by the staff (such as ready-reference works) should be spine-marked by the user before they are returned to the shelves.

4. If volumes are rebound, the spine-marking indication should be carried forward to the new binding. If such volumes have no spine mark on them, they should be left unmarked. (It is very likely that books not spine-marked should not be rebound.)

5. A program should be undertaken to make sure that clients do not remove the spine mark. Explain what is going on, what the dots mean, and their importance. Watch out for young children who might think that these dots were put on the books for their personal pleasure and who like to remove such dots.

6. Make sure that all volumes used are spine-marked. Carelessness in this activity will result in weeding out the very books that should be retained. Supervisors should check daily to make sure that the work is being done. When the routine is firmly established, monthly checks should still be made.

7. Overdue books, books kept out for very long periods of time (say all summer), books kept in staff offices, and other books not permitted to circulate normally should be spine-marked before shelving as if they were new acquisitions.

The Method Summarized

The spine-marking method measures and records the shelf-time period characteristics of that part of the collection being used. It involves applying two self-adhesive dots to the spine of each volume used. The spine mark establishes the beginning of a shelf-time period, which is then used to determine when weeding should occur.

If, for instance, after applying these dots for one year every subsequent volume used by library clients had been previously dotted, there would have been created a shelf-time period of one year, which would represent 100 percent of current usage. All of the volumes enjoying current use must have been dotted previously sometime during the last year, since that is when the dotting was being done. If one now removed all undotted volumes from the shelves, *100 percent* of all future usage will be retained by the remaining core collection.

In actual practice, the 100 percent keeping level is too high to result in substantial weeding. Therefore, as discussed elsewhere, some lower level is selected. Thus for example, when 96 percent (or whatever other level has been predetermined) of the volumes being used have been previously dotted, the weeding signal has been received and all undotted volumes on the shelves are weeded.

The Method Illustrated

The library may be weeded as one entity or weeded by class, and step-by-step instructions follow for both approaches. Ideally, all books experiencing use should be spine-marked before being reshelved, whether this use was in-library or a circulating use. However, the suggested methods still can be used if in-library use has not been indicated. Using the cut-point established at circulation will likely identify 20 percent to 30 percent of the volumes in the library as weeding candidates, and only those volumes need to be inspected by the weeder. If in-library use has not been recorded, the weeder must attempt to return to the collection, those volumes likely to have experienced recent in-library use.

The Procedure When Weeding the Library as an Entity

Step 1: Apply two self-adhering dots to the spine of every volume not already dotted as it circulates and, before reshelving, to every undotted volume experiencing in-library use. Since the dots tend to fall off, some materials with stronger glues have been used. One library is using cut-up colored library binding tape with considerable success. Only one set of dots is required on each volume, so that the dotting process becomes one of decreasing effort as time passes. For instance, on the first day all volumes experiencing use must be dotted. A few months later perhaps only half have to be dotted, since the rest were previously dotted. At one year, perhaps 90 percent are already dotted, so only the remaining 10 percent must be dotted. And just before the 96 percent weeding signal is received, only 4 percent of the volumes need be dotted.

The two dots are placed in a standardized, predetermined position, such as "centered on the spine, one-half inch from the bottom edge," as shown below:

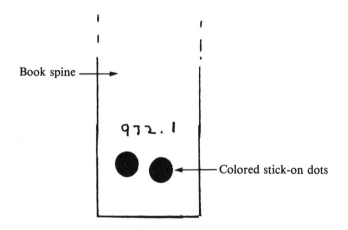

Make sure that the dots do not obscure the classification number. Two dots are used to improve the reliability and security of the system, that is, to prevent the loss of information in case one of the dots should fall off or be removed.

Step 2: If a volume is not already dotted, apply two dots to its spine as it comes back from the client. This step has two purposes. In the early stages of the procedure, it dots volumes which were out and are undotted because the spine-marking method had not yet begun. This speeds up the process somewhat. Second, and more importantly, it is a double check—to make sure that the books did not pass through the charge-out station without being dotted, or that dots have not fallen off or been removed. If step 1 has been applied rigorously, this second step will involve very few volumes after the first month.

Step 3: If the volume is not already dotted, apply two dots to the spine of each volume being reshelved. This is a triple check, since the volumes have been processed previously upon being charged and discharged. This step is essential if the core collection is to be identified properly. It is important that core-collection volumes are not weeded out because of careless spine-marking.

Step 4: One year after the dotting has been started, and monthly thereafter, tabulate whether the books being charged out have been previously dotted or not. Use the form in figure 11.1.

This is the basic information taken to establish the cut-off point used for weeding. It is essential that this be done carefully and regularly. The tabulation should consist of the books being charged out at all circulation stations and the books being reshelved after in-library use. The data indicate whether or not a volume has been dotted prior to this current use. The one-year waiting period has been chosen to prevent seasonal books from being weeded prematurely.

At this stage enter the information from 100 books, consecutively used, combining books circulating with those experiencing in-library use. After the tabulation, the form could look something like figure 11.2.

Fig. 11.1. Form: step 4.

SPINE-MARKING METHOD
(Form One: For Recognizing the Weeding Signal)

Summary of Method (see page 117 for complete details):

1. Apply two stick-on dots to the spine of every volume as it circulates, and every volume used in the library before reshelving, if not already dotted.
2. After one year of applying dots, tabulate, below, books being checked out and the books used in the library being reshelved, as having been previously "Dotted" or "Undotted."
3. Enter the "Total" number for each of these categories.
4. Enter these "Totals" on Form Two.

Class	Dotted	Total	Undotted	Total

Fig. 11.2. Form: step 4A.

SPINE-MARKING METHOD
(Form One: For Recognizing the Weeding Signal)

Summary of Method (see page 117 for complete details):

1. Apply two stick-on dots to the spine of every volume as it circulates, and every volume used in the library before reshelving, if not already dotted.
2. After one year of applying dots, tabulate, below, books being checked out and the books used in the library being reshelved, as having been previously "Dotted" or "Undotted."
3. Enter the "Total" number for each of these categories.
4. Enter these "Totals" on Form Two.

Class	Dotted	Total	Undotted	Total
Entire Collection	┼╫ ╫╫ ╫╫ ╫╫ ╫╫ ╫╫ ╫╫ ╫╫ ╫╫ ╫╫ ╫╫ ╫╫ ╫╫ ╫╫ |||		╫╫ ╫╫ ╫╫ ╫╫ ╫╫ ||	

Step 5: Add up the number of samples identified as "dotted" and "undotted," and enter the totals in the relevant columns. Here, 73 books had been previously dotted, 27 had not. See figure 11.3.

Fig. 11.3. Form: step 5.

SPINE-MARKING METHOD
(Form One: For Recognizing the Weeding Signal)

Summary of Method (see page 117 for complete details):

1. Apply two stick-on dots to the spine of every volume as it circulates, and every volume used in the library before reshelving, if not already dotted.

2. After one year of applying dots, tabulate, below, books being checked out and the books used in the library being reshelved, as having been previously "Dotted" or "Undotted."

3. Enter the "Total" number for each of these categories.

4. Enter these "Totals" on Form Two.

Class	Dotted	Total	Undotted	Total
Entire Collection	₩₩ ₩₩ ₩₩ ₩₩ ₩₩ ₩₩ ₩₩ ₩₩ ₩₩ ₩₩ ₩₩ ₩₩ ₩₩ ₩₩ III	73	₩₩ ₩₩ ₩₩ ₩₩ ₩₩ II	27

Step 6: Enter these totals on the new form in figure 11.4.

Fig. 11.4. Form: step 6.

SPINE-MARKING METHOD
(Form Two: For Recognizing the Weeding Signal)

Summary of Method (see page 117 for complete details):

1. Enter the totals from Form One, below.
2. Add the two totals together and enter under "Total Book Use."
3. Compute the percentage of volumes that were previously "Dotted."
4. Determine the "keeping percentage" (normally between 95 and 98%).
5. When that percentage is reached, remove all "Undotted" books from the collection.

Classification	Total Book Use	Total No. Dotted	Total No. Undotted	% Dotted
Entire Collection		*73*	*27*	

Step 7: Add these two totals together and enter on the form in the column headed "Total Book Use." The result (100) is shown in figure 11.5.

Fig. 11.5. Form: step 7.

SPINE-MARKING METHOD
(Form Two: For Recognizing the Weeding Signal)

Summary of Method (see page 117 for complete details):

1. Enter the totals from Form One, below.
2. Add the two totals together and enter under "Total Book Use."
3. Compute the percentage of volumes that were previously "Dotted."
4. Determine the "keeping percentage" (normally between 95 and 98%).
5. When that percentage is reached, remove all "Undotted" books from the collection.

Classification	Total Book Use	Total No. Dotted	Total No. Undotted	% Dotted
Entire Collection	100	73	27	

Step 8: Compute the percentage of volumes dotted and enter in the column heading "% Dotted." The computation is made by dividing the "Total No. Dotted" (73) by the "Total Book Use" (100). In this case, the result is 73 percent. The completed form should look like figure 11.6.

Fig. 11.6. Form: step 8.

SPINE-MARKING METHOD
(Form Two: For Recognizing the Weeding Signal)

Summary of Method (see page 117 for complete details):
1. Enter the totals from Form One, below.
2. Add the two totals together and enter under "Total Book Use."
3. Compute the percentage of volumes that were previously "Dotted."
4. Determine the "keeping percentage" (normally between 95 and 98%).
5. When that percentage is reached, remove all "Undotted" books from the collection.

Classification	Total Book Use	Total No. Dotted	Total No. Undotted	% Dotted
Entire Collection	100	73	27	73%

Step 9: Determine the keeping percentage to be used for weeding. This is an arbitrary decision to be made by the librarian, and is discussed at some length in chapter 7. In general, for circulating collections, percentages from 95 to 98 percent have been used successfully by the author. This percentage is the statistically computed percentage of circulation that should be retained after weeding. The higher this percentage, the fewer the number of books that will be weeded. Therefore, it is recommended that the keeping level not exceed 96 percent unless special conditions dictate a higher keeping level. If there is any doubt as to what percentage to select, use 96 percent.

Step 10: Continue to tabulate the data created by 100 consecutive circulations, once each month. During this tabulation period, continue the regular dotting procedures. These are not suspended until the weeding has been completed. When the 96 percent level is reached, go to step 11.

Step 11: When the 96 percent keeping level (or whatever other level was determined in step 9) is reached, tabulate the data from the next 400 consecutive circulations. When the weeding signal is received, your two forms should look like figures 11.7 and 11.8. If 400 cases do not produce the 96 percent or higher figure, wait one month and tabulate 400 cases again. Repeat this tabulating until the 96 percent keeping level is reached.

Fig. 11.7. Form: step 11A.

SPINE-MARKING METHOD
(Form One: For Recognizing the Weeding Signal)

Summary of Method (see page 117 for complete details):

1. Apply two stick-on dots to the spine of every volume as it circulates, and every volume used in the library before reshelving, if not already dotted.
2. After one year of applying dots, tabulate, below, books being checked out and the books used in the library being reshelved, as having been previously "Dotted" or "Undotted."
3. Enter the "Total" number for each of these categories.
4. Enter these "Totals" on Form Two.

Class	Dotted	Total	Undotted	Total
Entire Collection	(tally marks)	384	(tally marks)	16

Fig. 11.8. Form: step 11B.

SPINE-MARKING METHOD
(Form Two: For Recognizing the Weeding Signal)

Summary of Method (see page 117 for complete details):
1. Enter the totals from Form One, below.
2. Add the two totals together and enter under "Total Book Use."
3. Compute the percentage of volumes that were previously "Dotted."
4. Determine the "keeping percentage" (normally between 95 and 98%).
5. When that percentage is reached, remove all "Undotted" books from the collection.

Classification	Total Book Use	Total No. Dotted	Total No. Undotted	% Dotted
Entire Collection	400	384	16	96

Step 12: Go through the entire circulating collection and remove all undotted volumes from the shelves. This is the actual weeding process. You have removed the noncore volumes, all of which are candidates for weeding. The volumes remaining on the shelves after weeding will retain 96 percent or more of the current use. The volumes currently in circulation need not be checked or examined because all of them have been dotted.

This work can be done by nonlibrarians.

Step 13: Inspect all candidates for weeding and return to the shelves those volumes not to be weeded out. This is a professional job and should be done by the head librarian, the acquisitions librarian, or whoever is responsible for building the library collection and maintaining its integrity. Here, judgment is involved. If the in-library use has been recorded, it is axiomatic that the fewer books returned to the shelves the better the collection will be. If in-library use has not been recorded, it is important that librarians attempt to return to the shelves those volumes they judge to have experienced recent in-library use.

The Procedure for Weeding the Library by Class

In this case, the identical procedures, steps 1 through 13 above, are followed, with the modifications described below.

Modification 1: The form for identifying whether books are dotted or undotted is modified to identify the classes to be weeded. See figure 11.9. This example relates to a library using the Dewey Classification notation with certain arbitrary classes added: biographies, mysteries, science fiction, paperbacks. Any kind of logical classification is workable. Some that have been used in the field include fiction and nonfiction, adult and children's collections, and classes by type of material—books, CDs, periodicals, cassettes, etc.

Modification 2: Instead of 100 samples being recorded monthly, an attempt should be made to tabulate 100 samples for each class. However, if an early strong indication exists to show that more time is needed to reach 96 percent, fewer samples are acceptable. Figures 11.10 and 11.11 show actual data signaling that 96 percent is some months off, and further data collection can be put off for another month. The one exception is in class 400-499, where further tabulation should be continued at this time.

Modification 3: Continue the spine-marking procedure until all classes to be weeded have been weeded. When weeding the library as one entity, the first spine-marking process stops when the library is weeded. If spine-marking is continued in order to establish a new shelf-time period for the next weeding, the color of the dots is changed. In weeding by class, continue dotting with the same color until the last class is weeded. Since, after weeding a class, all volumes of that class are already dotted, the dotting task becomes progressively easier to perform.

Modification 4: When the weeding signal is received for any class, be sure to weed only that class. Figure 11.12 shows an actual result where three classes are ready to be weeded at the 95 percent level, although 400 samples should be obtained for each of these three classes.

(Text continues on page 133.)

Fig. 11.9. Form: M-1.

SPINE-MARKING METHOD
(Form One: For Recognizing the Weeding Signal)

Summary of Method (see page 117 for complete details):

1. Apply two stick-on dots to the spine of every volume as it circulates, and every volume used in the library before reshelving, if not already dotted.

2. After one year of applying dots, tabulate, below, books being checked out and the books used in the library being reshelved, as having been previously "Dotted" or "Undotted."

3. Enter the "Total" number for each of these categories.

4. Enter these "Totals" on Form Two.

Class	Dotted	Total	Undotted	Total
Fiction				
Mysteries				
Science Fiction				
Paper-backs				
000-99				
100-199				
200-299				
300-399				
400-499				
500-599				
600-699				
700-799				
800-899				
900-999				
Biogs				

Fig. 11.10. Form: M-2A.

SPINE-MARKING METHOD
(Form One: For Recognizing the Weeding Signal)

Summary of Method (see page 117 for complete details):

1. Apply two stick-on dots to the spine of every volume as it circulates, and every volume used in the library before reshelving, if not already dotted.

2. After one year of applying dots, tabulate, below, books being checked out and the books used in the library being reshelved, as having been previously "Dotted" or "Undotted."

3. Enter the "Total" number for each of these categories.

4. Enter these "Totals" on Form Two.

Class	Dotted	Total	Undotted	Total
Fiction		240		37
Mysteries				
Science Fiction				
Paper-backs		32		12
000-99		6		1
100-199		10		4
200-299		2		1
300-399		45		21
400-499		3		0
500-599		11		8
600-699		29		13
700-799		30		17
800-899		17		16
900-999		22		19
Biogs		12		4

Fig. 11.11. Form: M-2B.

SPINE-MARKING METHOD
(Form Two: For Recognizing the Weeding Signal)

Summary of Method (see page 117 for complete details):

1. Enter the totals from Form One, below.
2. Add the two totals together and enter under "Total Book Use."
3. Compute the percentage of volumes that were previously "Dotted."
4. Determine the "keeping percentage" (normally between 95 and 98%).
5. When that percentage is reached, remove all "Undotted" books from the collection.

Classification	Total Book Use	Total No. Dotted	Total No. Undotted	% Dotted
Fiction	277	240	37	89
Mysteries				
Science Fiction				
Paperbacks	44	32	12	73
000-99	7	6	1	86
100-199	14	10	4	71
200-299	3	2	1	67
300-399	66	45	21	68
400-499	3	3	0	100
500-599	19	11	8	58
600-699	42	29	13	69
700-799	47	30	17	64
800-899	33	17	16	52
900-999	41	22	19	54
Biographies	16	12	4	75
Total	612	459	153	75

Fig. 11.12. Form: M-2C.

SPINE-MARKING METHOD
(Form Two: For Recognizing the Weeding Signal)

Summary of Method (see page 117 for complete details):

1. Enter the totals from Form One, below.
2. Add the two totals together and enter under "Total Book Use."
3. Compute the percentage of volumes that were previously "Dotted."
4. Determine the "keeping percentage" (normally between 95 and 98%).
5. When that percentage is reached, remove all "Undotted" books from the collection.

Classification	Total Book Use	Total No. Dotted	Total No. Undotted	% Dotted	
Fiction	272	259	13	95	←
Mysteries	50	45	5	89	
Science Fiction					
Paperbacks	29	26	3	90	
000-99	3	2	1	67	
100-199	9	9	0	100	←
200-299	4	3	1	75	
300-399	42	34	8	81	
400-499	3	1	2	33	
500-599	14	12	2	86	
600-699	39	37	2	95	←
700-799	58	46	12	79	
800-899	72	59	13	82	
900-999	20	16	4	80	
Biographies	16	14	2	88	
Total	631	563	68	89	

Forms Used for the
Spine-Marking Method

Blank forms for reproduction begin on page 134.

SPINE-MARKING METHOD
(Form One: For Recognizing the Weeding Signal)

Summary of Method (see page 117 for complete details):

1. Apply two stick-on dots to the spine of every volume as it circulates, and every volume used in the library before reshelving, if not already dotted.
2. After one year of applying dots, tabulate, below, books being checked out and the books used in the library being reshelved, as having been previously "Dotted" or "Undotted."
3. Enter the "Total" number for each of these categories.
4. Enter these "Totals" on Form Two.

Class	Dotted	Total	Undotted	Total

SPINE-MARKING METHOD
(Form One: For Recognizing the Weeding Signal)

Summary of Method (see page 117 for complete details):

1. Apply two stick-on dots to the spine of every volume as it circulates, and every volume used in the library before reshelving, if not already dotted.
2. After one year of applying dots, tabulate, below, books being checked out and the books used in the library being reshelved, as having been previously "Dotted" or "Undotted."
3. Enter the "Total" number for each of these categories.
4. Enter these "Totals" on Form Two.

Class	Dotted	Total	Undotted	Total

SPINE-MARKING METHOD
(Form Two: For Recognizing the Weeding Signal)

Summary of Method (see page 117 for complete details):

1. Enter the totals from Form One, below.
2. Add the two totals together and enter under "Total Book Use."
3. Compute the percentage of volumes that were previously "Dotted."
4. Determine the "keeping percentage" (normally between 95 and 98%).
5. When that percentage is reached, remove all "Undotted" books from the collection.

Classification	Total Book Use	Total No. Dotted	Total No. Undotted	% Dotted

SPINE-MARKING METHOD
(Form One: For Recognizing the Weeding Signal)

Summary of Method (see page 117 for complete details):

1. Apply two stick-on dots to the spine of every volume as it circulates, and every volume used in the library before reshelving, if not already dotted.
2. After one year of applying dots, tabulate, below, books being checked out and the books used in the library being reshelved, as having been previously "Dotted" or "Undotted."
3. Enter the "Total" number for each of these categories.
4. Enter these "Totals" on Form Two.

Class	Dotted	Total	Undotted	Total
Fiction				
Mysteries				
Science Fiction				
Paper-backs				
000-99				
100-199				
200-299				
300-399				
400-499				
500-599				
600-699				
700-799				
800-899				
900-999				
Biogs				

SPINE-MARKING METHOD
(Form Two: For Recognizing the Weeding Signal)

Summary of Method (see page 117 for complete details):

1. Enter the totals from Form One, below.
2. Add the two totals together and enter under "Total Book Use."
3. Compute the percentage of volumes that were previously "Dotted."
4. Determine the "keeping percentage" (normally between 95 and 98%).
5. When that percentage is reached, remove all "Undotted" books from the collection.

Classification	Total Book Use	Total No. Dotted	Total No. Undotted	% Dotted
Fiction				
Mysteries				
Science Fiction				
Paperbacks				
000-99				
100-199				
200-299				
300-399				
400-499				
500-599				
600-699				
700-799				
800-899				
900-999				
Biographies				
Total				

Method 3: The Historical Reconstruction Method

When to Use It

This method can be used only when the book card method of circulation control is in effect, with the year of each use indicated. Ideally, both circulation use and in-library use should have been recorded. But if just circulation use has been recorded, this system may still be used. Since this also is true for the book card method of weeding, the historical reconstruction method can be used in place of the book card method. However, the book card method and the spine-marking method are preferred for at least 99 percent of libraries. Yet there are two situations in which the historical reconstruction method becomes the preferred method.

Situation 1: The two previous methods of weeding are applicable when the library can observe and record the current use being made of its resources. However, there are cases in which a major collection is used only as a feeder for local libraries. The use occurs at some distance from the main collection, and the central staff doing the weeding does not have ready access to current use records.

An example of a feeder library is the Bruce County Public Library in Port Elgin, Ontario. It is a central distribution library whose primary function is to stock branch libraries; the central library has no circulation of its own independent of the branches. The Bruce Library purchases books and distributes them to 21 branches and two deposit stations. Selected books are exchanged by the branches three or four times a year. In this situation, the historical reconstruction method is the best one available to determine candidates for weeding.

Situation 2: Another situation exists in which libraries are very small or have very little activity in the class of books to be weeded. The number of uses per day may be so few that a sample of 400 might take months to accumulate. For example, if in a preselected class of books only two uses occur per day, it would take 200 days to get a sample of 400, and the weeding would be delayed.

Advantages of the Method

1. *The historical reconstruction method might save time.* In the case of very little daily book use, no waiting time is required to accumulate 400 uses.

2. *In some cases, it is the only practical method available.* This is true for feeder libraries whose only clients are other libraries.

3. *It is a very complete method.* The book cards, theoretically, contain the entire use history of the volumes held by the library, and this is what is being sampled. While the book card method of weeding studies only a relatively few days of circulation to predict future use, this method looks at the entire history of past use, or at least the last 10 years of such use.

Steps to Be Taken
Before Weeding

Step 1: Appoint a weeding manager. Since this entire operation should take only a few days, a senior staff member should be permitted to spend full time organizing and supervising the operation.

Step 2: Organize the entire operation. A complete plan should be created, in writing, covering the following tasks:

Establish the date or dates that the actual weeding will take place.

Schedule the staff or volunteers who will do the work. A group of 10 assistants is sufficient for most libraries.

Acquire an adequate number of storage boxes to hold the volumes removed from the stacks. Try to estimate the number needed, figuring that between 10 and 30 percent of the volumes are likely to be removed.

Acquire tape or string to secure the packed boxes and marking pencils to note their content.

If possible, get one book truck for each worker so that there is a convenient place to put the books as they are removed from the shelves.

Schedule a person to physically move the books or boxes from the stack area to storage areas. Maintenance personnel can be used for this purpose.

Locate and prepare adequate storage space to hold the books removed from the shelves.

Have a half-hour training session with all involved personnel before the weeding starts. (See "Instructions for Weeding," which follows.)

Announce and publicize the fact that the library will be closed during the weeding period.

Schedule a day before the actual weeding for data collection and cut-off point determination.

Get 3 x 5-inch cards, two for each shelf involved in the weeding.

Get foot stools, tall stools, and short stools so weeders can work sitting down.

Step 3: Test out the system in a trial run. At least one week before the actual weeding, the weeding manager should make a trial run both to create the cut-off point and to identify candidates for weeding. This should work out any kinks and resolve any doubts in advance.

Training the Weeding Staff

As advised above, a training session should be set up in advance of the actual weeding. It is good practice to have this session immediately prior to the start of weeding.

Instructions for Weeding

Following are weeding instructions the author has used several times:

1. Weed in a fixed order, from top to bottom and from left to right.

2. Place a 3 x 5-inch card in the middle of a weeded shelf, between two books, clearly visible, to identify that shelf as having been weeded. This is done so that no shelf is unweeded or weeded more than once.

3. The cut-off date is _____. (Insert the cut-off date determined for your library.) Keep all volumes on the shelf that have been used once or more in _____. (List your cut-off date first, then list subsequent years up to the current year. For example, suppose your cut-off date is February 26, 1994. Fill in the space above: "Keep all volumes on the shelf which have been used since February 27, 1994, including all of 1995, 1996, 1997." The current year should be the last in the sequence.) Place on the book truck all volumes *last used* on the cut-off date or earlier.

4. Many cards have the due dates appearing out of chronological order. Search out the date reflecting the most recent use as the criterion for either leaving a book on the shelf or putting it on the book truck. If a Gaylord charging machine is being used, look at all four possible positions to find the most recent date.

5. If a quick glance at a card indicates any date listed in number 3 (1995, 1996, or 1997, in the example), the book is to remain on the shelf. In that case, it is not necessary to search out the most recent date on the book card.

6. If there is any doubt about whether a book should be retained or removed, keep that volume on the shelf.

7. If a book has no due date appearing on the book card, keep that volume if it seems to be a relatively new book or a book that has been given a new book card in the last five years. Remove books from the shelf if dusty, yellowed with age, or containing old-style book cards.

8. Treat duplicate titles as separate works. This means that one copy might be retained and another weeded out.

9. Keep local authors, gift books, or special books of local subjects if you happen to recognize them. Do not worry about discarding valuable works since the weeding manager will look at each book before it is discarded.

10. Do not make a subjective judgment about keeping a book because you think the author, subject, or title is important. If the book card indicates it should be removed, remove it. Do not do subjective weeding.

11. If you have any serious questions, ask the weeding supervisor.

12. Work as comfortably as possible. The use of different size stools will cut fatigue and increase productivity.

13. Your early selections will be double-checked by the weeding manager, who will give you any additional training you may need.

14. If for any reason you are interrupted in the middle of a shelf, turn the last book observed on its spine so that you can start from where you left off.

The Method Summarized

This method consists of collecting a meaningful sample of the book cards representing the entire circulating collection. Both the books on the shelves in the library and the books currently circulating outside the library are to be represented in this sample. The number of uses experienced over the last 10 years is then tabulated. This information is converted into shelf-time periods that have transpired between successive uses. The shelf-time periods, which describe the use pattern, are tabulated and a cut-off point for weeding is created. Then the book card of every volume not in circulation is examined, and those volumes that have not been used since the cut-off date become candidates for weeding.

In theory, the historical reconstruction method is based upon the concept that when book cards are date-stamped they contain the entire use history of the library. One weakness of the theory is that the collection is not intact—books and book cards have been lost, stolen, and weeded out. Therefore, just a part of the use record is available. To compensate for this weakness, the method concentrates on a recent time period. Instead of observing the entire use history, our method limits itself to usage during the last 10 years.

The Method Illustrated

Steps 1 through 6 describe a method for undertaking "systematic sampling." This method consists of using every "nth" book (say, every 200th book) as a sample. This technique assures sampling of all classes and locations proportionately. While attempting this method in the field, the aim was to tabulate 400 uses. It resulted in only 370 useful samples. This suggests that an attempt should be made to collect 500 useful samples instead of 400, as described below in step 2.

Step 1: Estimate the number of volumes in the circulating collection. In order to estimate the size of the circulating collection, count or estimate the number of book cards at the circulation stations representing books currently circulating. (This, of course, does not apply to feeder libraries, which disregard volumes now controlled by the branches.) To the circulating volumes add the number of volumes currently in the library—on the shelves, being reshelved, or awaiting reshelving.

To prevent a confusion of terms, "circulating collection" refers to all books permitted to circulate. The "circulating volumes" are that part of the circulating collection now actually out of the library in the hands of the clients—the volumes currently in circulation.

To estimate the number of volumes on the shelves, count the number of volumes on 10 shelves, divide the total by 10, and use this number as the average number of volumes on each shelf of the library. Then multiply the average number of volumes on each shelf by the number of shelves containing the collection to be weeded.

For example, the following number of books were found on 10 shelves, selected as average shelves: 21, 32, 29, 18, 30, 30, 22, 27, 34, 27. This totals 270. This number was divided by 10, so it was determined that the average shelf contained 27 volumes. There were 1,170 shelves containing the circulating collection in this library. This indicated approximately 31,600 books on the shelves.

It was found that when book cards were packed tight, there were 30 cards per inch. There were 100 inches of book cards representing the books circulating. Therefore, there were 8,000 volumes in circulation. By actual count, 400 volumes were being shelved or located at preshelving holding locations.

The total holdings of the circulating collection were:

On the shelves	31,600
In circulation	8,000
Being reshelved	400
TOTAL	40,000

The sample library had approximately 40,000 volumes in its circulating collection.

Step 2: Determine the size of the sample required. As in the other methods, 400 samples are used for computation purposes. Since in this procedure each sample represents one use, and not one volume, a check was made of the book cards. Ten book cards were selected, and a count of the number of uses per volume during the last 10 years was made. These sample book cards indicated an average of eight such uses. It was decided to take a sample of 50 volumes from this collection in order to get 400 samples of book use.

Step 3: Determine the number of volumes, separating sample volumes required for a systematic sampling. In the library cited above, the 40,000 volumes were divided by the number of samples desired (50). The resultant total was 800. In order to get 50 sample volumes evenly distributed throughout the collection, every 800th volume was selected from the collection.

Step 4: Determine the order in which the library will be sampled. A predetermined order should be established for the books on the shelves, the book cards of the books now circulating, and the books about to be reshelved. For example, the books on the shelves were to be sampled first, from top to bottom, from left to right, and the individual stacks were designated as to their successive order. Then the books being reshelved were to be counted in a predetermined order. Following these were the book cards for books circulating—by due date first, and then by call number.

Step 5: Select the first sample volume. Select at random any volume from the first 800 volumes on the shelf. In the sample library, the seventeenth volume on the top shelf in the first stack was chosen. Remove this volume and place it on a book truck.

Step 6: Select the remainder of the sample. In this library, an attempt was made to select every 800th book or book card in the circulating collection. The precise method of locating the sample volumes is to actually count out 800 volumes on the shelves or 800 book cards at circulation. Since precision was not deemed important, an estimate was made as to the approximate location of each successive sample volume. It was previously determined that there was an average of 27 volumes on each shelf. It was computed that the next sample was on shelf number 31, since 27 times 30 equals 810, and shelf number 31 is the thirtieth shelf after shelf number 1, the source of the first sample. To adjust for the extra 10 books in the 810, 10 was subtracted from sample number 17 used for the starting sample. The second sample was the seventh book on shelf number 31. Then volume 24 was taken from shelf number 60, volume number 14 from shelf number 90, etc.

For the book cards at the circulation desk, every 800th card was located by using a ruler to measure the thickness of the cards. It had been discovered previously that 80 cards measured one inch, therefore, 800 cards measured 10 inches. So a book card was selected by measuring successive 10-inch intervals and removing one card from each of those locations.

Each sample volume or book card was placed at a work desk. When the procedure was completed, 42 volumes and 10 book cards had been selected for the required sample.

Step 7: Tabulate the number of uses for each sample volume experienced in each year for the last 10 years. Use the form in figure 12.1.

Fig. 12.1. Form: step 7.

HISTORICAL RECONSTRUCTION METHOD
(Form One: For Computing the Cut-Date from the Entire Collection)

Summary of Method (see page 142 for complete details):

1. Select a "systematic sample" of 500 books and/or book cards.
2. From the first book card, tabulate, below, the number of uses recorded for each of the last ten years. You will need to use 25 copies of this form.
3. Take each successive book card and enter the number of uses, as in step 2.
4. When all 500 samples have been entered, enter data on Form Two for the Historical Reconstruction Method.

Sample #	Pre 1988	Year									
		88	89	90	91	92	93	94	95	96	97
1											
2											
3											
4											
5											
6											
7											
8											
9											
10											
11											
12											
13											
14											
15											
16											
17											
18											
19											
20											

*The current year should appear in the last column, and earlier years in each successive column.

This is a mechanical task. Remove the book cards from the first sample, and count the number of due dates for 1997. Enter this number in the line labeled "Sample 1" and in the column headed "97," as shown in figure 12.2.

Fig. 12.2. Form: step 7A.

HISTORICAL RECONSTRUCTION METHOD
(Form One: For Computing the Cut-Date from the Entire Collection)

Summary of Method (see page 142 for complete details):

1. Select a "systematic sample" of 500 books and/or book cards.
2. From the first book card, tabulate, below, the number of uses recorded for each of the last ten years. You will need to use 25 copies of this form.
3. Take each successive book card and enter the number of uses, as in step 2.
4. When all 500 samples have been entered, enter data on Form Two for the Historical Reconstruction Method.

Sample #	Pre 1988	Year									
		88	89	90	91	92	93	94	95	96	97
1											4
2											
3											
4											
5											
6											
7											
8											
9											
10											
11											
12											
13											
14											
15											
16											
17											
18											
19											
20											

This entry has been made from the book card reproduced in figure 12.3a-b. As can be seen, there were four 1997 dates, and the number "4" is entered on the form. Continue entering all of the relevant information from this book card related to use within the last 10 years. In the example, there were four uses indicated for 1996; two in 1995; and seven in 1994. The form now should look like figure 12.4.

Fig. 12.3a. Book card—front.

B Windsor

Ziegler, Philip

King Edward VIII.

DATE		ISSUED TO
JAN	12	1994
JAN	24	1994
FEB	1	1994
MAR	25	1994
MAY	28	1994
AUG	3	1994
OCT	30	1994
OCT	20	1995
MAR	3	1996
JUN	7	1996
JUN	27	1996

CAT. No. 23-115   PRINTED IN U. S. A.

Fig. 12.3b. Book card—back.

DATE		ISSUED TO
AUG	2	1995
SEP	1	1996
JAN	14	1997
FEB	3	1997
APR	20	1997
JUL	5	1997

Fig. 12.4. Form: step 7B.

HISTORICAL RECONSTRUCTION METHOD
(Form One: For Computing the Cut-Date from the Entire Collection)

Sample #	Pre 1988	Year									
		88	89	90	91	92	93	94	95	96	97
1								7	2	4	4
2											
3											
4											
5											
6											
7											
8											
9											
10											
14											
15											
16											
17											
18											
19											
20											

When all the data have been recorded, reslip the book card and remove the sample book from the work area. Now take each successive book card in the sample (52 for the library used as the model) and enter the data on the form. In the column headed "Pre 1988" record from each card the most recent date which predates 1988. This gives a starting date so that the first shelf-time period can be computed.

The raw data tabulated for the sample library appears in figure 12.5a-c.

Fig. 12.5a. Form: step 7C1.

HISTORICAL RECONSTRUCTION METHOD
(Form One: For Computing the Cut-Date from the Entire Collection)

Summary of Method (see page 142 for complete details):

1. Select a "systematic sample" of 500 books and/or book cards.
2. From the first book card, tabulate, below, the number of uses recorded for each of the last ten years. You will need to use 25 copies of this form.
3. Take each successive book card and enter the number of uses, as in step 2.
4. When all 500 samples have been entered, enter data on Form Two for the Historical Reconstruction Method.

Sample #	Pre 1988	Year									
		88	89	90	91	92	93	94	95	96	97
1				/							
2	87					/	/				
3			/		3		2		3		
4					/			/			
5						/	3		2		
6						3	2	6	4		
7							2	2	7		
8				/	4		2		3	3	
9				/	2	2	/	2			
10								3	/		
11				/							
12				/	2		/	3	5	2	
13									/	/	
14						2	9	9	7	2	
15	79						/	/	/	/	
16									2	2	
17									7	2	
18			/			/					
19			/			/		/			
20					/	/	3	/	/		/

(Text continues on page 151.)

Fig. 12.5b. Form: step 7C2.

HISTORICAL RECONSTRUCTION METHOD
(Form One: For Computing the Cut-Date from the Entire Collection)

Summary of Method (see page 142 for complete details):

1. Select a "systematic sample" of 500 books and/or book cards.
2. From the first book card, tabulate, below, the number of uses recorded for each of the last ten years. You will need to use 25 copies of this form.
3. Take each successive book card and enter the number of uses, as in step 2.
4. When all 500 samples have been entered, enter data on Form Two for the Historical Reconstruction Method.

Sample #	Pre 1988	Year									
		88	89	90	91	92	93	94	95	96	97
1	76							2			
2								12	3	1	
3							1				
4				1			1	2	1		
5					1						
6					1	3		1			
7					4	3	2	1	1	1	
8				1	1						
9			1					1	1		
10					1	1					
11					1		1	1	1	1	
12	no	use	indicated								
13	"	"	"								
14	"	"	"								
15					1	1	1	2			
16						1		1			
17				1	2			2			
18	no	use									
19		1				1	3				
20			1		4					1	

Fig. 12.5c. Form: step 7C3.

HISTORICAL RECONSTRUCTION METHOD
(Form One: For Computing the Cut-Date from the Entire Collection)

Summary of Method (see page 142 for complete details):

1. Select a "systematic sample" of 500 books and/or book cards.

2. From the first book card, tabulate, below, the number of uses recorded for each of the last ten years. You will need to use 25 copies of this form.

3. Take each successive book card and enter the number of uses, as in step 2.

4. When all 500 samples have been entered, enter data on Form Two for the Historical Reconstruction Method.

from circulating volumes

Sample #	Pre 1988	Year									
		88	89	90	91	92	93	94	95	96	97
1						7	5	5	7	2	
2					3	4	2	0	2	2	
3						4	3	6	2	2	
4						10	6	5	3		
5									16	6	
6										3	
7							1	2		1	
8						5	3	2	3	1	
9									11	3	
10								10	13	4	
11					1	2		4	5		
12						12	(volume misplaced)	7			
13											
14											
15											
16											
17											
18											
19											
20											

Step 8: Convert the data into shelf-time periods and tabulate. The converted data are tabulated in figure 12.6.

Fig. 12.6. Form: step 8.

HISTORICAL RECONSTRUCTION METHOD
(Form Two: For Computing the Cut-Date from the Entire Collection)

Summary of Method (see page 142 for complete details):

1. Convert the data from Form One into shelf-time periods. (See page 152.)
2. Total the number of uses for each shelf-time period and enter in "Total #" column.
3. Add up these totals in this column and enter at the bottom of the page.
4. Compute the percentage of use represented by each shelf-time period, and enter in the "%" column.
5. Compute the cumulated percentage for each successive period and enter under "Cum. %."
6. Select a keeping percentage to be used (normally between 95-98%).
7. Determine the cut-off date to be used for weeding.
8. Remove all volumes indicating no usage since cut-off date.

Under Years	Over Years	Summary of the Shelf-Time Periods		Total #	%	Cum. %
1						
2	1					
3	2					
4	3					
5	4					
6	5					
7	6					
8	7					
9	8					
10	9					
11	10					
	11					
			Total			

This is the most difficult and critical step of the historical reconstruction method of weeding. In order to simplify the computation of the shelf-time periods between successive uses, two rules have been created:

Rule 1: Assume that the use or uses recorded during a year occurred evenly distributed during that year. For example, if one use occurred, assume it happened on the 183d day of the year; two uses occurred on the 122d and 244th days; three uses on the 91st, 182d, and 273d days, etc. Normally, this detailed breakdown will not be needed, as the shelf-time periods become apparent without much computation.

Rule 2: Assume that books circulating on the same day of different years have the longest possible shelf-time period. Thus, if a book is used once in successive years, assume the shelf-time period to be "over one year."

Another point to note is that a shelf-time period requires a beginning and an end. This means that, if only one use is indicated, that sample cannot be tabulated and so must be disregarded. It also means that the *first* use indicated on any book card cannot be tabulated.

The computation of the data now proceeds. For practice, start computing the entries for the sample library made in figure 12.5a as follows:

1. Sample 1 has only one use in 1990, and it cannot be tabulated. Shelf-time periods need a beginning and an end.

2. Sample 2 had one use in 1987. The next use was in 1992. Applying rule 2, the shelf-time period should be entered as one use under six years but over five years. Enter as in figure 12.7.

Sample 2 had one use in 1992 and one use in 1993. Applying rule 2, the shelf-time period is entered as over one year and under two years. Figure 12.8 shows the entry.

Fig. 12.7. Form: step 8A.

HISTORICAL RECONSTRUCTION METHOD
(Form Two: For Computing the Cut-Date from the Entire Collection)

Summary of Method (see page 142 for complete details):

1. Convert the data from Form One into shelf-time periods. (See page 152.)
2. Total the number of uses for each shelf-time period and enter in "Total #" column.
3. Add up these totals in this column and enter at the bottom of the page.
4. Compute the percentage of use represented by each shelf-time period, and enter in the "%" column.
5. Compute the cumulated percentage for each successive period and enter under "Cum. %."
6. Select a keeping percentage to be used (normally between 95-98%).
7. Determine the cut-off date to be used for weeding.
8. Remove all volumes indicating no usage since cut-off date.

Under Years	Over Years	Summary of the Shelf-Time Periods			
			Total #	%	Cum. %
1					
2	1				
3	2				
4	3				
5	4				
6	5				
7	6	/			
8	7				
9	8				
10	9				
11	10				
	11				
		Total			

Fig. 12.8. Form: step 8B.

HISTORICAL RECONSTRUCTION METHOD
(Form Two: For Computing the Cut-Date from the Entire Collection)

Summary of Method (see page 142 for complete details):

1. Convert the data from Form One into shelf-time periods. (See page 152.)
2. Total the number of uses for each shelf-time period and enter in "Total #" column.
3. Add up these totals in this column and enter at the bottom of the page.
4. Compute the percentage of use represented by each shelf-time period, and enter in the "%" column.
5. Compute the cumulated percentage for each successive period and enter under "Cum. %."
6. Select a keeping percentage to be used (normally between 95-98%).
7. Determine the cut-off date to be used for weeding.
8. Remove all volumes indicating no usage since cut-off date.

Under Years	Over Years	Summary of the Shelf-Time Periods			
			Total #	%	Cum. %
1					
2	1	/			
3	2				
4	3				
5	4				
6	5				
7	6	/			
8	7				
9	8				
10	9				
11	10				
	11				
		Total			

Sample 3's first use in 1988, on the 183d day, is used only to establish the inception of a shelf-time period and cannot be tabulated. However, three uses occurred in 1991, the first on day 91, the second on day 182, and third on day 273. The shelf-time period between the day 183 in 1988 and day 91 in 1991 is under three years and over two years. The other two uses in 1991 are under one year. The first use in 1993 is over one year and under two. The next two uses are under one year. Figure 12.9 shows all the entries generated by the first three samples.

Fig. 12.9. Form: step 8C.

HISTORICAL RECONSTRUCTION METHOD
(Form Two: For Computing the Cut-Date from the Entire Collection)

Summary of Method (see page 142 for complete details):

1. Convert the data from Form One into shelf-time periods. (See page 152.)
2. Total the number of uses for each shelf-time period and enter in "Total #" column.
3. Add up these totals in this column and enter at the bottom of the page.
4. Compute the percentage of use represented by each shelf-time period, and enter in the "%" column.
5. Compute the cumulated percentage for each successive period and enter under "Cum. %."
6. Select a keeping percentage to be used (normally between 95-98%).
7. Determine the cut-off date to be used for weeding.
8. Remove all volumes indicating no usage since cut-off date.

Under Years	Over Years	Summary of the Shelf-Time Periods			
			Total #	%	Cum. %
1		2, 1, 2			
2	1	1 1 1			
3	2	1			
4	3				
5	4				
6	5				
7	6	1			
8	7				
9	8				
10	9				
11	10				
	11				
		Total			

This process is continued until all samples have been computed and tabulated. The entire tabulation for the sample library is shown in figure 12.10. The only entry that was unusual was made for sample 12, in figure 12.5c. Because the volume had been out of circulation for two years, 11 uses for 1992 were entered as having a shelf-time period of under one year, and six uses in 1995, as under one year. The seventh use in 1995 was not tabulated because of the special circumstance.

Fig. 12.10. Form: step 8D.

HISTORICAL RECONSTRUCTION METHOD
(Form Two: For Computing the Cut-Date from the Entire Collection)

Summary of Method (see page 142 for complete details):
1. Convert the data from Form One into shelf-time periods. (See page 152.)
2. Total the number of uses for each shelf-time period and enter in "Total #" column.
3. Add up these totals in this column and enter at the bottom of the page.
4. Compute the percentage of use represented by each shelf-time period, and enter in the "%" column.
5. Compute the cumulated percentage for each successive period and enter under "Cum. %."
6. Select a keeping percentage to be used (normally between 95-98%).
7. Determine the cut-off date to be used for weeding.
8. Remove all volumes indicating no usage since cut-off date.

Under Years	Over Years	Summary of the Shelf-Time Periods			
			Total #	%	Cum. %
1		2, 1, 2, 3, 1, 14, 10, 4, 1, 5, 7, 3, 2, 10, 28, 3, 8, 4, 1, 15, 3, 3, 6, 2, 2, 8, 3, 3, 25, 11, 16, 23, 21, 2, 2, 13, 13, 26, 2, 8, 11, 6			
2	1	~~HHH~~ ~~HH~~ ~~HHH~~ ~~HHH~~ ~~HHH~~ //			
3	2	~~HHH~~ //			
4	3	////			
5	4	//			
6	5	/			
7	6	//			
8	7				
9	8				
10	9	/			
11	10				
	11				
		Total			

Step 9: Total the number of uses tabulated for each shelf-time period. There were 326 uses under one year, 27 under two years, etc. These totals are entered in the column headed "Total #," as shown in figure 12.11.

Fig. 12.11. Form: step 9.

HISTORICAL RECONSTRUCTION METHOD
(Form Two: For Computing the Cut-Date from the Entire Collection)

Summary of Method (see page 142 for complete details):

1. Convert the data from Form One into shelf-time periods. (See page 152.)
2. Total the number of uses for each shelf-time period and enter in "Total #" column.
3. Add up these totals in this column and enter at the bottom of the page.
4. Compute the percentage of use represented by each shelf-time period, and enter in the "%" column.
5. Compute the cumulated percentage for each successive period and enter under "Cum. %."
6. Select a keeping percentage to be used (normally between 95-98%).
7. Determine the cut-off date to be used for weeding.
8. Remove all volumes indicating no usage since cut-off date.

Under Years	Over Years	Summary of the Shelf-Time Periods	Total #	%	Cum. %
1		2, 1, 2, 3, 1, 14, 10, 4, 1, 5, 7, 3, 2, 10, 28, 3, 8, 4, 1, 15, 3, 3, 6, 2, 2, 8, 3, 3, 25, 11, 16, 23, 21, 2, 2, 13, 13, 26, 2, 8, 11, 6	326		
2	1	HHT HHT HHT HHT HHT //	27		
3	2	HHT //	7		
4	3	////	4		
5	4	//	2		
6	5	/	1		
7	6	//	2		
8	7				
9	8				
10	9	/	1		
11	10				
	11				
		Total			

Step 10: Add up the "Total #" column entries and enter the total number of shelf-time periods in the sample in the indicated location on the bottom of the page. The form with the number "370" entered in the total box now looks like figure 12.12. Note that while only 370 useful samples were tabulated, this is close enough to 400 so that it was not necessary to resample the collection.

Fig. 12.12. Form: step 10.

HISTORICAL RECONSTRUCTION METHOD
(Form Two: For Computing the Cut-Date from the Entire Collection)

Summary of Method (see page 142 for complete details):

1. Convert the data from Form One into shelf-time periods. (See page 152.)
2. Total the number of uses for each shelf-time period and enter in "Total #" column.
3. Add up these totals in this column and enter at the bottom of the page.
4. Compute the percentage of use represented by each shelf-time period, and enter in the "%" column.
5. Compute the cumulated percentage for each successive period and enter under "Cum. %."
6. Select a keeping percentage to be used (normally between 95-98%).
7. Determine the cut-off date to be used for weeding.
8. Remove all volumes indicating no usage since cut-off date.

Under Years	Over Years	Summary of the Shelf-Time Periods	Total #	%	Cum. %
1		2,1,2, 3, 1, 14, 10, 4, 1, 5, 7, 3, 2, 10, 28, 3, 8, 4, 1, 15, 3, 3, 6, 2, 2, 8, 3, 3, 25, 11, 16, 23, 21, 2, 2, 13, 13, 26, 2, 8, 11, 6	326		
2	1	~~HHH~~ ~~HHH~~ ~~HHH~~ ~~HHH~~ ~~HHH~~ //	27		
3	2	~~HHH~~ //	7		
4	3	////	4		
5	4	//	2		
6	5	/	1		
7	6	//	2		
8	7				
9	8				
10	9	/	1		
11	10				
	11				
		Total	370		

Step 11: Compute the percentage of use represented by each shelf-time period, and enter the result in the column headed "%." This is done by dividing the total number of samples into the total number shown for each shelf-time period. First, 326 was divided by 370, giving 88 percent for the under one year shelf-time period. Then 27 was divided by 370, giving 7 percent, etc., until all shelf-time periods indicating some usage were tabulated. See figure 12.13.

Fig. 12.13. Form: step 11.

HISTORICAL RECONSTRUCTION METHOD
(Form Two: For Computing the Cut-Date from the Entire Collection)

Summary of Method (see page 142 for complete details):

1. Convert the data from Form One into shelf-time periods. (See page 152.)
2. Total the number of uses for each shelf-time period and enter in "Total #" column.
3. Add up these totals in this column and enter at the bottom of the page.
4. Compute the percentage of use represented by each shelf-time period, and enter in the "%" column.
5. Compute the cumulated percentage for each successive period and enter under "Cum. %."
6. Select a keeping percentage to be used (normally between 95-98%).
7. Determine the cut-off date to be used for weeding.
8. Remove all volumes indicating no usage since cut-off date.

Under Years	Over Years	Summary of the Shelf-Time Periods	Total #	%	Cum. %
1		2, 1, 2, 3, 1, 14, 10, 4, 1, 5, 7, 3, 2, 10, 28, 3, 8, 4, 1, 15, 3, 3, 6, 2, 2, 8, 3, 3, 25, 11, 16, 23, 21, 2, 2, 13, 13, 26, 2, 8, 11, 6	326	88	
2	1	~~HHT~~ ~~HHT~~ ~~HHT~~ ~~HHT~~ ~~HHT~~ //	27	7	
3	2	~~HHT~~ //	7	2	
4	3	////	4	1	
5	4	//	2	1	
6	5	/	1		
7	6	//	2	1	
8	7				
9	8				
10	9	/	1		
11	10				
	11				
		Total	370		

Step 12: Compute the cumulative percent for each successive shelf-time period and enter the results in the last column. This may be done by adding together the percentages already appearing in the next to last column starting from the top, or percentages can be recomputed by adding each successive number of cases to the previous total and dividing by 370. In the latter case, add 326 to the 27 cases for under two years. This equals 353. Now divide this by 370, and enter the result (95 percent) in the last column. Now add 7 more cases to the 353, divide by 370, and enter 97 percent in the next row, etc. See figure 12.14.

Fig. 12.14. Form: step 12.

HISTORICAL RECONSTRUCTION METHOD
(Form Two: For Computing the Cut-Date from the Entire Collection)

Summary of Method (see page 142 for complete details):

1. Convert the data from Form One into shelf-time periods. (See page 152.)
2. Total the number of uses for each shelf-time period and enter in "Total #" column.
3. Add up these totals in this column and enter at the bottom of the page.
4. Compute the percentage of use represented by each shelf-time period, and enter in the "%" column.
5. Compute the cumulated percentage for each successive period and enter under "Cum. %."
6. Select a keeping percentage to be used (normally between 95-98%).
7. Determine the cut-off date to be used for weeding.
8. Remove all volumes indicating no usage since cut-off date.

Under Years	Over Years	Summary of the Shelf-Time Periods	Total #	%	Cum. %
1		2, 1, 2, 3, 1, 14, 10, 4, 1, 5, 7, 3, 2, 10, 28, 3, 8, 4, 1, 15, 3, 3, 6, 2, 2, 8, 3, 3, 25, 11, 16, 23, 21, 2, 2, 13, 13, 26, 2, 8, 11, 6	326	88	88
2	1	~~HH HH HH HH HH~~ 11	27	7	95
3	2	~~HH~~ 11	7	2	97
4	3	1111	4	1	98
5	4	11	2	1	99
6	5	1	1		99
7	6	11	2	1	100
8	7				
9	8				
10	9	1	1		
11	10				
	11				
		Total	370		100

Step 13: Determine the keeping percentage to be used for weeding. This has been discussed on page 106 for the book card method of weeding. When the level has been determined, draw a line under the box containing this cumulative percentage level. If the 95 percent keeping level has been selected, draw a line as shown in figure 12.15. The form has now been completed.

Step 14: Determine the cut-off date to be used for weeding. This shelf-time period (over two years) is found in the second column on the left and is directly below the line drawn in step 13. In the sample library, the form indicates that all volumes used during the last two years be retained.

To establish the cut-off date, subtract these two years from the date the data were collected. In this case, the data were collected 2/27/96. Therefore, the cut-off point would be 2/27/94.

Fig. 12.15. Form: step 13.

HISTORICAL RECONSTRUCTION METHOD
(Form Two: For Computing the Cut-Date from the Entire Collection)

Summary of Method (see page 142 for complete details):
1. Convert the data from Form One into shelf-time periods. (See page 152.)
2. Total the number of uses for each shelf-time period and enter in "Total #" column.
3. Add up these totals in this column and enter at the bottom of the page.
4. Compute the percentage of use represented by each shelf-time period, and enter in the "%" column.
5. Compute the cumulated percentage for each successive period and enter under "Cum. %."
6. Select a keeping percentage to be used (normally between 95-98%).
7. Determine the cut-off date to be used for weeding.
8. Remove all volumes indicating no usage since cut-off date.

Under Years	Over Years	Summary of the Shelf-Time Periods	Total #	%	Cum. %
1		2,1,2,3,1,14,10,4,1, 5, 7, 3, 2,10, 28, 3, 8, 4, 1, 15, 3, 3, 6, 2,2, 8, 3, 3,25, 11, 16,23, 21, 2, 2, 13, 13, 26,2,8, 11, 6	326	88	88
2	1	~~HHT~~ ~~HHT~~ ~~HHT~~ ~~HHT~~ ~~HHT~~ //	27	7	95
3	2	~~HHT~~ //	7	2	97
4	3	////	4	1	98
5	4	//	2	1	99
6	5	/	1		99
7	6	//	2	1	100
8	7				
9	8				
10	9	/	1		
11	10				
	11				
		Total	370		100

Step 15: In the circulating collection, examine the book card of every book on the shelves, and remove all volumes whose most recent due date is the cut-off date or earlier. This is the actual weeding process. One book at a time is removed from the shelf, and the book card is examined. In the sample library, if the most recent date appearing on the book card was 2/27/94 or more recent, the book was returned to the shelf; if it was 2/26/94 or earlier, the book was removed from the shelf and considered a candidate for weeding.

Step 16: Inspect all candidates for weeding and return to the shelves those volumes not to be weeded out. This is a professional job and should be done by the head librarian, the acquisitions librarian, or whoever else is responsible for building the library collection and maintaining its integrity. Here, judgment is involved. If the in-library use has been recorded, it is axiomatic that the fewer books returned to the shelves the better the collection will be. If in-library use has not been recorded, it is important that librarians attempt to return to the shelves those volumes they judge to have experienced recent in-library use.

Weeding by Class

To weed by class, the identical procedure (steps 1 through 16) is followed, except that the collection to be weeded is only one part of the total circulating collection. For practical purposes, when applying these procedures, consider this part to be the whole collection. Four hundred samples of book use should be used to create the cut-off point of the class to be weeded.

Correcting a Distortion

The historical reconstruction method has been designed to collect the needed data from the entire circulating collection, including the volumes now circulating. In practice, occasionally, the method is being used where the book cards for books in circulation are not available to the weeder. A serious distortion is likely to be created when the sample is taken only from the books remaining in the library, since the most active books tend to be those in current circulation. This was observed in Larchmont, where a study was made of the books in circulation and the books on the shelves. The data from these two segments were computed separately and are summarized in table 12.1.

Table 12.1.
Percent of Use Having This Cumulative Shelf-Time Period

Shelf-Time Period Under:	Volumes on Shelves:	Volumes Currently Circulating	Volumes Circulating and on Shelves-Combined
1 year	81%	99%	88%
2 years	92%	100%	95%
3 years	95%		97%
4 years	97%		98%
5 years	98%		99%
7 years	99%		100%
10 years	100%		100%

The chart can be interpreted as follows: of the volumes on the shelves, 81 percent of the uses in the past had a shelf-time period of under one year, 92 percent under two years, etc. Of the books now out in circulation, 99 percent of their uses had shelf-time periods of less than one year, 100 percent under two years.

Based upon this information, if Larchmont used only the data from the shelves and selected a two-year shelf-time period as the cut-off point, it seems that it would retain 92 percent of the present usage when it actually would retain 95 percent of such usage. To compensate for this condition, when using data gathered only from the shelves, select a percentage cut-off point somewhat lower than would have been normally selected (say 90 to 93 percent).

Estimating Cut-Off Points

When a certain predetermined cut-off point percentage does not appear on the form in the last column (see step 13), the cut-off point can be estimated by interpolation. For example, if one wanted to weed at the 96 percent level in Larchmont, one would use two and one-half years as the shelf-time cut-off point, the period half way between 95 and 97 percent, which does appear on the form.

Methods to Improve Future Weeding

For libraries that intend to make continued use of the historical reconstruction method, the following procedures should be followed:

1. All new books being processed should have an initial date stamped on the book card. This gives a starting date to assist in measuring the shelf-time period, and prevents the weeding of a new acquisition that hasn't had an adequate opportunity to circulate.

2. Whenever books are rebound and new book cards are inserted, the old book card should be stored in the book pocket along with the new card.

3. Whenever a book is weeded out of a collection, its book card should be saved for future use in reconstructing the use history of the library.

4. Whenever a book card is used up and a new card created, the old book card should be stored in the book pocket along with the new card. All old book cards should be retained in this way for at least 10 years.

5. When books are returned to the library after a long overdue period, the date of reshelving ought to be entered on the book card. This prevents a book which had no chance to circulate from being weeded prematurely.

6. When books have been held in the librarian's office or taken out of normal use by the staff, the date of shelving the book in publicly accessible areas should be entered on the book card.

7. When books in the circulating collection experience in-library use, they should be date-stamped before reshelving.

8. Due dates should be stamped on book cards in chronological order, instead of random order, so that date information can be tabulated more easily.

Forms Used for the
Historical Reconstruction Method

Blank forms for reproduction begin on page 165.

HISTORICAL RECONSTRUCTION METHOD
(Form One: For Computing the Cut-Date from the Entire Collection)

Summary of Method (see page 142 for complete details):

1. Select a "systematic sample" of 500 books and/or book cards.
2. From the first book card, tabulate, below, the number of uses recorded for each of the last ten years. You will need to use 25 copies of this form.
3. Take each successive book card and enter the number of uses, as in step 2.
4. When all 500 samples have been entered, enter data on Form Two for the Historical Reconstruction Method.

Sample #	Pre 1988	Year									
		88	89	90	91	92	93	94	95	96	97
1											
2											
3											
4											
5											
6											
7											
8											
9											
10											
11											
12											
13											
14											
15											
16											
17											
18											
19											
20											

HISTORICAL RECONSTRUCTION METHOD
(Form Two: For Computing the Cut-Date from the Entire Collection)

Summary of Method (see page 142 for complete details):

1. Convert the data from Form One into shelf-time periods. (See page 165.)
2. Total the number of uses for each shelf-time period and enter in "Total #" column.
3. Add up these totals in this column and enter at the bottom of the page.
4. Compute the percentage of use represented by each shelf-time period, and enter in the "%" column.
5. Compute the cumulated percentage for each successive period and enter under "Cum. %."
6. Select a keeping percentage to be used (normally between 95-98%).
7. Determine the cut-off date to be used for weeding.
8. Remove all volumes indicating no usage since cut-off date.

Under Years	Over Years	Summary of the Shelf-Time Periods			
			Total #	%	Cum. %
1					
2	1				
3	2				
4	3				
5	4				
6	5				
7	6				
8	7				
9	8				
10	9				
11	10				
	11				
		Total			

13

Method 4: Computer Assisted Weeding

Background

A majority of the libraries in the United States are using computers today, and there are at least 31 companies selling some $5 billion worth of their computer products to libraries every year.[1] Every day more libraries are going online. Computerization can involve almost every library operation—high speed computers, relational databases, and sophisticated programs are helping librarians select and catalog their new acquisitions, register their borrowers, control all aspects of circulation, permit self check-out, collect fines, provide access to the Internet, do the accounting, prepare useful reports, take book inventory and do shelf-reading, and perform dozens of other functions. Librarians can now rid themselves of much of the drudgery of librarianship. As might be expected, computers have been simplifying and improving the quality of the weeding process, perhaps the most onerous of all the tasks that librarians are called upon to perform.

Computer-Produced Use Information

It is the main point of this book that *use information* is the basic information needed for confident and simplified weeding. As Bertland reported, "The (circulation) analysis has helped to identify some of the parameters for weeding based upon circulation history. . . ."[2] Line reports, "Libraries tend not to collect data on use before weeding . . . automated systems should now make it possible to gather relevant data."[3] Wallace makes an even stronger statement: "Most automated circulation systems provide faculties for generating reports on the nature of the collection, including data necessary for a study of obsolescence."[4] Reed and Erickson add, "With the advent of machine readable circulation records, studies of the pattern of circulation were easier to perform because the records of use could be analyzed by computer."[5]

Among the computerized library systems studied, the following use-oriented aids to weeding were found:

1. Shelf list reports. (See figure 13.1. The shelf list. Page 169.)

    The most frequently used report found in the field survey was a printout of the entire library or selected sections of the library sorted by shelf list order, the order of the books on the shelves. Such reports contained varying amounts of information, which could include such items as author, title, bar code number, call number, date of acquisition, number of uses to date, date of last use, status, date due and much more.

However, all of the systems did not include all of this information. For example, a DRA installation showed the date of last use but not the total number of uses of each volume on this report, although that information was available on the printout for each individual book. These printouts were then used by the librarians to make decisions as to whether to weed a specific volume. The most influential piece of information was the number of uses a volume had experienced. When they were in doubt about weeding a volume, weeders were more likely to retain volumes that experienced more use and weed out volumes with little or no use.

The next most important piece of information was the date of last use. A book used recently was more likely to be retained than a book that had not been used in a long time. Weeders did consider other factors shown on such reports: the number of copies of the title in the collection, the date of acquisition, the date of publication, the imprint, etc. Almost all libraries having these lists available made some use of them in the weeding process. Larger libraries tended to divide their collections into sections and assign each section to a different librarian, giving them printouts and permitting them to decide how to employ them. All the libraries using the computer-created shelf lists found them valuable tools for weeding.

There were a number of problems experienced in the use of such reports. They were frequently very lengthy, bulky, and awkward to handle in the stacks. In addition, since substantial parts of the collection were in circulation and others misshelved, there was a lot of time spent trying to identify the volumes that weeders wished to inspect—the weeding candidates.

In several libraries these reports had to be created off-site: at a centralized computer location for consortiums sharing the facility, at remote centralized computer locations run by the supplier of both programs and the hardware, or out-sourced to a private company when computers were overworked and computer resources were not available. This involved some additional cost and time waste. A number of libraries had such reports available only once a year or less frequently, and as time passed, the librarians were using information that might have been out-of-date.

There were secondary advantages to going through the shelves with shelf-list printouts. Missing volumes often were identified by a lack of recorded use, especially if another copy of the same title had enjoyed heavy use, or if the records showed that the book was not in circulation and not on the shelves. In addition, some librarians bought more books of the classes being heavily used, as this fact showed up rather clearly in the shelf list. On the other hand, lightly used classes often signaled that fewer of these books should be purchased.

Fig. 13.1. The shelf list.

03/26/95 LBN108			PUBLIC LIBRARY BOOK COLLECTION REPORT-- LOCATION: CALL NO: CREATED BEFORE: CREATED AFTER:		NO USE SINCE;		PAGE 9,620
REC-NO	LOCATION	CALL-NO	AUTHOR/TITLE	ITEM-ID	CR-DATE	LAST-USE	CHARGES
AAM9106	NONF	508.94 E	Evans, Howard Ensign / Australia, a natural history /	31544084077783	10/11/87	12/23/90	2
AAT7442	NONF	509 A	Alic, Margaret / Hypatia's heritage :	31544086239894	10/11/87	11/05/93	8
AAE5031	NONF	509 A	Anderson, Clifford N / Fertile crescent;	31544075041475	10/11/87	03/29/93	3
AA28893	NONF	509 A	Asimov, Isaac. / Asimov's chronology of science	31544089186993	12/26/89	10/04/94	7
AA20814	NONF	509 A	Asimov, Isaac. / Science past, science future /	31544075055699	07/06/89	01/27/94	2
AAW5505	NONF	509 B	Bettex, Albert W / Discovery of nature.	31544066037771	02/11/88	11/25/94	4
ABE8189	NONF	509 B	Biagioli, Mario / Galileo, courtier :	31544092417914	09/01/93	05/19/94	7
AAU4122	NONF	509 B	Bruce, Robert V / Launching of modern American s	31544087033882	10/11/87	01/24/93	2
AAU4122	NONF	509 B	Bruce, Robert V / Launching of modern American s	31544087065256	06/06/88		
ABA2151	NONF	509 B	Bruno, Leonard C / Landmarks of science :	31544089297576	06/26/90	03/23/94	4
AAW2618	NONF	509 B	Bruno, Leonard C / Tradition of science :	31544087242830	12/30/87	05/26/92	6
AAT4093	NONF	509 B	Burke, James. / Day the universe changed /	31544086211984	10/11/87	04/23/94	15
AAT4093	NONF	509 B	Burke, James. / Day the universe changed /	31544086189479	10/11/87	01/17/95	9
AAT4093	NONF	509 B	Burke, James. / Day the universe changed /	31544086211992	10/11/87	02/24/95	17
AAA0809	NONF	509 C	Cohen, I. Bernard. / From Leonardo to Lavoisier, 14	31544081553646	04/25/88	11/22/94	7
AAQ2351	NONF	509 C	Cohen, I. Bernard. / Revolution in science /	31544085080109	10/11/87	05/17/94	12
AAE5030	NONF	509 D	Daniels, George H / Science in American society:	31544072042997	10/11/87	01/27/94	4

2. Uncirculated book lists. (See figure 13.2. Inactive items report.)

   Of more value are "dusty book lists"—lists of books that have not circulated, either from the inception of the record keeping or from a time period arbitrarily selected. For example, one may generate a list of all volumes not circulated for three years, or five years, or some other such date. These lists are often used to develop candidates for weeding and, obviously, are much shorter than the printouts of the whole collection. While they can be arranged in a variety of ways (by author, publisher, date of publication, etc.), the most useful sort is by classification number, so that the books can be found sequentially on the shelves.

   Again, the reports cost money to produce, take time, and are bulky and awkward to handle. Most libraries produce these lists yearly or less often, but weeding rarely proceeds rapidly unless some pressing space problem arises or some major change is contemplated. Therefore, yearly lists serve the weeders well.

   These reports, in fact, reflect shelf-time periods, periods books remain on the shelves unused. On the other hand, the period used was not computed in advance as to its validity or its impact on the collection or on the future usage of that collection. However, these lists generally identify a subset of volumes that can be weeded out without any reduction in the future use of the library.

   Another advantage of the lists is that most systems total the number of volumes in such a list, and by comparing it to the number of volumes in the library, can predict what percentage of the library would be weeded out if all of these volumes were removed. When that number seems to be too high, the cut-date can be extended back further to produce a smaller number of weeding candidates.

   In cases where the number of books on the list is not computed, the pages of the printout are usually numbered and the number of volumes per page can be multiplied by the number of pages to compute the number of weeding candidates.

3. The percentage of usage compared to the percentage of holdings—reports of circulation by class. (See Figure 13.3. Item utilization report.)

   Since computers often can produce lists of books by classification, broad or narrow, along with the total circulations of these volumes, such information has been used to weed. For example, on this report the Dewey 219's classification (drawing) represents 2.34 percent of this library's holdings but only 1.66 percent of the library's circulation. This might signal the advisability of weeding some of the 219's. On the other hand, class 209 (galleries, museums) represents 0.33 percent of the holdings but 1.28 percent of the circulation. This might discourage weeding of that class. With this system the classes selected can be as large or small as the librarian wishes. For example, all of the 200's could be considered one class, if such a class were considered useful.

Fig. 13.2. Inactive items report: not used after Dec. 31, 1991, Gaylord.

GALAXY   INACTIVE ITEMS REPORT   14-FEB-1995 23:50:07.12   PAGE 42

ITEM ID	CIRC LIFE	DATE LAST CIRCULATED	AUTHOR	TITLE	CALL NUMBER
000100 3142 5301	1	4-OCT-91	ZENKER, HAZEL G.	CAKE BAKERY.	641.8653ZEN
000100 1375 8001	1	23-OCT-91	LAUGHLIN, RUTH.	NATURAL SWEETS & TREATS :	641.86LAU
000100 5017 8801	1	13-NOV-91	BATTERBERRY, ARIANE RUSK	BLOOMINGDALE'S BOOK OF ENTERTAINING /	642.41 BATTERBURY 15
000100 0211 8501	2	20-OCT-91	JANIK, CAROLYN.	THE HOUSE HUNT GAME :	643-12 JANIK
000100 0716 0401	0	7-APR-90		COMPLETE HANDYMAN DO-IT- YOURSELF ENCYCLOPED	643-7 COMPLE V.1
000100 9716 1101	0	19-MAR-80		COMPLETE HANDYMAN DO-IT- YOURSELF ENCYCLOPED	643-7 COMPLE V.2
000100 9716 1701	0	25-JAN-88		COMPLETE HANDYMAN DO-IT- YOURSELF ENCYCLOPED	643-7 COMPLE V.6
000100 6453 4101	0	18-APR-90	SCIENCE AND MECHANICS	COMPLETE HANDYMAN DO-IT-YOURSELF ENCY	643-7 COMPLE V.8
000100 5793 0701	1	25-OCT-91	DANIELS, M. E.	HOW TO REMODEL AND ENLARGE YOUR HOME /	643-7 DANIELS
000102 0242 1610 1	1	11-NOV-91	FELDMANN, CARL.	MANAGE YOUR OWN RENOVATION PROJECT /	643-7 MFL
000101 3934 5403	1	26-DEC-91	HUGHES, HERB.	HOME REMODELING DESIGN & PLANS /	643-7 HUGHES
000101 4326 4901	0	18-MAY-89	MARSHALL CAVENDISH CORP.	KNOW HOW	643-7 KNOW
000101 4326 5101	0	17-MAY-89	MARSHALL CAVENDISH CORP.	KNOW HOW	643-7 KNOW
000101 4326 4501	0	18-MAY-89	MARSHALL CAVENDISH CORP.	KNOW HOW	643-7 KNOW
000101 4326 5201	0	12-OCT-91	MARSHALL CAVENDISH CORP.	KNOW HOW	643-7 KNOW
000101 4326 4801	0	18-MAY-89	MARSHALL CAVENDISH CORP.	KNOW HOW	C43-7 KNOW
000101 4326 5001	0	17-MAY-89	MARSHALL CAVENDISH CORP.	KNOW HOW	643-7 KNOW
000101 4451 4601	6	13-OCT-91	MYEPS, STANLEY.	CREATIVE HOME REMODELING /	643-7 MYE
000104 2538 4201	1	18-JUN-91		THE OLDER HOUSE.	643-7 OLD
000104 2502 2501	2	20-JUN-91	SPERLING, PHYLLIS.	HOW TO REDESIGN & RENOVATE YOUR HOUSE OR APA	643-7 SPE
000101 3376 8001	1	13-OCT-91	WATKINS, A. M.	THE NEW COMPLETE BOOK OF HOME REMODELING, IM	643-7 WATKINS
000100 4105 3201	1	12-JUN-91	DALZELL, J. RALPH	REPAIRING AND REMODELING GUIDE FOR HOME INTE	643-7DALZELL
000100 9762 2101	1	3-JUN-91	BRANN, DONALD R.	HOW TO BUILD OUTDOOR PROJECTS /	643-8 BRANN
000100 6602 8201	1	3-NOV-91	BUTCHER, LEE.	THE CONDOMINIUM BOOK :	643BUTCHE
000100 3779 0201	1	10-NOV-91	MENCHER, MELVIN.	THE FANNIE MAE GUIDE TO BUYING, FINANCING, A	643MEN
000102 1703 7301	2	17-DEC-91	MALACY, DAN	HOME ENERGY YOUR BEST OPTIONS FOR SOLAR HEAT	644-1 HAL
000100 5516 8001	1	21-NOV-91	SUNSET	GARDEN ART & DECORATION EMINENTLY SUITABLE /	645.85U
000104 1779 2201	0	20-NOV-91	BOYER, G. BRUCE.	THE CUSTOM LOOK,	646.32 BOY
000100 3770 7802	2	17-SEP-91	JOHNSON, MARY	MARY JOHNSON'S GUIDE TO ALTERING AND RESTYLI	646-4JOHNSO
000100 4002 9202	2	8-OCT-91	PARISH, PEGGY.	COSTUMES TO MAKE.	646-4PARISH
000100 1170 7901	1	25-OCT-91	WYSE, LOIS.	BLONDE, BEAUTIFUL BLONDE :	646.7 WYS
000101 7503 1403	3	7-JUN-91	STERLING, WENDY.	THIN THIGHS IN 30 DAYS :	646.75 STE
000101 7150 0701	3	9-SEP-91	RUNDBACK, BETTY REVITS &	BED AND BREAKFAST USA	647.047301 RUNDBAC 1
000103 0755 2001	1	10-JUN-91		STATE BY STATE GUIDE TO BUDGET MOTELS.	647.047302 BRE'86/87
000100 3982 9750 01	2	10-DEC-91	CHIM, WANDA.	AMERICA'S WONDERFUL LITTLE HOTELS AND INNS.	647.047A AMER
000104 2413 3001	2	17-SEP-91	GISLER, PEGGY	OPPORTUNITIES IN FAST FOOD CAREERS	647.95 CHIN
000103 0984 0901	3	10-OCT-91	UNTERMAN, PATRICIA.	ZAGAT NEW YORK CITY RESTAURANT SURVEY.	647.957471 ZAGAT 199
000101 0000 3124	1	15-DEC-91		BEST RESTAURANTS OF SAN FRANCISCO :	647.05704 UNT
000101 0000 1503	1	11-NOV-91	ALTH, MAX.	THE STAIN REMOVAL HANDBOOK /	648 ALT
000100 8412 0701	3	10-AUG-91	ASLETT, DON.	DON ASLETT'S STAINBUSTER'S BIBLE :	648.1 ASLETT
000104 0771 0702	3	25-NOV-91		HOW TO CLEAN PRACTICALLY ANYTHING /	648.5 HOW
000103 2110 6202	1	17-OCT-91	KUZMA, KAY.	PRIME-TIME PARENTING /	649.1 KUZ 1ST
000101 4148 0101	1	16-DEC-91	PLUTZIK, RORERTA	THE PRIVATE LIVES OF PARENTS	649.1 PLU
000101 9151 0301	2	10-OCT-91	LIEDERMAN, ADRIENNE B.	THE PREMIE PARENTS' HANDBOOK :	649.122 LIE
000102 2212 3901	1	4-JUN-91	AMES, LOUISE BATES.	DON'T PUSH YOUR PRESCHOOLER,	649.123 AMES
000100 1524 3501	1	29-NOV-91	YURA, MICHAEL T.	RAISING THE EXCEPTIONAL CHILD /	649.15 YUR

Fig. 13.3. Item utilization report: Gaylord.

GALAXY   AGE_LEVEL = 0 ALL   ITEM UTILIZATION REPORT   16-JAN-1936 00:59   PAGE 5

STATISTICAL CLASS

STATISTICAL CLASS	H BOOK PBK / AUDIO OF C.	VIDEO RE C.	FRAMED P RINTS	MISC.	TOTAL
206 – DICTIONARIES	0.37	2.03			0.03
207 – GALLERIES, MUSEUMS	0.43	1.41			1.28
210 – HISTORY & GEOGRAPHY	2.23	0.75			0.77
211 – LANDSCAPING	1.06	1.64			1.84
212 – ARCHITECTURE	0.43	0.70			0.65
213 – SCULPTURE	1.06	0.83			0.86
214 – CARVING	3.12	1.56			2.21
215 – NUMISMATICS	0.48	0.32			0.57
216 – CERAMICS	1.17	0.41			0.52
217 – ART METALWORK	1.18	2.06			0.75
218 – MINOR ART		1.00	4.00		1.00
219 – DRAWING	2.34	1.27	1.50		1.66
220 – DECORATIVE	1.30	1.07	1.76		1.13
221 – TEXTILE ARTS	1.10	0.75	2.75		0.31
222 – INTERIOR DECORATION	1.73	1.56			1.52
223 – GLASS	1.24	1.30			1.78
224 – FURNITURE	0.50	0.55			0.74
225 – PAINTING	1.87	1.34	6.40		1.50
226 – GRAPHIC ARTS	0.60	0.65	3.00		0.64
227 – PRINTS-STAMPS	0.74	0.45	0.36		0.62
224 – PHOTOGRAPHY	0.55	0.44	1.27		0.47
229 – MUSIC	0.53	0.56	1.45		0.58
231 – GENERAL	0.44	0.59	3.01		0.70
231 – DRAMATIC MUSIC	0.84	0.71			0.93
232 – SACRED MUSIC	0.90	0.53	3.07		0.57
233 – VOCAL	0.30	0.72			0.76
234 – INSTRUMENTAL ENSEMBLE	0.75	0.30			0.30
235 – KEYBOARD	0.43	0.58		1.50	0.41
236 – STRINGS	2.14	0.87			0.03
237 – WIND	0.14	1.13	6.00		1.46
238 – PRECUSSION	0.42	0.45			0.20
239 – RECREATION & PERFORMING A	0.86	0.57	1.95		0.51
240 – PUBLIC PERFORMANCE	0.56	0.52	2.00		0.04
241 – THEATRE	1.11	0.35	7.42		0.48
242 – INDOOR GAMES	1.93	1.04	3.15		1.57
243 – GAMES OF SKILL	2.22	2.75	4.50		1.47
244 – GAMES OF CHANCE	0.84	1.14	2.53		1.70
245 – ATHLETICS	0.92	0.64			0.74
246 – AQUATIC & AIR SPORTS	0.84	0.41			0.55
247 – EQUESTRIAN	0.87	0.78			0.80
248 – FISHING, HUNTING, SHOOTIN	2.00	0.53			0.01
249 – LITERATURE	0.25	1.40			1.50
250 – PHILOSOPHY	0.14	0.12			0.13
251 – DICTIONARIES	0.87	0.13			0.13
252 – RHETORIC & COLLECTION	0.84	0.50			0.66
253 – HISTORY, DESCRIPTION & CR	0.20	0.05			0.03
254 – AMERICAN LITERATURE	0.70	0.09			0.10
255 – POETRY	0.60	0.31			0.80
256 – DRAMA	0.41	2.47			0.53
257 – FICTION	0.62	2.55			0.52
258 – ESSAYS		0.80			0.77
PAGE TOTALS	0.91	0.70	3.42	0.75	0.90

4. The age of the materials in relationship to usage. (See Figure 13.1. The shelf list.)

   Computers have proven themselves useful in combining diverse information. Since the book information and the circulation control systems are generally integrated, one may be able to observe the date of last use and the date the book was added to the collection on the same report. While research has shown age to be a difficult criterion to use in the weeding process (see page 24), there is no doubt that the age and usage of a book have a strong inverse relationship. For example in Figure 13.1, Anderson's *Fertile Crescent* was entered into the system 10/11/87 and last used 3/29/93. Burke's *The Day the Universe Changed,* entered the same date, was last used 2/24/95. This difference was meaningful to the weeders.

5. Use patterns at the circulation stations. (See Figure 13.4. Circulating items listed by date of last use.)

   Most of the systems observed retain the date of last use of each volume (as well as the total number of uses). This information can be collected electronically at the circulation desk, creating a pattern of shelf-time periods for the books circulating, and then entering these intercepted circulations into the regular system at a later time. This is not a very common procedure, but would produce the best cut-point for creating a list of candidates for weeding.[6]

6. Records of in-library use.

   A number of programs incorporate systems for recording the in-library use of materials, usually with hand-held equipment that can scan identification numbers and make the appropriate entry into the records. Such information is an essential element in computer weeding cut-points and shelf-time periods of the collection.

Fig. 13.4. Circulating items listed by date of last use.

page 1

Coll	CALL#	Title [from BIB record]	Barcode	Date added	Date of Last Use	USE
T	Hall	Seen the red sky	33005005220664	19 APR 1982		0
NF	R08.82 F487	Film scripts four	33005001401355	30 APR 1986		0
NF	814 T391	Approaches to Walden	33005001444629	23 JUN 1986		0
NF	332.024 B813	A second start : a widow's guide to financial survival at a time of emotional crisis	33005001469204	17 OCT 1986		0
NF	741.235 H83	How to draw in pastels, pencils and pen & ink	33005001577949	30 JUL 1987		0
NF	745.5 M766	Indian crafts and skills : an illustrated guide for making authentic Indian clothing, shelters, and ornaments	33005001584440	23 JUN 1987		0
NF	338.644 N125	The big boys : power and position in American business	33005001591072	02 JUL 1987		0
F	<R> Peters	Die for love	33005001600907	11 JUL 1988		0
P	<R> Dubanevich	Pigs in hiding	33005001608538	21 JUN 1988		0
P	Sheldon	Master of the game	33005001608900	29 JUN 1988		0
F	Drury	The hill of summer : a novel of the Soviet conquest	33005001608918	29 JUN 1988		0
NF	343.07 8152	The law and legislation of credit cards : use and misuse	33005001702117	21 OCT 1987		0
RC	688.722 D516	The collectors encyclopedia of Barbie dolls and collectibles	33005001801349	26 JUL 1988		0
NF	647.94 S158	Country Inns and back roads : North America	33005001288919	06 MAR 1985	09 SEP 85	2
NF	200.973 023	Hist atlas religion in America	33005000093476	19 FEB 1984	08 FEB 86	13
NF	200.973 023	Hist atlas religion in America	33005000093476	19 FEB 1984	08 FEB 86	13
F	Miller	Bright tomorrow	33005000050310	18 FEB 1984	15 APR 86	8
F	Gann	In the company of eagles	33005000634212	14 DEC 1984	20 MAY 86	6
F	Frankel	The Aleph solution	33005000020883	19 FEB 1984	22 JUL 86	11
NF	917.3 J418	A walk across America	33005001403013	23 APR 1986	09 AUG 86	1
F	White	The solid mandala	33005001087337	28 NOV 1983	18 OCT 86	8
NF	647.94 R156	Lodgings for less : Eastern states	33005001148311	18 APR 1984	08 DEC 86	3
F	<M> Coffey	The wall of masks	33005006616854	19 FEB 1984	03 MAR 87	23
F	Coetzee	Foe	33005015304R4	17 APR 1987	19 MAY 87	1
F	Coetzee	Foe	33005015304R4	17 APR 1987	19 MAY 87	1
NF	550 As42e	Exploring the earth and the cosmos	33005000807420	07 JUN 1982	09 JUN 87	20
NF	636.72 H41	The complete Lhasa Apso	33005000181982	18 FEB 1984	07 JUL 87	26
NF	709.7 T42	Primitives & folk art	33005000229950	16 MAR 1982	04 AUG 87	8
F	<R> Roby	The broken key	33005000804948	20 MAY 1982	06 OCT 87	21
NF	120 B835	On knowing : essays for left hand	33005000075408	15 MAR 1982	08 OCT 87	2
T	Hall	Another kind of courage	33005000522185	19 APR 1982	08 OCT 87	7
F	<R> Benzoni	Catherine's quest	33005001117134	24 MAY 1984	24 OCT 87	10
LPN	050 R22	Reader's Digest--large type edition	33005000766595	06 AUG 1982	05 NOV 87	4
LPN	050 R22	Reader's Digest--large type edition	33005000766595	06 AUG 1982	05 NOV 87	4
NF	809 Am35	American Heritage history of the writers' America	33005001489008	18 FEB 1984	06 NOV 87	10
F	Aldrich	In a dark garden	33005000000117	18 FEB 1984	06 NOV 87	9
F	<M> York	Death to my killer	33005000087171	15 JAN 1982	08 NOV 87	11
NF	M773.5 M61	Hole in the rock	33005001370593	13 FEB 1984	09 NOV 87	31
NF	155.232 K521	Chancing it : why we take risks	33005001305341	13 MAY 1985	09 NOV 87	5
NF	394.268282 M58	The Victorian Christmas book	33005000128157	19 FEB 1984	17 NOV 87	21
NF	155.924 R225s	The sibling bond	33005000815357	21 SEP 1982	30 NOV 87	20
NF	709.72 F983	Pre-Columbian art of Mexico	33005001215631	07 AUG 1985	07 DEC 87	7
NF	551 H15	Encyclopedia of the planet Earth	33005001172709	17 SEP 1984	14 DEC 87	23
NF	709.72 P269	Aztec art	33005001215417	07 AUG 1985	16 DEC 87	4
F	Geary	Goodbye to Poplar haven : recollections of a Utah boyhood	33005001658574	19 AUG 1987	29 DEC 87	3
F	Geary	Goodbye to Poplar haven : recollections of a Utah boyhood	33005001658574	19 AUG 1987	29 DEC 87	3

Computer Assisted Weeding—A Few Examples

A Suburban Public Library Using NOTIS

This library, in a prosperous suburb of a major U.S. city, has approximately 270,000 volumes and circulates about 640,000 volumes per year. For many years it had a NOTIS System, which it recently replaced. With the NOTIS System both the shelf list and uncirculated book list included the same information, except that the uncirculated book list was of books not used since 1992. (See Figure 13.1. The shelf list, and Figure 13.5. The uncirculated book list.) The shelf list is, theoretically, a list of all their volumes, printed in the order of the classification or call number. The uncirculated book list, also in call number order, lists every volume that has not been used since 12/31/92, as of March 26, 1995. In other words, it reflects an open-ended shelf-time period of a little over two years. These books had remained on the shelf, unused, for two years and three months or longer.

The mainframe computer used for this system was also the computer used by the city's other departments and was not located inside the library but at city hall. Thus, whatever printouts were required could not be produced in-house but had to be requested from the city. Because of their length, these lists were printed only once a year and were out-sourced—printed by an outside agency. The last printout of the shelf list was 16,708 pages and filled 15 large volumes. The list of uncirculated books, which are considered the candidates for weeding, contained 5,089 pages, also a rather bulky printout. It is apparent that if all these volumes were weeded out, just about 30 percent of the collection would be removed. From the author's experience, this is just about right for a useful weeding program that would optimize the future use of the collection.

The uncirculated book list had been divided among the library staff members, and they were informed that these books were likely candidates for weeding and that the librarians should proceed to weed the library. For all the reasons mentioned earlier in this book, the project has been lengthy, with time restraints and subjective weeding criteria slowing down the final results. The principal data used for weeding were the factors of non-use during this period, the total number of previous uses, and the acquisition date of the book (labeled "RC Date," standing for "Record Created Date"). Of the 50,000 books on this printout, thousands of books have been removed, but the entire project has not yet been finished. On the positive side, the librarians' work has been simplified. They are examining only 30 percent of the library's collection, and this 30 percent is the proper subset of books to weed—every time one of these volumes is removed, the usefulness of the library is improved, provided the volume did not experience in-library use only.

Fig. 13.5. Uncirculated book list: NOTIS.

| 03/26/95 | LBN108 | BOOK COLLECTION REPORT-- | LOCATION: CALL NO: CREATED AFTER: CREATED BEFORE:12/31/92 LOCATED BEFORE:12/31/92 | | NO USE SINCE: 12/31/92 | | PAGE 2,507 |
REC-NO	LOCATION	CALL-NO	AUTHOR/TITLE	ITEM-ID	CR-DATE	LAST-USE	CHARGES
AAJ7326	NONF	640.43 H	Hirsch, Gretchen / Womanhours :	3154469349377	10/11/87	02/08/91	4
AAM1260	NONF	640.73 H	Hayward, Mike / Baby-proofing your home /	2154408105Z890	10/11/87	09/04/91	3
AAF3767	NONF	640.73 L. 1976	Levy, Leon, / Consumer in the marketplace /	3154408211Z459	10/11/87		1
AAH4909	NONF	640.73 M	Maynes, Edwin Scott, / Decision-making for consumers	3154408211Z483	10/11/87	11/18/89	1
AAA6385	NONF	640.73 M	McLachlan, Christoph / Inflation-wise:	2154408104Z428	10/11/87	11/15/88	1
AAH4911	NONF	640.73 M	Myerson, Bess / Complete consumer book :	3154408085Z390	10/11/87	04/14/89	2
AAE7718	NONF	640.73 P	Papanek, Victor J / How things don't work /	3154407711B684	10/11/87	09/24/90	1
AAV9145	NONF	640.73 P	Passell, Peter / Best /	3154408072431Z	11/16/87	06/09/90	14
AAE7719	NONF	640.73 R	Rinzler, Carol Ann / Consumer's brand-name guide to	2154408055Z900	10/11/87	05/11/89	1
AAG4446	NONF	640.73 S	Sellers, Nancy / Comparison shopping and caring	3154408304Z005	10/11/87	11/15/88	1
ABD4718	NONF	640.73 T	Teitel, Martin / Rain forest in your kitchen :	3154409299Z045	05/12/92	12/28/92	7
ABA5576	NONF	640.73 T	Troelstrup, Archie W / Consumer in American society :	3154408935B0T6	07/25/90		
AAH4921	NONF	640.73 T	350 ways to save energy (and m	3154409049H072	10/11/87	06/11/90	1
AAL5645	NONF	640.8 C	Chaback, Elaine / Official kids' survival kit :	2154408159Z982	10/11/87	01/21/89	3
AAX6556	NONF	640.973 C	Carter, Mary Randolp / American family style /	3154408830S904-	10/26/88	03/10/92	16
AAE7725	NONF	641 A	American heritage cookbook.	3154469014698	10/11/87	02/24/92	4
AAE7731	NONF	641 B	Berkeley Co-op food book :	3154408041A98.	10/11/87	11/30/90	4

One interesting aspect can be seen in the shelf list (figure 13.1). Two copies of the same book by Robert V. Bruce were owned by the library—one experienced 2 uses, the other had no use at all. It seems possible to assume that this second volume was stolen or, at the very least, was never put on the shelf in the correct location. Of course, an inspection of the books on the shelves would indicate whether such a conjecture is true. However, there were several other cases where one of two copies had 20 or more uses and the other had no uses. This is a more dramatic indication of some serious problem.

A Public Library Using Gaylord

The library has a collection of 123,000 volumes and an annual circulation of about 340,000 volumes. In a community of 15,400 people this is 22 volumes per year per resident, an extraordinarily high number. The mainframe computer, operated by Gaylord in Syracuse, New York, is located at a considerable distance from the library. Every night, all daily information is read by Gaylord's system. Gaylord provides all the services a stand-alone system would provide, and for these services the library pays somewhat more than $50,000 per year. This fee seems reasonable since it saves the costs of much more sophisticated equipment and programs, the cost of a full-time computer specialist, and upgrading the programs on a regular basis. Since Gaylord is able to upgrade all of their many clients with one program, the cost benefits to one library must be substantial.

All reports, including an annual shelf-list printout and an annual inactive book list, are sent to the library from Syracuse. The inactive book list is customized for each library, and this one has chosen three years of non-use as their criterion (see Figure 13.2. Inactive items report). In addition, it produces the item utilization report (Figure 13.3) comparing the percentage of use with the percentage of the library's holdings for 550 Dewey classifications. This is customized for each library, and the number of classes can be increased or reduced.

The Inactive Items Report, historically, has contained between 6,500 and 8,000 books. These books are removed from the stacks by pages and relocated in a non-public area. The head librarian then examines them and returns between 10 and 15 percent of them to the circulating collection. He observes that when most librarians are asked to return weeding candidates to the shelves, they return too many volumes, so he does the work himself. The yearly weeding begins in May and is finished by June or July. This library had a freshness and vibrancy about it.

A Public Library Consortium Using GEAC

This is the central site for an eight library consortium using GEAC Plus System, an integrated system. Among many other things, the library is producing reports requested by the members as well as trying to advise them as to changes in the reports they think would be beneficial. Because the central computer services all the libraries, and because all of them request reports, the system is rather slow. When finished, the reports are delivered to the member libraries.

As with most systems, the menus are relatively easy to use and offer plain language choices. In addition, hundreds of easily selected options are available so that reports can emphasize different aspects, such as date, usage, class of book, location, etc.

The system creates two reports that are being used to assist the weeding process. An item list report (Figure 13.6), lists volumes which on April 18, 1996 had not circulated since 12/31/91. This is an uncirculated book list showing an open-end shelf-time period of a predetermined duration. Since there are only four volumes per page in this format, the printouts are much more voluminous than those produced in the first library discussed above. The installation began in 1980 with CLSI and was updated in 1990 by GEAC. At the present time the system is being replaced. Nevertheless, the current system gives considerable information, and weeders were given the lists and encouraged to weed from "these candidates for weeding." The information used by the weeders is the "last activity date" and the "times circulated."

Figure 13.7 shows the "Sort order," the menu used to order the "Item list" report and illustrates the ease of using this program:

"Collection" is the field which selects one of the eight libraries in the consortium.

"Call Number Range" selects the part of the collection to be included in the list, in this case the Dewey 600's.

"Last Circ Act" stands for "last circulation activity" and requests all volumes not used since 12/31/91.

A Consortium Using DRA

A sophisticated system was installed in August 1995, cost over $700,000, and serves 52 libraries with 5,700,000 volumes and 10,000,000 circulations per year. Much of the data from the old CLSI system employed from 1970 to 1995, and upgraded during that period, was easily converted into the new DRA system. As one would expect, the menus are user friendly and offer a wide range of reports with useful options. The printing is extremely fast and clear.

The book information (Figure 13.8. Item record) contains 30 fields, including "# TRANS:" (number of transaction or circulations to date) and "LST TRNS DATE:" (last transaction date, or date of last circulation). The "Items uncirculated since" report (Figure 13.9. Items uncirculated) gives more useful information than the other systems reported on so far. Of value to a weeder are the last two columns:

"LCB" stands for "last copy in branch."

"LCS" stands for "last copy in system."

Fig. 13.6. Item list report: GEAC.

04/18/1996   Page 21

636.71/MIL   MILCSB097000
Miller, Harry Herman, 1900-
The Common sense book of puppy and dog care.
Item Barcode: 3 1974 00331 0629
Item Call No.: 636.71/MIL
Format: Book
Loan Cat: B
Stat. Cat: 54
Cost: $3.95
Last Activity: 03/27/1991 00:00:00
Status: On Shelf
Times Circulated: : 7

641.22/ADA   ADAWOAM95000
Adams, Leon David, 1905-
The wines of America / Leon D. Adams with Bridgett Novak.
Item Barcode: 3 1974 00431 5627
Item Call No.: 641.22/ADA
Format: Book
Loan Cat: B
Stat. Cat: 56
Cost: $14.95
Last Activity: 12/23/1991 00:00:00
Status: On Shelf
Times Circulated: : 0

641.3/TA   TANFIHI99000
Tannahill, Reay.
Food in history.
Item Barcode: 3 1974 00025 1362
Item Call No.: 641.3009/TAN
Format:
Loan Cat:
Stat. Cat: 56
Cost: $0.00
Last Activity: 10/26/1991 00:00:00
Status: On Shelf
Times Circulated: : 3

641.5/MCG R641.5/MCG   MCGOFAC99000
McGee, Harold.
On food and cooking : the science and lore of the kitchen / Harold McG
Item Barcode: 3 1974 00302 2182
Item Call No.: 641.5/MCG
Format: Book
Loan Cat: B
Stat. Cat: 56
Cost: $30.00
Last Activity: 08/28/1991 00:00:00
Status: On Shelf
Times Circulated: : 9

Fig. 13.7. Sort order: GEAC.

```
x   Admin      Help      Compile Report      Go To

x                        Item List Report - Search Criteria
x

x       Criteria             Operator          Value
x

x   Collection:              MEL
x   Collection Range:
x   Scat:
x   Scat Range:
x   Barcode Range:
x   Call Number Range:       600        to        659.9999
x   Format Code:
x   Loan Cat:
x   Cost:
x   Last Circ Act:           <= 12/31/91
x   Times Circulated:
x   Status: Enter 1 for On Shelf or 5 for Checked Out:  |
x   Circulating items only?

x

x
mqqqqqqqqqqqqqqqqqqqqqqqqqqqqqqqqqqqqqqqqqqqqqqqqqqqqqqqqqqqqqqqqq
```

Obviously, a weeding decision, assuming non-use is not the exclusive criterion, is easier to make if the book is neither the last copy in the library nor the last copy in the system. An additional feature is that if a book has experienced no circulation, the system substitutes the "status date" or the "inventory date" so that newer books are not weeded out unintentionally.

The system also has the ability to compute rapidly how many volumes will be listed when any specific uncirculated volume cut-date is selected. This can assist librarians in deciding if a different cut-date should be selected because too many or too few volumes are on the list.

There are two other features of value. First, as with most systems, the programs offer a way to purge the catalog of weeded or lost volumes, with the "Withdrawn items report." This simplifies what used to be an arduous procedure.

Secondly, there is a field that will record in-house use of books not reshelved by the patrons. If all volumes experiencing in-library use had such use recorded, the circulating collection could be weeded with greater confidence. Since in-library use is rarely recorded in current practice, librarians must use their judgment when examining weeding candidates, to retain those volumes experiencing in-library use but not circulating.

The system cannot create a report on the shelf-time periods of the books as they circulate. (See page 206 for the author's suggestion for changes in computer programs.) However, the author contacted DRA and the company offered to create the necessary program for a fee of $7,500. This example of the availability of a strong support system is one of the strengths of this DRA installation.

A System Using CARL

A group of 38 cooperating libraries recently converted from UTLAS to CARL. The new system greatly simplified and expanded the entire operation. All member libraries are now internetworked, all workstations have access to the Internet, and all the members can print out their own reports, either in full or in part.

As with the other systems, the reports are able to include date of last circulation and the total number of circulations (Figure 13.10. Shelf list: CARL). However, laser printing is available and the quality and legibility of this shelf list is outstanding. In addition, it shows the date of publication in the last column, a valuable piece of information to many weeders.

Book information is available in detail (Figure 13.11. Holding edit) or in a compressed form (Figure 13.12. Compressed). One of the great strengths of this system is that in-library use can be entered by scanning the book with a handheld reader. An example of this is illustrated in Figure 13.12, for Danielle Steel's book *Lightning,* which indicates 21 cumulative circulations and 3 in-house uses. The in-house use is a critical and useful piece of information and essential to all of the weeding methods proposed in this book.

(Text continues on page 186.)

Fig. 13.8. Item record: DRA.

```
Network Cataloging Utility    --Item Record (Screen 1 of 2)--    Tue 04/02/199
BIB DBCN: ADA-5148                                 BORROWER DBCN: AAA-0000
  Conroy, Pat. Beach music. 1st ed. New York: N.A. Talese. 1995.

ITEM NUMBER: 31299004173739

 1. OWNING AGENCY: 010101     2. PERM LOC: 010101     3. NEXT LOC: 010101
 4. LAST LOC: 010101          5. HOLD LOC: 010101     6. MAT CODE: 12
 7. DATE BORROWED: 03/20/1996 8. DATE DUE:            9. HOUR DUE: 0:00
10. LST TRNS DATE: 04/02/1996 11. # TRANS: 14        12. TRANS MTD: 0

13. LOAN OUT DATE:           14. LOAN PERIOD:        15. RENEWALS: 0
16. LOAN RET DATE:           17. PRICE: $27.50       18. RENEW LIMIT: 0
19. NOTICE SENT:             20. STAT CAT 1: 51      21. STAT CAT 2:
22. STATUS DATE: 02/27/1996  23. STATUS: 524288      24. ITEM LEVEL: A
25. SHELF DATE:              26. INV DATE: 08/15/1995

27. SHELF LOC:                                       O=MARION
28. CALL NO: FIC Conroy
29. ENUMERATION:
30. CIRC NOTE:
>>
```

Fig. 13.9. Items uncirculated: DRA.

03/24/1996

Items uncirculated since 03/01/1995
for Library System 11.

*** DEPARTMENT 110100 ***

Page 231

Call Number	Vol.	Title	Author	Lng	Item Number	Mat Code	P. Loc	Last Trans	LCB	LCS
[BIOGRPHY] B Morri		Will's boy :	Morris, Wright.	eng	31219000968262	BOOK	110100	10/16/1994	Yes	Yes
[BIOGRPHY] B Morri		White rabbit :	Morrison, Marth	eng	31219001965309	BOOK	110100	11/12/1993	Yes	Yes
[BIOGRPHY] B MORRO		Cousin Bruciel :	Morrow, Cousin	eng	31219001819955	BOOK	110100	01/09/1995	No	No
[BIOGRPHY] B Moste		Zero Mostel :	Brown, Jared.	eng	31219002180742	BOOK	110100	02/28/1991	Yes	No
[BIOGRPHY] B Mowre		Hadley :	Diliberto, Giol	eng	31219002664497	BOOK	110100	08/11/1994	No	No
[BIOGRPHY] B Muham		Muhammad :	Armstrong, Kare	eng	31219002734787	BOOK	110100	04/17/1993	Yes	Yes
[BIOGRPHY] B Muham		Muhammad: prophet an	Watt, William M	eng	31219000291202	BOOK	110100	12/23/1994	Yes	Yes
[BIOGRPHY] B Mulca		My lips are sealed :	Mulcahy, Susan.	eng	31219002101615	BOOK	110100	01/31/1995	Yes	Yes
[BIOGRPHY] B Murdo		Citizen Murdoch /	Kiernan, Thomas	eng	31219001785796	BOOK	110100	05/23/1992	Yes	Yes
[BIOGRPHY] B Murra		Jim Murray :	Murray, Jim.	eng	31219002892007	BOOK	110100	10/19/1994	Yes	Yes
[BIOGRPHY] B Murro		Murrow, his life and	Sperber, A. M.	eng	31219001745511	BOOK	110100	12/15/1993	Yes	Yes
[BIOGRPHY] B Murro		Miss America, 1945 :	Dworkin, Susan.	eng	31219001800011	BOOK	110100	06/06/1994	Yes	Yes
[BIOGRPHY] B MYERS		Queen Bess :	Preston, Jennif	eng	31219002344017	BOOK	110100	07/02/1993	Yes	Yes
[BIOGRPHY] B Myrda		Another world :	Myrdal, Jan.	eng	31219003073672	BOOK	110100	12/06/1994	Yes	Yes
[BIOGRPHY] B Nabok		Vladimir Nabokov :	Boyd, Brian.	eng	31219002612546	BOOK	110100	08/21/1993	Yes	Yes
[BIOGRPHY] B Nabok		Vladimir Nabokov :	Boyd, Brian.	eng	31219002433273	BOOK	110100	08/21/1993	Yes	Yes
[BIOGRPHY] B Nast		The man who was Vogu	Seebohm, Caroli	eng	31219001447903	BOOK	110100	01/20/1995	Yes	Yes
[BIOGRPHY] B Nelso		Defending the devil	Nelson, Polly.	eng	31219003109905	BOOK	110100	01/19/1995	Yes	Yes
[BIOGRPHY] B Ness		Torso :	Nickel, Steven.	eng	31219002170644	BOOK	110100	09/08/1994	Yes	Yes
[BIOGRPHY] B Newha		Focus :	Newhall, Beaumo	eng	31219002891868	BOOK	110100	12/12/1994	Yes	Yes
[BIOGRPHY] B Nicho		Jack Nicholson :	Shepherd, Donal	eng	31219002590494	BOOK	110100	05/24/1994	Yes	No
[BIOGRPHY] B Nietz		Friedrich Nietzsche,	Frenzel, Ivo.	eng	31219020470368	BOOK	110100	07/04/1994	Yes	No
[BIOGRPHY] E Nijin		Vaslav Nijinsky :	Ostwald, Peter	eng	31219002552775	BOOK	110100	10/01/1993	No	No
[BIOGRPHY] B NIN M		Henry and June :	Nin, Anais,	eng	31219001776003	BOOK	110100	01/22/1992	Yes	Yes
[BIOGRPHY] B Oakle		Annie Oakley /	Kasper, Shirl,	eng	31219002726049	BOOK	110100	04/19/1993	Yes	Yes
[BIOGRPHY] 3 O'CAS		Sean O'Casey :	O'Connor, Garry	eng	31219002119500	BOOK	110100	01/03/1994	Yes	Yes
[BIOGRPHY] E O'CON		The hereditary bonds	MacDonagh, Oliv	eng	31219002066515	BOOK	110100	12/07/1992	Yes	Yes
[BIOGRPHY] B O'CON		John Cardinal O'Conn	Hentoff, Nat.	eng	31219020466661	BOOK	110100	10/27/1992	Yes	Yes
[BIOGRPHY] B O'Kee		O'Keeffe and Stiegli	Eisler, Benita.	eng	31219002334492	BOOK	110100	10/01/1993	Yes	Yes
[BIOGRPHY] B Olivi		Laurence Olivier :	Holden, Anthony	eng	31219001599989	BOOK	110100	08/17/1992	Yes	Yes
[BIOGRPHY] B Olivi		Laurence Olivier :	Spoto, Donald.	eng	31219002675048	BOOK	110100	06/09/1993	Yes	Yes
[BIOGRPHY] B Onass		Jacqueline :	Galella, Ron.	eng	31219000553718	BOOK	110100	09/19/1991	Yes	Yes
[BIOGRPHY] B Onass		A Woman named Jackie	Heymann, C. Dav	eng	31219002162672	BOOK	110100	01/04/1994	Yes	Yes
[BIOGRPHY] B Onass		A Woman named Jackie	Heymann, C. Dav	eng	31219002122664	BOOK	110100	01/20/1992	No	No
[BIOGRPHY] B Onass		A Woman named Jackie	Heymann, C. Dav	eng	31219002161179	BOOK	110100	12/24/1990	No	No
[BIOGRPHY] B ONASS		A Woman named Jackie	Heymann, C. Dav	eng	31219001987600	BOOK	110100	03/08/1993	No	No
[BIOGRPHY] B Onass		All the pain that mo	Wright, William	eng	31219002559710	BOOK	110100	02/16/1995	Yes	Yes
[BIOGRPHY] B O'Nei		O'Neill	Gelb, Arthur.	eng	31219002112976	BOOK	110100	01/13/1994	Yes	Yes
[BIOGRPHY] B O'Nei		Man of the House :	O'Neill, Tip.	eng	31219001688816	BOOK	110100	07/11/1994	Yes	Yes
[BIOGRPHY] B Orwel		Orwell, the transfor	Stansky, Peter.	eng	31219000749621	BOOK	110100	05/07/1992	Yes	Yes
[BIOGRPHY] B Otis		Upside your head :	Otis, Johnny.	eng	31219002973773	BOOK	110100	04/23/1994	Yes	Yes
[BIOGRPHY] B O'Too		Peter O'Toole :	Freedland, Mich	eng	31219001365401	BOOK	110100	12/02/1991	Yes	Yes
[BIOGRPHY] B Paar		P.S. Jack Paar /	Paar, Jack.	eng	31219001320935	BOOK	110100	09/30/1994	Yes	Yes
[BIOGRPHY] B Pack		Cast no shadow /	Lovell, Mary S.	eng	31219002674884	BOOK	110100	12/09/1993	Yes	Yes
[BIOGRPHY] B Paige		Don't look back. :	Ribowsky, Mark.	eng	31219003016663	BOOK	110100	09/19/1994	Yes	Yes
[BIOGRPHY] B Paley		Empire :	Paper, Lewis D.	eng	31219001889228	BOOK	110100	03/07/1991	Yes	Yes
[BIOGRPHY] B Parke		Elvis and the colone	Vellenga, Dirk.	eng	31219002060720	BOOK	110100	10/30/1991	Yes	Yes
[BIOGRPHY] B Parks		Rosa Parks :	Parks, Rosa.	eng	31219002677887	BOOK	110100	09/26/1994	Yes	Yes
[BIOGRPHY] B Pasca		La popessa / Paul I.	Murphy, Paul I.	eng	31219001322337	BOOK	110100	01/25/1995	Yes	Yes
[BIOGRPHY] B PATTO		Patton, the man behi	Blumenson, Mart	eng	31219002512274	BOOK	110100	07/20/1989	No	No
[BIOGRPHY] B Paul		Paul VI :	Hebblethwaite,	eng	31219002577919	BOOK	110100	10/30/1993	Yes	Yes
[BIOGRPHY] B Paul		Les Paul :	Shaughnessy, Ma	eng	31219002838753	BOOK	110100	09/07/1993	No	No
[BIOGRPHY] E FAULI		Linus Pauling :	Serafini, Antho	eng	31219002211117	BOOK	110100	07/29/1991	Yes	Yes

Fig. 13.10. Shelf list: CARL.

```
April 1, 1996                    SHELF LIST BY BRANCH                              PAGE: 100
     Free Library
PUR    BRANCH
==================================================================================================

              LCCN:  66020725   ISBN:              BID:    125145
              Birmingham, Stephe  Our crowd"; the gr            Harper & Row                  1967
              404p.                              SHELF          ITEM LOAN PERIOD: 9999
PUR STA    301.451 924 B                         31027009682853   $0.00      DISCHG NOTE:
              MEDIA: BK      CIRCULATIONS:    1  LAST CIRC DATE: 02/21/92    ITEM NOTE:
        ----------------------------------------------------------------------------------

              LCCN:           ISBN:              BID:    198199
              Bennett, Lerone, 1  Before the Mayflow   Rev. ed.   Penguin Books               1964
              435p.                              SHELF          ITEM LOAN PERIOD: 9999
PUR STA    301.451 B                             31027100037072   $2.45      DISCHG NOTE:
              MEDIA: BK      CIRCULATIONS:    0  LAST CIRC DATE: 03/13/91    ITEM NOTE:
        ----------------------------------------------------------------------------------

              LCCN:  61005368   ISBN:              BID:    595303
              Griffin, John Howa  Black like me      Updated, wit  Signet/New American Library :  1976
              188 p. ;                           N/A           ITEM LOAN PERIOD: 9999
PUR STA    301.451 G                             31027100049523   $1.00      DISCHG NOTE:
              MEDIA: PBK     CIRCULATIONS:    2  LAST CIRC DATE: 02/18/95    ITEM NOTE:
        ----------------------------------------------------------------------------------

              LCCN:  66012544   ISBN:              BID:    441422
              Woodward, C. Vann   The strange career  2d rev. ed.  Oxford University Press,      1966
              xiii, 205 p.                       SHELF          ITEM LOAN PERIOD: 9999
PUR STA    301.451/W/1966                        31027100049473   $1.50      DISCHG NOTE:
              MEDIA: PBK     CIRCULATIONS:    0  LAST CIRC DATE: 05/07/92    ITEM NOTE:
        ----------------------------------------------------------------------------------

              LCCN:  89049000   ISBN:              BID:    549021
              Tannen, Deborah.    You just don't und            Morrow,                       1990
              330 p. ;                           SHELF          ITEM LOAN PERIOD: 9999
PUR STA    302/T                                 31027100030754   $18.45     DISCHG NOTE:
              MEDIA: BK      CIRCULATIONS:   17  LAST CIRC DATE: 03/12/94    ITEM NOTE:
        ----------------------------------------------------------------------------------

              LCCN:  90046188   ISBN:              BID:    579408
              Halberstam, David.  The next century             Morrow,                        1991
              126 p. ;                           SHELF          ITEM LOAN PERIOD: 9999
PUR STA    303.4909 H                            31027100036140   $16.45     DISCHG NOTE:
              MEDIA: BK      CIRCULATIONS:    0  LAST CIRC DATE: 03/05/91    ITEM NOTE:
        ----------------------------------------------------------------------------------

              LCCN:  89031502   ISBN:              BID:    527626
              Berger, Gilda.      Violence and the m            F. Watts,                     1989
              176 p. ;                           SHELF          ITEM LOAN PERIOD: 9999
PUR STA    303.6/B                               31027100018726   $13.40     DISCHG NOTE:
              MEDIA: BK      CIRCULATIONS:    0  LAST CIRC DATE: 05/01/90    ITEM NOTE:
        ----------------------------------------------------------------------------------
```

Fig. 13.11. Holding edit, full information: CARL.

```
*************************************     HOLDINGS  EDIT     *************************************

Item #| 3102210006607024    | Item # |          | Boundwith|        |

Current Branch| PKS    | Loc| STACKS |  Owning Branch| PKS    | Loc| STACKS |

Call#| Fiction
                       |--|            |--|         —        |--|     —      —

LC Card #| 94043651                    Control #| 0000741806  |

Status| C |Status Date| 040196 | Media | 7D  | Price| 24.95 |Type|

Circ History|  3  | Hold History|  0  | Cum History|  21  |

Notes |  |                        ( Edit date 072595  staff EIT )

TITLE LEVEL:
Author| Steel, Danielle.
Title| Lightning                                   Date| 1995  |
Branch| PKS    | Loc| STACKS |  Call#|

F1=RECOVER  F2=NOTES  F3=NEXT  F4=PREV  F5=MOVE  F6=DEL  F9=WRITE
```

Fig. 13.12. Item report, compressed: CARL.

Steel, Danielle,
    Lightning
Fiction

Branch: PKS   Loc: STACKS   Item: 31022100607024
                         Item:

Media: 7D   CumCirc: 21   InHouse: 3   Holds: 0

Last Action Date: 04/01/96

Charged: 04/01/96 13:07   Due: 04/08/96 at PKS   : OA3

               H -- to HOLD (item level)
               Q -- to QUIT
               >

Some Observations in the Field

1.   Unless a library had just changed its system, almost every one of them felt that much better computer systems and programs were now available. The almost daily changes in computerization were evident everywhere. There was a feeling of being out of date in face of the availability of more sophisticated systems, which include Internet accessibility at all terminals, the availability of union catalogs, LC Catalog and other important catalogs, CD-ROMs, multimedia computers, high-speed printers, higher quality printing with laser printers, improvements in color reproduction, and dozens of other capacities announced almost daily.

2.   Local libraries wanted more control over the system and the ability to print out reports locally instead of having to use off-site services. The present time lag and delay was not acceptable to many librarians.

3.   The slowness of the response of computer systems in producing the requested reports frustrated a number of users. This was due primarily to the fact that many reports and processes were in demand by different libraries at the same time, and any job had to queue up to wait its turn for computer time.

4.   The ease of transferring information from one vendor's system to a completely different vendor's system was impressive.

5. The excellent support efforts by most vendors were appreciated.

6. The difficulties in learning how to use new systems and the long time it takes to get them fully implemented was a common complaint.

7. The menus offer a large number of choices, but only a few of them are used. As with most computer programs, they offer vastly more than what is needed by the library.

8. The bulk of the printouts and their complexity often made it slow and difficult to extract the information desired. In almost half the libraries visited, further information had to be sent to the author later, information that should have been readily available, such as total circulation figures, the number of volumes in the collection, etc. In some cases the library could not find the data requested without considerable effort.

9. Some useful data was difficult to recover because of the nature of the programs. For example, in one library, an attempt was made to get an uncirculated book list that would identify 25 percent of the total collection. Even with a very sophisticated installation this could be done only by trial and error, by altering the date being used. Then the computer had to display the entire list on the screen before the number of entries on this list was available. The same awkward process had to be repeated using different cut-dates until a list representing 25 percent of the collection could be produced.

10. While most library administrators and librarians felt that computers were helping them, a large number of librarians still resist computers and feel computer illiterate.

11. Commercial providers of computers and programs for libraries have manifested little interest in the weeding process and its needs.

How to Weed Today, Using Computer Assistance

Unfortunately, computers do not give the information needed in an easy, painless manner. There are two possible methods available today, depending upon the programming of the computers.

Summary of the Methods

In order to weed with the greatest confidence, the in-library use of books must be recorded. This means that books must not be reshelved by the users, and their use must be recorded by the computer system before they are reshelved.

At the present time, all computer systems observed retained "the date of last circulation" (or in-library use, when such use is recorded as a "circulation") until the book is used again, when they replace that date with a new date. They erase that piece of information and add one use to the number in the field showing the total number of uses experienced by that volume. For proper weeding, it is necessary to record and tabulate the date of last use (before it is destroyed), in order to determine a weeding cut-date.

A method of intercepting the information before it disappears must be used. A backup computer is frequently available for listing circulations in the event that the main system is down. Four hundred consecutive uses, both in-library and circulation uses, are recorded outside the regular system and tabulated either by computer or manually to show what cut-date, or shelf-time period, would retain 95 to 98 percent of the future use. These books are then removed from the collection, and librarians examine them to determine if any volumes should be returned to the shelves.

Step 1: Intercept approximately 400 consecutive uses, both in-library and circulation uses, and record them on a computer system by-passing the regular system. This should be done on a back-up computer at the circulation station. Handheld computers or a PC can be employed.

Step 2: Have these volumes printed out by the regular system, in order of the date of last use. Most systems are programmed to use different fields as the primary sort. (See Figure 13.4. Circulating items listed by date of last use.) When the printout has been completed, dump the intercepted circulations into the regular system so that they then will be charged out normally.

Step 3: Determine the percentage of future circulation to be retained (between 95 to 99 percent). If in doubt, the author's projects have shown that 96 percent has given good results, with an increase rather than a 4 percent loss in circulation.

Step 4: Determine the cut-off point to be used for weeding. This is done in the following manner:

1. Starting from the top of the list count down until locating the space between two volumes which has 4 percent of the volumes above it and 96 percent of the volumes below it. Just multiply the number of volumes in the sample by four, round the answer to the next higher whole number, and count down that number of volumes. In this case, $437 \times .04 = 17.48$, so count down 18 volumes and indicate the space with a small arrow. The arrow is located between the dates "20 May 86" and "22 Jul 86" (see figure 13.13).

2. Count the number of volumes above this arrow which were added to the collection after the date immediately below the arrow—May 1986 (see the column headed "Date added"). Eleven such volumes were added since that date and therefore did not have ample opportunity to be used during the full time period.

Fig. 13.13. List of 437 items checked out on 23 Aug 1988 with date of last use.

page 1

cut-off point

Coll	CALL#	Title [from BIB record]	Barcode	Date added	Date of Last Use	USE
T	Hall	See the red sky	33005000527664	19 APR 1982		0
NF	808.82 F487	Film scripts four	33005001401355	30 APR 1986		0
NF	814 T391	Approaches to Walden	33005001444629	23 JUN 1986		0
NF	332.024 B813	A second start : a widow's guide to financial survival at a time of emotional crisis	33005001469204	17 OCT 1986		0
NF	741.235 H83	How to draw in pastels, pencils and pen & ink	33005001577949	30 JUL 1987		0
NF	745.5 W766	Indian crafts and skills : an illustrated guide for making authentic Indian clothing, shelters, and ornaments	33005001584440	23 JUN 1987		0
NF	338.644 N125	The big boys : power and position in American business	33005001591072	02 JUL 1987		0
F	<R> Peters	Die for love	33005001600907	11 JUL 1988		0
P	Dubamevich	Pigs in hiding	33005001608538	21 JUN 1988		0
F	Sheldon	Master of the game	33005001608900	29 JUN 1988		0
F	Drury	The hill of summer : a novel of the Soviet conquest	33005001608918	29 JUN 1988		0
NF	343.07 B152	The law and legislation of credit cards : use and misuse	33005001702117	21 OCT 1987		0
RC	688.722 D516	The collectors encyclopedia of Barbie dolls and collectibles	33005001801349	26 JUL 1988		0
NF	647.94 S158	Country Inns and back roads : North America	33005001288919	06 MAR 1985	09 SEP 85	2
NF	200.973 023	Hist atlas religion in America	33005000093476	19 FEB 1984	08 FEB 86	13
NF	200.973 023	Hist atlas religion in America	33005000093476	18 FEB 1984	08 FEB 86	13
F	Miller	Bright tomorrow	33005000050310	14 DEC 1984	15 APR 86	8
F	Gann	In the company of eagles	33005000634217	19 FEB 1984	20 MAY 86	6
NF	Frankel	The Aleph solution	33005000020883	23 APR 1986	22 JUL 86	11
F	917.3 J418	A walk across America	33005001403013	28 NOV 1983	09 AUG 86	1
NF	White	The solid mandala	33005001087337	18 APR 1984	18 OCT 86	8
F	647.94 R156	Lodgings for less : Eastern states	33005001148311	19 FEB 1984	08 DEC 86	3
F	<M> Coffey	The wall of masks	33005000616854	17 APR 1987	03 MAR 87	23
F	Coetzee	Foe	33005001530404	17 APR 1987	19 MAY 87	1
F	Coetzee	Foe	33005001530484	07 JUN 1982	19 MAY 87	1
NF	550 As42e	Exploring the earth and the cosmos	33005000807420	18 FEB 1984	09 JUN 87	20
NF	636.72 H41	The complete Lhasa Apso	33005000181982	16 MAR 1982	07 JUL 87	26
F	709.7 T42	Primitives & folk art	33005000222950	20 MAY 1982	04 AUG 87	8
F	<R> Roby	The broken key	33005000080494	15 MAR 1987	06 OCT 87	21
NF	120 B835	On knowing : essays for left hand	33005000075408	19 APR 1982	08 OCT 87	2
T	Hall	Another kind of courage	33005000522185	24 MAY 1984	08 OCT 87	7
F	<R> Benzoni	Catherine's quest	33005001117134	06 AUG 1982	24 MAY 87	10
LPN	050 R22	Reader's Digest--large type edition	33005000076695	06 AUG 1982	05 NOV 87	4
LPN	050 R22	Reader's Digest--large type edition	33005000076695	19 FEB 1984	05 NOV 87	4
NF	809 Am35	American Heritage history of the writers' America	33005000148908	18 FEB 1984	05 NOV 87	10
F	Aldrich	In a dark garden	33005000000117	15 JAN 1982	06 NOV 87	9
F	<M> York	Death to my killer	33005000087171	13 MAY 1985	07 NOV 87	11
NF	M273.5 W61	Hole in the rock	33005001137059	19 FEB 1984	09 NOV 87	31
NF	155.232 K521	Chancing it : why we take risks	33005001305341	21 SEP 1982	17 NOV 87	5
NF	394.268282 M58	The Victorian Christmas book	33005001028157	07 AUG 1985	30 NOV 87	21
NF	155.924 B225s	The sibling bond	33005000815357	17 SEP 1984	07 DEC 87	20
NF	709.72 F983	Pre-Columbian art of Mexico	33005001215631	07 AUG 1985	14 DEC 87	7
NF	551 H15	Encyclopedia of the planet Earth	33005001172709	19 AUG 1987	16 DEC 87	23
NF	709.72 P269	Aztec art	33005001215417	19 AUG 1987	29 DEC 87	4
F	Geary	Goodbye to Poplar haven : recollections of a Utah boyhood	33005001658574	19 AUG 1987	29 DEC 87	3
F	Geary	Goodbye to Poplar haven : recollections of a Utah boyhood				3

Step 5: Create an uncirculated book list using the date just established. All computer systems observed were able to produce a list showing all volumes that had not been used since any specific date desired.

Step 6: Have clerks and volunteers remove all volumes from the shelves that were on this uncirculated book list and store them on shelves away from the main collection. These are the candidates for weeding. This completes the most arduous part of the weeding process and relieves librarians of what is basically a manual task. In a library, because of space limitations, perhaps 10 percent of the weeds should be placed in this "weeding storage area" at one time.

Step 7: Give the librarians one week to examine these volumes and suggest books that should be returned to the stacks. A book recommended for retention should have a written justification for such retention and the weeding manager should make the final decision. Since few books should be returned to the shelves, this work should be done fast and painlessly. There is statistical evidence that the removal of these volumes will improve the value and the use of the library.

However, if the in-library usage has not been recorded, this method still can be employed. Then it becomes important that the librarians attempt to retain in the collection those books experiencing recent in-library use.

A Manual Computer Assisted Method

There are computer systems that are not programmed to print out a list of books in order of the date of last use, but are able to print out a list of the books which includes a field indicating the date of last use. In this method, such a list is used to compute manually a weeding shelf-time period.

Step 1: Intercept approximately 400 consecutive uses, both in-library and circulation uses, and record them on a computer system not presently connected to the regular circulation control system. This should be done by using the backup system if one is provided. If not, some systems have a switch to disconnect them from the mainframe normally used for circulation control. In other cases, libraries have PCs not normally used for circulation control but which can be used for this purpose. Some libraries have hand-held computers that could be used.

Step 2: Feed this list of 400 volumes into the regular computer system, and obtain a printout of these volumes, including the date of last use.

Step 3: Manually, enter the year of last use for each volume in the column "Volumes With This Date of Last Use," as shown in Figure 13.14. Figure 13.16 shows the entry of the 17 volumes listed in Figure 13.15. It should be noted that for the book showing no usage, 1988, the year this book was accessioned, is the date used. If this accession date is not available, no entry should be made for the book. The system using a crossed line for every fifth entry makes counting easier.

When all 407 entries (actual sample size taken in a public library) have been completed (see Figure 13.17. Special form: Step 3a), the intercepted data should be fed into the regular charge-out system so that the books will be charged out normally.

(Text continues on page 195.)

Fig. 13.14. Computer assisted method: Special form.

COMPUTER ASSISTED METHOD
(Form for Computing Cut-Date)

Summary of Method (see page 187 for complete details):

1. By-passing the regular system, record 400 consecutive uses, combining both books being circulated and books having in-library use, using a standby computer system.
2. Have the regular system print out a list of these books, showing the date of last use.
3. Manually, enter the year of last use for each volume in the column "Volumes With This Date of Last Use."
4. In the column "TOTAL #" enter the total number of cases in each row.
5. Add up the "TOTAL #" column and enter the total at the bottom of the page.
6. Compute the percentage of usage represented by each year. Enter in column headed "TOTAL %."
7. Compute and enter under "CUM. %" the cumulative percentage, starting from the top of the form.
8. Determine the keeping percentage to be used for weeding.
9. Determine the cut-off date to be used for weeding.
10. Have the computer produce a list of all books which have not been used since that cut-off date and remove them from the collection.

Date	Volumes With This Date of Last Use	TOTAL		CUM
		#	%	%
1997*				
1996				
1995				
1994				
1993				
1992				
1991				
1990				
1989				
1988				
1987				
Pre 1986				
	Total			

*Note: The current year should appear in the top row and earlier years in each successive row.

Fig. 13.15. Simulated date of last use report: At circulation.

03/28/95   LIB108   BOOK COLLECTION REPORT--   LOCATION: CALL NO: CREATED AFTER: NO USE SINCE:
CREATED BEFORE:

REC-NO	LOCATION	CALL-NO	AUTHOR/TITLE	ITEM-ID	CR-DATE	LAST-USE	CHARGES
AAR9106	NONF	508.94 E	Evans, Howard Ensign / Australia, a natural history /	31544084077783	10/11/87	12/23/90	2
AAT7442	NONF	509 A	Alic, Margaret / Hypatia's heritage :	31544086239894	10/11/87	11/05/93	8
AAE5031	NONF	509 A	Anderson, Clifford N / Fertile crescent;	31544075041475	10/11/87	03/29/93	3
AA28893	NONF	509 A	Asimov, Isaac. / Asimov's chronology of science	31544089186993	12/26/89	10/04/94	7
AAZO814	NONF	509 A	Asimov, Isaac. / Science past, science future /	31544075065699	07/08/89	01/27/94	2
AAW5505	NONF	509 B	Bettex, Albert W / Discovery of nature.	31544066037771	02/11/88	11/25/94	4
ABE8189	NONF	509 B	Biagioli, Mario / Galileo, courtier :	31544092417914	09/01/93	05/19/94	7
AAU4122	NONF	509 B	Bruce, Robert V / Launching of modern American s	31544087033882	10/11/87	01/24/93	2
AAU4122	NONF	509 B	Bruce, Robert V / Launching of modern American s	31544087065256	06/06/88		
ABA2151	NONF	509 B	Bruno, Leonard C / Landmarks of science :	31544089297576	06/26/90	03/23/94	4
AAW2618	NONF	509 B	Bruno, Leonard C / Tradition of science :	31544087242830	12/30/87	05/26/92	6
AAT4093	NONF	509 B	Burke, James. / Day the universe changed /	31544086211984	10/11/87	04/23/94	15
AAT4093	NONF	509 B	Burke, James. / Day the universe changed /	31544086189479	10/11/87	01/17/95	9
AAT4093	NONF	509 B	Burke, James. / Day the universe changed /	31544086211992	10/11/87	02/24/95	17
AAA0809	NONF	509 C	Cohen, I. Bernard. / From Leonardo to Lavoisier. 14	31544081553646	04/25/88	11/22/94	7
AAQ2351	NONF	509 C	Cohen, I. Bernard. / Revolution in science /	31544085080109	10/11/87	05/17/94	12
AAE5030	NONF	509 D	Daniels, George H / Science in American society:	31544072042997	10/11/87	01/27/94	4

Fig. 13.16. Special form: Step 3.

COMPUTER ASSISTED METHOD
(Form for Computing Cut-Date)

Summary of Method (see page 187 for complete details):

1. By-passing the regular system, record 400 consecutive uses, combining both books being circulated and books having in-library use, using a standby computer system.
2. Have the regular system print out a list of these books, showing the date of last use.
3. Manually, enter the year of last use for each volume in the column "Volumes With This Date of Last Use."
4. In the column "TOTAL #" enter the total number of cases in each row.
5. Add up the "TOTAL #" column and enter the total at the bottom of the page.
6. Compute the percentage of usage represented by each year. Enter in column headed "TOTAL %."
7. Compute and enter under "CUM. %" the cumulative percentage, starting from the top of the form.
8. Determine the keeping percentage to be used for weeding.
9. Determine the cut-off date to be used for weeding.
10. Have the computer produce a list of all books which have not been used since that cut-off date and remove them from the collection.

Date	Volumes With This Date of Last Use	TOTAL		CUM
		#	%	%
1997				
1996				
1995	//			
1994	// // //			
1993	///			
1992	/			
1991				
1990	/			
1989				
1988	/			
1987				
Pre 1986				
	Total			

Fig. 13.17. Special form: Step 3a.

COMPUTER ASSISTED METHOD
(Form for Computing Cut-Date)

Summary of Method (see page 187 for complete details):

1. By-passing the regular system, record 400 consecutive uses, combining both books being circulated and books having in-library use, using a standby computer system.
2. Have the regular system print out a list of these books, showing the date of last use.
3. Manually, enter the year of last use for each volume in the column "Volumes With This Date of Last Use."
4. In the column "TOTAL #" enter the total number of cases in each row.
5. Add up the "TOTAL #" column and enter the total at the bottom of the page.
6. Compute the percentage of usage represented by each year. Enter in column headed "TOTAL %."
7. Compute and enter under "CUM. %" the cumulative percentage, starting from the top of the form.
8. Determine the keeping percentage to be used for weeding.
9. Determine the cut-off date to be used for weeding.
10. Have the computer produce a list of all books which have not been used since that cut-off date and remove them from the collection.

Date	Volumes With This Date of Last Use	TOTAL		CUM
		#	%	%
1997				
1996	(tally marks)			
1995	(tally marks)			
1994	(tally marks)			
1993	(tally marks)			
1992	(tally marks)			
1991	(tally marks)			
1990	(tally marks)			
1989	(tally marks)			
1988	(tally marks)			
1987				
Pre 1986				
	Total			

Step 4: Total the number of books indicated for each year. In the column "TOTAL #" enter this number. Figure 13.18 shows these entries for all 407 books. It can be seen that 299 books were previously used in 1996 and entered in the proper row and column. Likewise, the 59 books used in 1995 were entered in the same column and the next row. This process was continued until all the samples were tallied in accordance with their shelf-time periods (as expressed in terms of the date of their previous use).

Step 5: Add up the column that was just tabulated in Step 4. The sum represents the total number of books used in the sample. Enter this number on the bottom line alongside the word "Total." Here the number 407 was entered, and the form now looks like Figure 13.19.

Step 6: Compute the percentage of usage represented by each year. This percentage figure should be entered in the column directly to the right of the "TOTAL #" column headed "TOTAL %." To compute the percentage for each year, divide the total number of uses in that year by the total number of cases in the entire sample as indicated in Step 5. In Figure 13.20, 299 books for 1996 were divided by the total number of books in the sample, 407. This equaled 73.5 percent, figured to the nearest half percent. Repeat this process for each successive year. In this library, it produced 14.5 percent for 1995, 4 percent for 1994, etc. Obviously, this computation can be made only for years in which some previous use was recorded.

Step 7: Compute the cumulative percentage starting from the most recent year. Enter these figures in the column headed "CUM %." *Cumulative percentage* results from the successive percentages being added together from the top to the bottom of the form. The form now looks like Figure 13.21. In our example, in the row designated "1996," 73.5 percent is carried over from the "TOTAL %" column and entered alongside in the "CUM %" column. Going down one row, the 73.5 percent is added to the 14.5 percent, and 88 percent is written in the 1995 row. For the next year, 4 percent is added to the 88 percent, giving 92 percent, and so forth, until all percentages have been added together. The total always should equal 100 percent. If, because of rounding, the resultant figure is not 100 percent, cumulate the total number of books, year by year, and recompute the cumulative percentages. Thus, add the 299 books to the 59 books, and divide this new number (358) by the total number of books (407). Enter this percentage in the "CUM %" column. Now add the 16 books in 1994 to the 358 (giving 374) and divide this number by 407. Continue this process until 100 percent of the books have been cumulated and tabulated.

(Text continues on page 200.)

Fig. 13.18. Special form: Step 4.

COMPUTER ASSISTED METHOD
(Form for Computing Cut-Date)

Summary of Method (see page 187 for complete details):

1. By-passing the regular system, record 400 consecutive uses, combining both books being circulated and books having in-library use, using a standby computer system.
2. Have the regular system print out a list of these books, showing the date of last use.
3. Manually, enter the year of last use for each volume in the column "Volumes With This Date of Last Use."
4. In the column "TOTAL #" enter the total number of cases in each row.
5. Add up the "TOTAL #" column and enter the total at the bottom of the page.
6. Compute the percentage of usage represented by each year. Enter in column headed "TOTAL %."
7. Compute and enter under "CUM. %" the cumulative percentage, starting from the top of the form.
8. Determine the keeping percentage to be used for weeding.
9. Determine the cut-off date to be used for weeding.
10. Have the computer produce a list of all books which have not been used since that cut-off date and remove them from the collection.

Date	Volumes With This Date of Last Use	TOTAL		CUM
		#	%	%
1997				
1996	＃＃＃ (tally marks)	299		
1995	(tally marks)	59		
1994	(tally marks)	16		
1993	(tally marks)	17		
1992	IIII	4		
1991	IIII	4		
1990	II	2		
1989	＋＋＋	5		
1988	I	1		
1987				
Pre 1986				
	Total			

Fig. 13.19. Special form: Step 5.

COMPUTER ASSISTED METHOD
(Form for Computing Cut-Date)

Summary of Method (see page 187 for complete details):

1. By-passing the regular system, record 400 consecutive uses, combining both books being circulated and books having in-library use, using a standby computer system.
2. Have the regular system print out a list of these books, showing the date of last use.
3. Manually, enter the year of last use for each volume in the column "Volumes With This Date of Last Use."
4. In the column "TOTAL #" enter the total number of cases in each row.
5. Add up the "TOTAL #" column and enter the total at the bottom of the page.
6. Compute the percentage of usage represented by each year. Enter in column headed "TOTAL %."
7. Compute and enter under "CUM. %" the cumulative percentage, starting from the top of the form.
8. Determine the keeping percentage to be used for weeding.
9. Determine the cut-off date to be used for weeding.
10. Have the computer produce a list of all books which have not been used since that cut-off date and remove them from the collection.

Date	Volumes With This Date of Last Use	TOTAL		CUM
		#	%	%
1997				
1996	(tally marks)	299		
1995	(tally marks)	59		
1994	(tally marks)	16		
1993	(tally marks)	17		
1992	(tally marks)	4		
1991	(tally marks)	4		
1990	(tally marks)	2		
1989	(tally marks)	5		
1988	(tally marks)	1		
1987				
Pre 1986				
	Total	407		

Fig. 13.20. Special form: Step 6.

COMPUTER ASSISTED METHOD
(Form for Computing Cut-Date)

Summary of Method (see page 187 for complete details):

1. By-passing the regular system, record 400 consecutive uses, combining both books being circulated and books having in-library use, using a standby computer system.
2. Have the regular system print out a list of these books, showing the date of last use.
3. Manually, enter the year of last use for each volume in the column "Volumes With This Date of Last Use."
4. In the column "TOTAL #" enter the total number of cases in each row.
5. Add up the "TOTAL #" column and enter the total at the bottom of the page.
6. Compute the percentage of usage represented by each year. Enter in column headed "TOTAL %."
7. Compute and enter under "CUM. %" the cumulative percentage, starting from the top of the form.
8. Determine the keeping percentage to be used for weeding.
9. Determine the cut-off date to be used for weeding.
10. Have the computer produce a list of all books which have not been used since that cut-off date and remove them from the collection.

Date	Volumes With This Date of Last Use	TOTAL #	TOTAL %	CUM %
1997				
1996	𝍸𝍸𝍸𝍸... (tally marks)	299	73.5	
1995	𝍸𝍸𝍸... (tally marks)	59	14.5	
1994	𝍸𝍸𝍸 I	16	4	
1993	𝍸𝍸𝍸 II	17	4	
1992	IIII	4	1	
1991	IIII	4	1	
1990	II	2	.5	
1989	𝍸	5	1	
1988	I	1	.5	
1987				
Pre 1986				
	Total	407		

Fig. 13.21. Special form: Step 7.

COMPUTER ASSISTED METHOD
(Form for Computing Cut-Date)

Summary of Method (see page 187 for complete details):

1. By-passing the regular system, record 400 consecutive uses, combining both books being circulated and books having in-library use, using a standby computer system.
2. Have the regular system print out a list of these books, showing the date of last use.
3. Manually, enter the year of last use for each volume in the column "Volumes With This Date of Last Use."
4. In the column "TOTAL #" enter the total number of cases in each row.
5. Add up the "TOTAL #" column and enter the total at the bottom of the page.
6. Compute the percentage of usage represented by each year. Enter in column headed "TOTAL %."
7. Compute and enter under "CUM. %" the cumulative percentage, starting from the top of the form.
8. Determine the keeping percentage to be used for weeding.
9. Determine the cut-off date to be used for weeding.
10. Have the computer produce a list of all books which have not been used since that cut-off date and remove them from the collection.

Date	Volumes With This Date of Last Use	TOTAL		CUM
		#	%	%
1997				
1996	＃＃＃＃＃ (tally marks) IIII	299	73.5	73.5
1995	＃＃＃＃ (tally marks) ＃＃ IIII	59	14.5	88
1994	＃＃＃ I	16	4	92
1993	＃＃＃ II	17	4	96
1992	IIII	4	1	97
1991	IIII	4	1	98
1990	II	2	.5	98.5
1989	＃	5	1	99.5
1988	I	1	.5	100
1987				
Pre 1986				
	Total	407		

Step 8: Determine the keeping percentage to be used for weeding. This is an arbitrary decision to be made by the librarian and is discussed at some length in chapter 7. In general, for circulating collections; percentages from 95 to 98 percent have been used successfully by the author to determine how much of the use of the present collection should be retained after weeding. The higher this percentage, the fewer the number of books that will be weeded. Therefore, it is recommended that the keeping level not exceed 96 percent unless special conditions dictate a higher number. If there is any doubt as to what percentage to select, use 96 percent. And remember, in fact, usage is likely to increase, not decrease, after weeding.

Step 9: Determine the cut-off date to be used for weeding. Run your eye down the "CUM %" column and draw a line under the box that contains the keeping percentage level just selected in step 8. The form has been completed (see Figure 13.22). Now read in the left-hand column the years divided by the line just drawn. This is interpreted as follows: Keep all the volumes last used in 1993 or more recently; weed all the volumes last used in 1992 or before. The cut point has now been determined: December 31, 1992.

Step 10: Have the computer produce a list of all books that have not been used since that cut-date.

Step 11: Have clerks and volunteers remove all volumes from the shelves that are on this unused book list. These volumes should be stored on shelves away from the main collection. They are the weeding candidates. This completes the most arduous part of the weeding process and relieves librarians of what is basically a manual task. In a library, because of space limitations, perhaps 10 percent of the weeding candidates should be placed in this "weeding storage area" at one time.

Step 12: Give the librarians one week to examine these volumes and suggest which ones should be returned to the collection. A book recommended for retention should have a *written* justification for such retention, and the weeding manager should make the final decision. There is statistical evidence that the removal of these volumes will improve the value and the use of the library.

Even if the in-library usage has not been recorded, this method still can be employed. Then it becomes important that the librarians attempt to retain in the collection those books from the weeding candidates that have experienced recent in-library use.

Fig. 13.22. Special form: Step 9.

COMPUTER ASSISTED METHOD
(Form for Computing Cut-Date)

Summary of Method (see page 187 for complete details):

1. By-passing the regular system, record 400 consecutive uses, combining both books being circulated and books having in-library use, using a standby computer system.
2. Have the regular system print out a list of these books, showing the date of last use.
3. Manually, enter the year of last use for each volume in the column "Volumes With This Date of Last Use."
4. In the column "TOTAL #" enter the total number of cases in each row.
5. Add up the "TOTAL #" column and enter the total at the bottom of the page.
6. Compute the percentage of usage represented by each year. Enter in column headed "TOTAL %."
7. Compute and enter under "CUM. %" the cumulative percentage, starting from the top of the form.
8. Determine the keeping percentage to be used for weeding.
9. Determine the cut-off date to be used for weeding.
10. Have the computer produce a list of all books which have not been used since that cut-off date and remove them from the collection.

Date	Volumes With This Date of Last Use	TOTAL		CUM
		#	%	%
1997				
1996	ᚱᚱᚱᚱᚱᚱᚱᚱᚱᚱᚱ (tally marks) IIII	299	73.5	73.5
1995	(tally marks) IIII	59	14.5	88
1994	(tally marks) I	16	4	92
1993	(tally marks) II	17	4	96
1992	IIII	4	1	97
1991	IIII	4	1	98
1990	II	2	.5	98.5
1989	ᚱᚱᚱ	5	1	99.5
1988	I	1	.5	100
1987				
Pre 1986				
	Total	407		

Another Variation of the Manual Method

There are systems that are not programmed satisfactorily for using either of these methods without some changes. While all the systems observed were able to intercept the circulation records, even some sophisticated and complex systems were not programmed to print lists of the records intercepted. Some ingenuity must be used in this situation. In one installation, the list of 400 books had to be fed into the main computer one book at a time, a rather onerous task. The manual method just described can be used by entering the dates of last use on the form. As an alternative, instead of printing out the information for each book, the records can be brought up on the computer screen and, without printing them out, the date of last use entered on the form. Again, use this data with the manual method just described.

An Unscientific Way of Selecting a Cut-Date

There exist two quick-and-dirty methods of selecting a cut-date for weeding which should be used only as a last resort, since they lack statistical verification, precision, and certainty. Nevertheless, crude as they are, they are a vast improvement over arbitrarily selecting the cut-date for a "dusty book" list printout. While, by some miracle, the cut-date arbitrarily chosen might be a valuable and useful date, more often it is way off the target. To get a quick check to see if the date is anywhere near being valid, use one of the following methods.

Method 1

Compute the number of circulations your average volume experiences in a year. For example, if your collection has 100,000 volumes and your circulation is 300,000 you would have three circulations per year per volume. Check Table 13.1, below. Look down the column called "Number of Circulations Per Year Per Volume" and find the next lowest amount of circulation. Then use the "Shelf-Time Period" associated with that "Number of Circulations." In the example, Briarcliff has 3.5 and Tarrytown 2.8 circulations per year per volume. Use the cut-date found in the next column—17 months from a library having 2.8 circulations per book per year, slightly lower than your figure of 3 uses per volume. The author suggests, on a first major weeding of a library, not to use a cut-date of less than one year.

Note that there is not a direct one-to-one correlation between circulations per year and cut-date, but there is a very strong statistical correlation.

Table 13.1.
Shelf-Time Period Cut-Off Points Related to Rate of Circulation.

Library	Number of Circulations Per Year Per Volume	Shelf-Time Period Cut-Off Point at 96 Percent Keeping-Level
Trenton	1.4	36 months
Newark	1.5	25 months
Fox Meadow	1.6	39 months
Tarrytown—1980	2.3	45 months
Larchmont	2.6	29 months
Tarrytown—1969	2.8	17 months
Briarcliff	3.5	6 months
Orem	5.0	10 months
Harrison	5.0	9 months
Morristown	6.2	2 months

Method 2

In the Five Libraries Study (see page 63) the following percentages of books would have been weeded out at the 95 percent keeping level.

Briarcliff	44%
Tarrytown	25%
Morristown	44%
Trenton	33%
Newark	40%

It appears that unless a library recently has been weeded heavily, at least 25 percent of the collection should be weeded. If the printout of books that did not experience use does not contain at least 25 percent of the collection, the author would recommend using a more recent cut-date to establish this list. For example, in one library a three year cut-date indicated that only 9 percent of the collection was listed on the uncirculated book list. This library should try a cut-date of two years, or even one year, in order to obtain a list including 25 percent or more of the collection.

There is a natural tendency on the part of library directors to fear that such a large weeding will be too noticeable and generate a backlash against the library (see page 64). But a substantial increase in book use experienced after deep weeding should win back any such backlash.

Steps to Be Taken Before Weeding

Step 1: Appoint a weeding manager. A senior staff member should be appointed to be in full charge of organizing and supervising this operation. For the time it takes to remove the volumes from the shelves, this manager should be relieved of all other duties.

Step 2: Organize the entire operation. A complete plan should be created, in writing, covering the following:

1. Determine the date on which the weeding procedure will start.

2. Schedule the staff or the volunteers who will do the work. The size of the group of assistants is limited to the number of terminals available, unless a printout of books to be weeded is to be used. About 10 weeders are sufficient for most medium-sized libraries.

3. Acquire an adequate number of storage boxes to hold the volumes removed from the stacks. Try to estimate the number needed by weeding a small section as a sample.

4. Acquire tape or string to secure the packed boxes and marking pencils to note their contents.

5. If possible, allocate a book truck for each worker to handle the weeding candidates removed from the stacks.

6. Schedule a sufficient number of people to physically move the books or boxes from the stack area to storage areas. One "mover" for each two or three weeders would suffice.

7. Locate and prepare adequate storage space to hold the books being weeded.

8. Establish computer workstations for the weeders who are checking the collection for weeding candidates, unless a printout of weeding candidates is used to weed the collection.

9. Have a half-hour training session with all involved personnel before the weeding starts. (See "Instructions for Weeding," page 205.)

10. As weeding normally can be completed in a day or two, it would be helpful to close the library during the weeding period.

11. Schedule a day before the actual weeding for data collection and cut-off point determination.

12. Get 3 x 5-inch cards, one for each shelf involved in the weeding.

13. If weeding from a printout book list, get foot stools, tall stools, and short stools so that the weeders can work sitting down.

Step 3: Test out the system in a trial run. At least one week before the actual weeding, the weeding manager should make a trial run both to create the cut-off point and to identify candidates for weeding. This should work out any kinks and resolve any doubts in advance.

Training the Weeding Staff

As advised above, a training session should be set up in advance of the actual weeding. It is good practice to have this session immediately prior to the start of weeding. Following are weeding instructions the author has used several times.

Instructions for Weeding

1. Weed in a fixed order, from top to bottom and from left to right.

2. Place a 3 x 5-inch card in the middle of a shelf, between two books, clearly visible, to identify a shelf that has been weeded. This is done so that no shelf goes unweeded and is helpful in assigning the work load.

3. Inform the weeders of the cut-off point as follows: "The cut-off point is _____. (Insert the cut-off point determined for your library.) Keep all volumes on the shelf that have been used once or more in _____ *or more recently.* If the volume has experienced no use, *retain it if it was added to the collection in the above year or more recently.*"

4. If there is any doubt about whether a book should be retained or removed, keep that volume.

5. Treat duplicate titles as separate works. This means that one copy might be retained and a similar copy removed.

6. Keep local authors, gift books, or special books of local subjects, if you happen to recognize them. Do not worry about discarding valuable works, since the weeding manager will look at each book before it is discarded.

7. Do not make a subjective judgment about keeping a book because you think the author, subject, or title is important.

8. If you have any serious questions, ask the weeding supervisor.

9. Work as comfortably as possible. The use of different size stools will cut fatigue and increase productivity.

10. Your early selections will be double-checked by the weeding manager, who will give you any additional training you may need.

11. If for any reason you are interrupted in the middle of a shelf, turn the last book observed on its spine so that you can start from where you left off.

How Computers Could Simplify Weeding

Computers, properly programmed, have the capacity to produce all the information necessary for rapid, effective, painless, meaningful, and safe weeding. Two things may prevent this from happening:

1. Librarians, as a rule, find it difficult to give up their belief that they must use judgment in weeding and that their judgment gives more valid selection than the statistics of book usage. At this time, most librarians with a valid "dusty book" list in hand, which would actually retain 95 to 99 percent of the predicted future use, refuse to simply remove these candidates for weeding. They often spend months applying the unproven, confusing, and invalid criteria and techniques found in chapter four. The author has observed librarians checking publication dates, publishers, condition, duplication, standard lists, indexes, etc., spending perhaps a half hour on one book that hasn't been used in 20 years. Each librarian seems to have a different definition of what "a classic to be retained" is. Everything by Charles Dickens is not being used, and even with the popular Dickens titles, certain old, unappealing copies of these titles remain unused on the shelves. From a library's point of view, "a classic" is not a title but a volume. A classic is an older work that is enjoying frequent current use. It can be identified most surely by its shelf-time period—the length of time it remains on the shelves unused.

2. Computer programs, to date, have not produced the reports of the shelf-time periods of the volumes as they experience use—reports that would make weeding almost automatic. As Day and Revill suggest, library suppliers should ". . . provide collection management information at a more sophisticated level."[7] They all produce the number of uses a volume has experienced and the date of its last use, but what librarians need is a compilation of the shelf-time characteristics of volumes as they experience use. Each library has two almost separate collections—that which is used and that which remains on the shelf unused. The variable shelf-time period identifies the differences between these two collections. A perfect library would have all of its volumes experiencing use, and the books on the shelves would have the same average shelf-time period as the books being used.

    Until librarians and the vendors of computerized circulation control systems accept this fact and make the relevant programs available, librarians are forced to guess at the proper cut-date or to improvise a method for creating the date to be used to produce "dusty book" lists.

Furthermore, creating the proper cut-date is relatively simple. Computers could easily create a list such as this, taken from an actual library, as the books experienced use.

If you weed books not used since:	You will retain this percentage of the future use of the current collection:
1996	73.5%
1995	88%
1994	92%
1993	96%
1992	97%
1991	98%

The librarian could then make an arbitrary selection of either 1993, 1994, or 1995, as the cut-date. The computer could print out a "dusty book" list of volumes not used since the selected date. And better still, all volumes should have a computer readable identification code on the spine enabling a hand-held computer to indicate the books to be weeded. A clerk could go through the collection, remove all candidates for weeding, and relocate them very temporarily in some non-public area. Librarians could return some of them to the shelves if they find a valid reason, write it up, and get the head librarian to approve the decision.

Summary

It is important to realize that weeding has become an expensive, time-consuming procedure in almost every library. Many libraries have rarely been weeded. Some weeding programs go on for years without ever terminating. Librarians, in general, have neither the time nor the enthusiasm for a book by book, decision-making process. It is this author's suggestion that weeding be done using only one objective criterion.

Most of us weed as if our decisions are going to make a major difference to clients. Most of our clients accept our already incomplete libraries as being unable to satisfy every whim and desire.

Conclusion

Stand-alone computer circulation control programs sell for under $1,000 and centralized computer systems shared by a number of libraries can cost $1 million or more. Yet both types of systems retain valuable use information that can help make weeding efficient and rational. But librarians must insist that the systems are "open" enough to permit user requests to be implemented in order to maximize the benefits that computers are capable of providing.

Notes

1. Jeff Barry, Jose-Marie Griffiths, and Peiling Wang, "Automated System Market Place 96: Jockeying for Supremacy in a Networked World," *Library Journal* 121 (1 April 1996): 40.

2. Linda H. Bertland, "Circulation Analysis as a Tool for Collection Development," *School Library Media Quarterly* (Winter 1991): 96.

3. Maurice B. Line, "Changes in the Use of Literature with Time-Obsolescence Revisited," *Library Trends* 41, no. 4 (Spring 1993): 165.

4. Danny P. Wallace, "The Young and the Ageless: Obsolescence in Public Library Collections," *Public Libraries* 29 (March/April 1990): 104.

5. Lawrence L. Reed and Rodney Erickson, "Weeding: A Quantitative and Qualitative Approach," *Library Acquisitions: Practice and Theory* 17 (1993): 175.

6. If computers were programmed to retain the last two dates of circulation, this second field could be used to create the cut-point needed by weeders.

7. Mike Day and Don Revill, "Towards the Active Collection: The Use of Circulation Analysis in Collection Evaluation," *Journal of Librarianship and Information Science* 27 (September 1995): 149.

Form Used for the Computer Assisted Method
COMPUTER ASSISTED METHOD
(Form for Computing Cut-Date)

Summary of Method (see page 187 for complete details):

1. By-passing the regular system, record 400 consecutive uses, combining both books being circulated and books having in-library use, using a standby computer system.

2. Have the regular system print out a list of these books, showing the date of last use.

3. Manually, enter the year of last use for each volume in the column "Volumes With This Date of Last Use."

4. In the column "TOTAL #" enter the total number of cases in each row.

5. Add up the "TOTAL #" column and enter the total at the bottom of the page.

6. Compute the percentage of usage represented by each year. Enter in column headed "TOTAL %."

7. Compute and enter under "CUM. %" the cumulative percentage, starting from the top of the form.

8. Determine the keeping percentage to be used for weeding.

9. Determine the cut-off date to be used for weeding.

10. Have the computer produce a list of all books which have not been used since that cut-off date and remove them from the collection.

Date	Volumes With This Date of Last Use	TOTAL		CUM
		#	%	%
1997				
1996				
1995				
1994				
1993				
1992				
1991				
1990				
1989				
1988				
1987				
Pre 1986				
	Total			

Some Practical Considerations

Background

A number of experiences in library weeding have produced information and procedures that can assist in improving the results obtained when applying the recommended methods of weeding. Some of this information can be used also as a standard for comparison, for planning purposes, and to increase confidence in your findings.

Shelf-Reading

Shelf-reading is one of the oldest of conventional library routines. It involves returning the books on the shelves to their proper sequence. For all of the recommended weeding methods, decisions for weeding are based upon the use or non-use of a volume during a given period of time. Volumes that have not been used because they were misshelved distort the results. It is common practice in university libraries that students purposely misshelve books so that they will always be available to the only student who knows their improper secret location. It is imperative that shelf-reading be done for the entire library at least once every six months.

Weeding the Book Catalog

The advent of computer catalogs has simplified the task of conforming the catalog to the actual holdings of a library. The records of weeded works can be removed rather easily. With card catalogs the removal of records is an arduous task, often more difficult than placing the cards in the catalog in the first place.

If the catalog is to be accurate and up-to-date, all entries should represent materials available to the user. This is never true. Libraries, even with sophisticated, electronic security systems, experience a great deal of theft (2 to 5 percent per year, on an average). The records of stolen books that remain in the catalog represent a major distortion.

The best way to improve this situation is by taking inventory regularly and removing the records of the works no longer a part of the collection. This is not a popular practice, but a well-weeded collection calls for a well-weeded catalog.

Duplicates to Be Considered Individually

From the point of view of the weeder, duplicate titles of different editions or duplicate copies of the same edition should be considered as if they were separate works. There are four reasons for this decision:

1. Such a decision simplifies weeding. It can be extremely difficult to treat multiple copies as one. For example, such volumes can be located in widely dispersed places and difficult to bring together. At the moment of weeding, they might be in circulation, on the shelf, being reshelved, in reserve, or in special displays. In addition, volumes located in different places are likely to experience different use patterns.

2. Even if multiple copies are found in one location, different use patterns might develop because of physical characteristics of the volume— whether or not it has a dust jacket, been rebound, is torn, etc. Such differences can cause the future use pattern to vary. Little is known of the causes of book use, so to assume that similar titles will experience similar usage is not justified.

3. It may seem unusual to weed one copy of a book and retain an identical copy. However, as long as one copy remains in the collection, the library has changed very little compared with removing all copies of one title. If all copies are removed, it is because of lack of use. If all remain, it indicates steady use. If only one copy is retained, it indicates relatively light use and that one copy will be adequate for the demands likely to be made on that title.

4. If the same title exists in different editions, it is not unusual for there to be heavy use of the newer editions and little or no use of the older editions. Certainly such older editions should be weeded out.

Weeding the Collection as an Entity or by Class

No matter which weeding method is to be used, a decision must be made in advance whether to weed the collection as a whole, to weed one or more segments or classes, or to weed the entire collection by class. It is not uncommon to treat fiction and nonfiction as two distinct classes, with different cut-off points and different shelf-time period characteristics. However, any other subdivision can be made. In the example shown on page 129, the classes have been separated into the Dewey hundreds, fiction, short stories, biographies, mysteries, and paperbacks. These divisions, or even much smaller divisions, can be used and should be predetermined by each library depending upon the precision desired and the objectives of the library. Libraries that are attempting to satisfy some of the recreational and informational needs of small communities should not consider weeding by minute classes. Serious research libraries should break down the classes to reflect differences in use patterns.

It was found that different classes of books tend to have different shelf-time periods and different patterns of usage. For instance, fiction generally has a shorter average shelf-time period than nonfiction, and such classes as religion and travel showed a great variation from each other, with religion almost always having much longer average shelf-time periods than travel. Obviously, the supply of any class of books, the use being made of the library, and the type of user all affect shelf-time period.

If a library were weeded as an entity, a somewhat different collection of books would be weeded than if the same library were weeded by class. For instance, if weeded as an entity, a library might retain 96 percent of the total future usage. This might result in keeping 98 percent of the fiction usage, 90 percent of the travel usage, and only 80 percent of the usage of religious works. If each class were weeded separately, 96 percent of the usage of each class would be retained, but the shelf-time period cut-off point would have to be developed for each class independently. This is an onerous task and is worth the effort only when some meaningful purpose might be served. Weed the largest classes that can be reasonably justified.

One reason that different classes have different shelf-time periods is illustrated in chapter 8 (page 63), which shows that collections might not contain volumes in proportion to their usage. When proportionately fewer volumes are held in a class, the shelf-time period shortens; when proportionately more volumes are held, the shelf-time period gets longer. If the library is weeded as one entity, the library holdings will be evened out so that each class will contain a number of volumes proportionate to that class's usage. In the case of Harrison, the adult fiction collection contained 24 percent of the library's volumes. Those volumes experienced 48 percent of the total library usage. To optimize the library's investment in books, more fiction should be acquired until the fiction holdings represent 48 percent of the total holdings. Even this percentage is probably on the low side, since as more fiction is purchased fiction use will increase. Nevertheless, weeding the collection as a whole and weeding by class are equally valid approaches.

How Long Does It Take to Weed?

Records have been kept on the actual time it takes to create a cut-off point and to weed a library. Each method has its own problems, and there are substantial differences between libraries. Individual work output varies greatly. In addition, the libraries described below were closed to the public, during the day or two books were being removed from the shelves, to prevent clients from interfering with the weeding process.

Book Card and Historical Reconstruction Methods

1. *To accumulate the basic information.*

    The time needed to accumulate the 400 to 500 book cards used to create the cut-off point in the book card method of weeding has been from one to seven days. While no substantial effort is required, the time is needed to permit 400 to 500 books to be used either in the library or circulated. The historical reconstruction method of weeding takes about one to two hours to remove the volumes from the shelves, tabulate the data from their book cards, and reslip and reshelve the volumes.

2. *To compute the cut-off point.*

The time needed to compute the cut-off points in both methods is under one hour.

3. *To weed the library.*

The time needed to do the actual weeding varied considerably. Each book must be removed from the shelf, and the book card must be scrutinized carefully to see if the last date entered indicates a core-collection book or one to be weeded. Careful records were kept in several recent weedings.

Public Library A: A collection of 17,175 volumes was weeded in three hours and 15 minutes by the equivalent of nine and one-half workers, all experienced employees of this library. Removed from the shelves were 1,980 fiction volumes (13.5 percent of the collection) and 648 biographies (26 percent of the collection). The average worker handled 554 volumes per hour. These employees were working on their day off and wasted little time. In addition, it took five worker-hours to move the books and pack them into cardboard cartons (52 to a carton).

School Library A: The collection consisted of approximately 10,000 volumes, of which 1,019 were removed from the shelves. It took 25 worker-hours, and each person (there were 11) handled 400 volumes per hour. This work was done by two regular staff members, 10 volunteers, and the author. Putting the books into the storage area and into cartons took four worker-hours.

School Library B: The collection of 9,000 in-library volumes was weeded by a group of inexperienced volunteers. They removed 2,965 volumes. They were slowed down by certain written entries on the book cards, which confounded easy decision making. The 10 volunteers handled an average of 200 volumes per hour, including the loading, moving, and boxing of the books.

It can be seen from the above data that a range of 200 to 554 volumes were being handled per hour per worker. While this variability makes planning more difficult, it is good practice to weed a library in one day in order to minimize the disruption of the normal library service. This is possible since almost any number of workers can be accommodated when each works in a very restricted area.

Spine-Marking Method

1. *To accumulate the basic information.*

The time needed to receive the weeding signal is between one and five or more years. The total number of worker-hours involved has not been recorded since the work was spread out over such a long time period and was performed as an auxiliary effort relating to the normal, routine circulation, processing, and shelving procedures.

2. *To compute the cut-off point.*

The time needed to do the computation is about 10 minutes.

3. *To weed the library.*

The time required to remove 1,200 volumes of one class was under one hour, in one case. Most of this time was spent in moving the volumes to the storage area.

Computer Assisted Method

1. *To accumulate the basic information.*

The time needed to accumulate the date of last use from the last 400 volumes experiencing in-library use or being circulated depends upon the amount of client activity. This is likely to vary from a few hours to four or five days.

2. *To compute the cut-off point.*

The time needed to compute the cut-off point, whether done manually or by computer, should be less than one hour.

3. *To weed the library.*

The time needed to do the actual weeding can vary considerably, depending upon the method used and the programming of the computer. If each volume on the shelves must be read into the computer, hundreds of worker-hours can be involved. If the computer produces a finished weeding list, either a "dusty book" list of volumes unused, or a list of volumes not used since the cut-off point, a library could be weeded in a day or two, provided adequate assistance is available.

How Deeply Should Weeding Be Done?

One of the fears librarians have about weeding is that so much will be weeded that the library will look empty. Neither the clients nor the trustees are likely to accept this condition with pleasure. And, in many cases, the fear is a real one—especially when weeding is long overdue. For example, in one junior college library, 75 percent of the volumes had never been used. In this library, to weed at any level would have removed at least this 75 percent.

There are two practical solutions to this problem. First, if too many books are going to be weeded at the selected keeping-level, increase this level to 98, 99, or even 100 percent. Second, if this higher keeping-level still weeds too many volumes, return a percentage of the candidates for weeding to the shelves. Try to return those volumes with the most recent imprint dates.

Under normal conditions, weed out between 10 and 30 percent of a collection, depending upon the ready availability of shelf space or the need for additional space. A library can be weeded more deeply the next time around. In order to accomplish weeding at a level that retains 70 to 90 percent of the collection, estimate the likely amount of weeding by the following methods:

1. *Sampling the entire collection.* Apply the computed cut-off point to a sample of 100 volumes, selected periodically from the collection. For example, if there are 100 stacks in the library, take the first volume in each stack and compute the percentage of volumes being weeded.

2. A simpler method is to *weed one stack* and compute the percentage of the collection being weeded. This method has the weakness that different sections of the library tend to contain different percentages of noncore volumes. However, as weeding progresses, adjustments can be made to correct over-weeding.

3. If the spine-marking method is being used, it is easy to *see how much weeding will occur,* since all the unmarked volumes are to be removed.

Cut-Off Points Found in Libraries

The cut-off points appearing in table 14.1 are given in order that you may compare your results with the results obtained by others.

Cut-Off Points Related to the Rate of Circulation Per Volume

A spread of cut-off points from two months to over 30 years has been reported in table 14.1. A further study into the likely cause of this diversity revealed an interesting phenomenon. The cut-off point relates rather closely to the rate of the circulation of a collection, meaning the relationship of the circulation to the size of the collection. This ratio is a useful predictor of the approximate length of the shelf-time period needed to weed. It was observed that large, highly specialized collections have much smaller usage per book than popular fiction collections in suburban public libraries. Table 14.2 illustrates the relationship. While it is obvious that these variables are not related one-to-one, a rough prediction of shelf-time period cut-off point can be made at the 96 percent keeping-level.

Although the weeding techniques recommended involve observing both the circulation activity and simultaneous in-library use of volumes, it seems clear that these two items are closely related. In general, the greater the circulation, the greater the in-library use. These tables considered only circulation use, but might have been improved if in-library use also had been considered.

Table 14.1.
Shelf-Time Period Cut-Off Points at the 96 Percent Keeping-Level.

Library	Shelf-Time Period in Months
Morristown Public—Fiction	2 months
Briarcliff Public—Fiction	6 months
Harrison Public—Fiction	9 months
Orem Public	10 months
Minot Public	12 months
Tarrytown Public—Fiction	17 months
Garland County Library	19 months
St. Laurent Public	24 months
Greenacres Elementary School	25 months
Newark Public—Fiction	25 months
Larchmont Public	29 months
Tech University	32 months
North York Board of Education	34 months
Trenton Public	36 months
Columbia Special	36 months
Fox Meadow Elementary School	39 months
Louisiana State Library	60 months
Deering University	60+months
Grand Rapids—Fiction	120 months
Cowles Special	252 months
Chemistry—University	324 months
Physics & Pharmacy—University	360+months

Table 14.2.
Shelf-Time Period Cut-Off Related to Rate of Circulation.

Library	Number of Circulations Per Year Per Volume	Shelf-Time Period Cut-Off Point at 96 Percent Keeping-Level
Trenton	1.4	36 months
Newark	1.5	25 months
Fox Meadow	1.6	39 months
Tarrytown—1980	2.3	45 months
Larchmont	2.6	29 months
Tarrytown—1969	2.8	17 months
Briarcliff	3.5	6 months
Orem	5.0	10 months
Harrison	5.0	9 months
Morristown	6.2	2 months

Part 3
THE WEEDING PROCESS FOR NONCIRCULATING COLLECTIONS

15

Weeding Reference Collections

Reference collections generally do not circulate. They are collections of books, serials, and other types of materials limited to use within the library in order to provide a higher level of service to the average user. They offer easier access to frequently consulted materials. Even though reference books generally are consulted for specific items of information rather than read cover to cover, what is a reference book in one library, is a circulating book in another.

Types of Reference Collections

The problems involved in weeding such materials are made more complex by the fact that there are different types of reference collections which might respond to different kinds of weeding. The following reference collections most readily lend themselves to weeding:

1. *General Reference Collections.* In many libraries they often consist of books kept in a special area and marked in some fashion indicating that they are reference works, not to be circulated. The main branch of the New York Public Library is an example of an entire collection of millions of volumes that basically do not circulate outside the library confines.

2. *Indexes, Abstracts, Yearbooks, etc.* They are often found in special sections that have desk or table space available for the convenience of the users.

3. *Ready Reference Collections.* These usually are kept near to where reference librarians attempt to answer their patrons' questions. The librarians themselves are often the only direct users of this material.

4. *Reserve Collections.* Usually found in academic libraries or school media centers, these are a special subset of course-related materials thought to be needed by the students, are checked out for in-library use, and returned to the shelves or files quickly. Some libraries permit short-term circulation privileges, but generally the material is thought to be accessible to more students if it does not circulate.

5. *Serials, Periodicals, Newspapers, etc.* These normally do not circulate outside the library. There is an entire literature on the problems of weeding serials, since their growth is usually at a rate faster than the growth of the space where they are stored. Weeding serial titles offers its own set of difficulties.

Background

"Evidence suggests that many titles in what were designed to be lean 'working' reference collections are rarely if ever consulted."[1] ". . . librarians are now aware that: (a) bigger is not better if access is reduced, and (b) less is more if accuracy is guaranteed."[2] "Although systematic weeding of library reference collections has repeatedly been recommended . . . few practical guides have been put forth . . ."[3] The present generally accepted criteria and techniques for weeding are presented below. However, it is the aim of this book to find easier and more reliable methods of making weeding decisions. What is wanted is ". . . an objective method for identifying materials for weeding."[4]

Present Methods of Weeding Reference Materials

In general the criteria used to weed reference collections are:[5]

1. Usage of the material is the primary consideration of most reference librarians in deciding whether to weed reference materials. Such usage might be limited to usage within one's own library or reported by other libraries. Usage data might also include interlibrary loans, the number of times an item has been used in one year, the amount of time between transactions, circulation counts, and in-library use.[6] While user-need is the criterion of choice for most reference librarians,[7] ". . . identifying what sources have been used in the past is difficult, since there are no circulation records."[8]

2. The age of the material has been a standard criterion for weeding much material, especially where new editions or up-to-date editions appear regularly (in such works as yearbooks, almanacs, and encyclopedias). Scheduled replacement, especially on a predetermined basis, is a commonly accepted technique used by reference librarians.[9]

3. The presence or absence of the library's holdings in the indexes serving the clients of the library.

4. The lack of citations for specific reference material in citations indexes used in the library,[10] although Line points out that "No one has yet successfully studied how far citations reflect use."[11]

5. The convenient availability of the reference works elsewhere.

6. The validity of the information in the reference works.

7. The presence or absence of reference works on standard lists of recommended holdings. Truett reports ". . . most libraries conducted systematic evaluation of the reference collection, primarily by means of comparisons to checklists or standard lists of recommended titles."[12] Titles mentioned as used in the evaluation included the *Public Library Catalog*, recommended reference book lists from *Library Journal, Best Reference*

Books, Booklist, Sheehy's *Guide to Reference Books, Books for College Libraries, ARBA,* and even the most current edition of *Books in Print.*[13]

Suggested Methods of Weeding Reference Works

While each type of reference collection lends itself to different weeding treatment, it is suggested that all of the above types of collections could be improved if the usage of the collections were known. Biggs observes that, "Systematically-gathered use data are needed to guide selection and weeding."[14] Since current common practice rarely records or tabulates in-library use, some method of recording usage must be devised. Substantial use information could be obtained by:

1. Dotting the spine (or some other place) of each book as it is used, over a period of time of at least one year, and preferably four to five years.

2. Using this visible means of recording circulation as a tool of weeding. This might mean removing all undotted books, removing some of the dotted but less used works, or *not* considering dotted books for removal (except where more current editions are available). The use of "spine-marking" is really a method of determining shelf-time periods. In addition, different colored dots could be used each year, for example, to show which books have been used more recently. As with circulating collections, when the shelvers find that 96 to 99 percent of the books they are reshelving had previously been dotted, the rest of the collection—the undotted books—might be considered candidates for weeding. (See chapter 11 on spine marking.)

3. Establishing a weeding criterion based upon little or no use of the reference material. Such a criterion may be, for example, to consider all books not used in 18 months to be serious candidates for weeding.

4. As an additional value to this system, buying more works in classifications where heavy usage is indicated by the concentration of dotted works, and reducing acquisitions in classes where little or no use is indicated.

Special Weeding Suggestions for Reference Collections

1. *The General Reference Collections.* These collections, especially in many public libraries, lend themselves to deep weeding. Many of the volumes remain on the shelves for years unused and unwanted.[15] When weeded, the unused materials should be discarded or moved into the circulating collection.

   One problem is that identifying and dotting books used in-library takes additional work. It means that the users must be instructed and trained not to reshelve books once they are removed from the shelves. Then the library workers who do the reshelving must be trained to apply stick-on dots to the books. Adding one dot for each usage helps determine the number of usages and should be done if such information would help make weeding decisions. Perhaps the first dot should be applied to the spine and all subsequent dots inside the cover.

This technique demands discipline and extra time to apply the dots but saves months of work during the actual weeding.

2. *Indexes, Abstracts, Yearbooks, etc.* These offer a special challenge. At what point may one safely remove the older volumes, and how many years of back runs must be retained in primary use areas? It has been suggested that libraries use some form of relatively inconspicuous marking or other indicator so that any movement of the volume would show usage. Fussler and Simon suggested using " . . . infrared dust, beads on the top of the book or unexposed photographic paper inserted between the pages."[16] Harris suggested putting a slip in the book that cannot be seen while the book is on the shelf but is clearly visible when the book is removed. The user is asked to remove the slip, but it is placed in such a fashion that even if the user doesn't remove it, there will be an obvious indication that the slip was disturbed.[17] Some such method should be used for at least one year to discover if patterns of usage indicate at what point older volumes become weedable. These older runs might be removed to less accessible areas or weeded out.

3. *Ready Reference Collections.* Reference librarians have first-hand knowledge of the usefulness of these collections since they are handling them regularly. Aside from the problem of how often they should be replaced with new editions, or updated in some other way, individual titles are vulnerable to remaining unused for long periods of time even though the rest of the collection enjoys considerable use. It is suggested that librarians use the spine-marking system (placing two small self-adhering dots on the spine) the first time the volume is used, to uncover *non-use* of these works. While at first many volumes might have to be dotted, that number will decline rapidly as they need not be redotted after the first usage. The task of dotting is one which becomes easier each day. Again, this takes willingness on the part of the reference librarians to cooperate. Any ready reference work not used in one year is likely to be a reasonable candidate for weeding and/or returning to the circulating collection.

4. *Reserve Collections.* The reserve collections, with works selected by the teaching staff, often are full of unused materials for courses no longer taught, courses being taught by new staff, and outdated materials long forgotten. The spine-marking method should be used to show non-use. Many teaching cycles are of one year in duration, that is, the courses are taught annually. Under those conditions, the materials not used during that year are unlikely to be used at all. When courses are taught less frequently, longer periods should be used in making weeding judgments.

Dots should be applied to any books being used and not already dotted. All books not dotted at the end of the proper teaching cycles should be removed and either returned to the circulating collection or discarded. The teaching staff should be given the opportunity, in writing, to support its desire to keep unused works in the reserve collection.

5. *Serials, Periodicals, Newspapers, etc.* There is no simple overall solution to the problem of serials. Possibly someday soon, all serials will be available on computer terminals, and libraries won't have to dedicate so much space to them. Again, the spine-marking system should be used, prohibiting users from reshelving the work. As non-use is indicated, the earlier unused runs of periodicals can be sold off, replaced with microfilm or CD-ROMs, or moved into storage away from primary areas. As with all types of reference material, it is important to observe usage patterns if intelligent weeding programs are to be undertaken.

Three Experiences Using the Spine-Marking Method

The following are three reports of reference collections being weeded using dots affixed to the materials to indicate usage.

In 1978, Shaw reported on a technique that " . . . can be used in a wide variety of libraries for an indefinite period of time and with minimal expense."[18] In the Case Western Reserve University Libraries, on the spine of the bound journal volumes, a small pressure sensitive label was applied the first time each was reshelved. The users were encouraged not to reshelve. Data were collected periodically, counting the total number of volumes and titles that had been tagged. The result of the study was that it identified those volumes that were used and those volumes that were not used. ". . . Thus decisions regarding the disposition of volumes or titles can be made with confidence that they will stand the test of time."[19] (See page 68.)

Biggs reports "affixing a small pressure sensitive label to a book's spine the first time it is reshelved" in the reference collection at Bowling Green State University (Ohio). A different colored dot was used for each of the three semesters the dotting took place. At the end of a year and a half, subject specialists scanned the shelves, and if they wished to retain an undotted volume, they had to write a supporting rationale and have their requests approved by the head of reference.[20]

In a longer term project, over a period of five years, Engeldinger's staff placed stick-on dots inside the back cover of every reference book reshelved. When five dots had been applied no new ones were added. After five years it was found that 34.8 percent of the reference collection had received no usage, and 51.4 percent had received only one use during that period.[21] (See page 69.)

A Current Weeding Program

In September 1995, the Roscoe L. West Library at Trenton State College (New Jersey) began a weeding program of the reference collection using spine marking. There are a number of clearly visible signs posted around the library which state:

> A usage study of Reference Books
> is underway. Books *must* be
> reshelved by Library Staff to
> ensure accurate findings.
> Thank you.

Mary Biggs is the dean of the library and is being assisted by Patricia Butcher. Because of their previous experience in this process, they have taken steps to ensure that books are not reshelved by patrons. There are strong indications that they have succeeded in this effort.

They pointed out three specific aspects of general interest:

1. Patrons are less likely to reshelve if there is plenty of desk and table space on which to leave the books once they are used.

2. Self-adhering dots sold in stationery stores tend to fall off so they have cut up ordinary Brodart library mending tape, which has a much stronger adhesive. These are very difficult for the patrons to remove.

3. It is often difficult to find tape of such a color that it will not blend in with the cover of the volumes and, thus, be difficult to identify or see.

Each semester a different colored tape is to be used, and at the time of our visit, in April 1996, two different colors had been applied. So far these colored markings have not been used for weeding, but after two years the information they supply will be considered. However, at present the markings have been helpful to indicate areas of heavy usage and light usage, and that information currently is being taken into consideration in the acquisition process.

Computer Assisted Weeding

A number of library computer systems are programmed in such a way that they may be used as a substitute for applying dots to the spines of volumes.[22] Reference books marked with computer readable codes, when not reshelved by the user, can be scanned and entered easily into the computer system. Then, at any later date, the number of uses, the date of last use, and the lack of any use can be indicated in a print out. However, this author has not been able to find a library using this method of weeding.

Another source of information produced by computer circulation modules is the information recorded in Reserve Collections. NOTIS has a reserve room capacity which records the title, author, instructor, course number, and hourly loan periods of reserve room materials.[23] The charging out of these volumes creates the basis for identifying non-use of specific titles and could substitute for the dotting system recommended above.

Conclusion

The knowledge of the use of library materials is a vital factor, but not the only one, in the weeding and retention of reference collections. While the knowledge of past use patterns is valuable, their greatest value seems to be in indicating materials that have enjoyed no use at all during the test periods. It is assumed that the public would be better served by returning such reference materials to the circulating collections.

Notes

1. Mary Biggs, "Discovering How Information Seekers Seek: Methods of Measuring Reference Collection Use," *The Reference Librarian,* 29 (1990): 103.

2. Kathleen E. Joswick and John P. Steirman, "Systematic Reference Weeding: A Workable Model," *Collection Management* 18 (1/2) (1993): 104.

3. Amrita J. Burdick, "Science Citation Index Data as a Safety Net for Basic Science Books Considered for Weeding," *Library Resources and Technology Service* 33 (4) (October 1989): 368.

4. Joswick, 103.

5. Eleanor Mathews and David A. Tyckson, "A Program for the Systematic Weeding of the Reference Collection," *The Reference Librarian* 29 (1990): 135.

6. Ibid.

7. Sydney J. Pierce, "Introduction" to "Weeding and Maintenance of Reference Collections," *The Reference Librarian* 29 (1990): 3.

8. Ibid., 6.

9. Elizabeth Futas and Jonathan S. Tyron, "Scheduled Reference Collection Maintenance: The Rhode Island Experience," *The Reference Librarian* 29 (1990): 69-75.

10. Joswick, 104.

11. Maurice B. Line, "Changes in the Use of Literature with Time-Obsolescence Revisited," *Library Trends* 41 (4) (Spring 1993): 673.

12. Carol Truett, "Weeding and Evaluating the Reference Collection: A Study of Policies and Practices in Academic and Public Libraries," *The Reference Librarian* 29 (1990): 53.

13. Ibid., 64.

14. Biggs, 103.

15. Eugene A. Engeldinger, "Use as a Criterion for Weeding of Reference Collections: A Review and Case Study," *The Reference Librarian* 29 (1990): 124-125.

16. Herman H. Fussler and Julian L. Simon, *Pattern in the Use of Books in Large Research Libraries* (Chicago: University of Chicago Press, 1969), 108.

17. C. Harris, "A Comparison of Issues and In-Library Use of Books," *Aslib Proceedings* 29 (1977): 118-126.

18. W. M. Shaw Jr., "A Practical Journal Usage Technique," *College and Research Libraries* 39(6) (November 1978): 479.

19. Ibid., 481.

20. Biggs, 106.

21. Engledinger, 124-125.

22. For example, *DRA's (Date Research Associates) Circulation User Manual*, (1993): 13–33, under the heading of "Count In-House Use of Items" says, " . . . at the end of the day all items left on tables could be scanned for in-house use statistics. This could be especially useful to generate statistics for reference materials that do not circulate at all."

23. American Library Association, Library Technology Reports 30/1 (Jan/Feb 1994): 86.

Glossary

Better Predictor. The criterion that will yield a core collection of fewer volumes that will still satisfy a given level of future use.

Classic. An older book that exhibits the same use pattern of new books.

Closed-End Shelf-Time. The time period between the last two uses of a volume.

Compact Storage. Various methods of storage that will accommodate more books in a given area than will a conventional stack arrangement.

Core Collection. Subset of the holdings that can be identified with reasonable assurance as being able to fulfill a certain predetermined percentage of the future demand on the present collection.

Current Circulation Method. The sampling of books as they circulate in order to determine use patterns. This is done by examining books or book cards at the circulation desk to obtain data. It assumes that current patterns of use at circulation are a valid sample of the total use pattern.

Cut-Off Period or Point. The exact time point that determines whether a book is in the core or the noncore collection, i.e., the criterion to be used for weeding—the most recent use date describing volumes to be weeded.

Cut-Point. Same as "cut-off period or point."

Dusty Book List. A computer report of the books in the library that have not been used since a preselected date. This list measures the open-end shelf-time period of the books listed—the time that has elapsed since the last use of the book.

First Shelf-Time Period. Shelf-time period for a book before its first use; this can be determined only if one records the date the newly acquired book was first shelved.

"Five Libraries Study." A 1969 research project undertaken by the author in five libraries: Briarcliff and Tarrytown, in New York, and Morristown, Trenton, and Newark, in New Jersey.

Harrison Study. A research project in which the theoretical findings of the Five Libraries Study were put to practical use in weeding the Harrison Public Library.

Historical Reconstruction Method. Ideally, this means reconstructing the entire usage history of each volume in a collection by using the recorded dates of either circulation on in-library use.

Historical Reconstruction Method, Modified. Reconstructing history of usage over a shorter period of time.

Imprint Date. Age of a book as indicated by the most recent date printed on the title page or verso.

Keeping-Level. The percentage of predicted use to be maintained after weeding.

Level of Future Use. Predicted percentage of use to be retained by the core collection; likelihood of future use of a work, based on its past use.

Noncore Collection. Subset of the holdings identified as representing a very small amount of the likely future use of a collection.

Open-End Shelf-Time Period. The description of the characteristics of the whole collection; the time that has elapsed between the last use of the book and the date of the study. It measures the most recent length of time in which no use has been made of the volume.

Primary Collection Areas. Open stack areas, accessible to users, which house the regularly used collection.

Secondary Collection Areas. Storage areas less accessible than primary collection areas; normally not open to the user.

Shelf-Time Period. The length of time a book remains on the shelf between uses.

Spine Mark. Coded mark on the spine of a volume that indicates use.

Weeding. Removing the noncore collection from the primary collection area.

Weeding Signal. The first indication that the core collection has been identified, when using the spine-marking method of creating weeding criteria.

Bibliography

Bertland, Linda H. "Circulation Analysis as a Tool for Collection Development." *School Library Media Quarterly* (Winter 1991): 90-97.

Biggs, Mary. "Discovering How Information Seekers Seek: Methods of Measuring Reference Collection Use." *The Reference Librarian* 29 (1990): 103-117.

Engeldinger, Eugene A. "Use as a Criterion for Weeding of Reference Collections." *The Reference Librarian* 29 (1990): 119-128.

Evans, G. E. *Developing Library and Information Center Collections,* 2d ed. (Littleton, CO: Libraries Unlimited, 1987), 291-309.

Lancaster, F. W. "Obsolescence, Weeding, and the Utilization of Space." *Wilson Library Bulletin* 62, no. 9 (May 1988): 47-49.

Line, Maurice B. "Changes in the Use of Literature with Time-Obsolescence Revisited." *Library Trends* 41, no. 4 (Spring 1993): 665-683.

McKee, Penelope. "Weeding the Forest Hill Branch of Toronto Public Library by the Slote Method: A Test Case." *Library Research* 3 (1981): 283-301.

Reed, Lawrence L. and Rodney Erickson. "Weeding: A Quantitative and Qualitative Approach." *Library Acquisitions: Practice and Theory* 17 (1993): 175-181.

Roy, Loriene. "Does Weeding Increase Circulation? A Review of the Related Literature." *Collection Management* 10, 1/2 (1988): 141-153.

――――. "Weeding." *Encyclopedia of Library and Information Science*, Allen Kent, ed., vol. 54, sup. 17 (1994): 352-398.

――――. "Weeding Without Tears: Objective and Subjective Criteria Used in Identifying Books to be Weeded in Public Library Collections." *Collection Management* 13, 1/2 (1990): 83-92.

Selth, Jeff, Nancy Koller, and Peter Briscoe. "The Use of Books Within the Library." *College and Research Libraries* 53, no. 3 (May 1992): 197-295.

Wallace, Danny P. "The Young and the Ageless: Obsolescence in Public Library Collections." *Public Libraries* 29 (March/April 1990): 102-105.

Winche, E., and B. Molesworth. "Collection Weeding: York Regional Library." *APLA Bulletin* 44, no. 4 (January 1981): 38-39.

Epilogue

"In the futile attempt we all make to tidy up our lives
and our surroundings,
nothing is more difficult than throwing out a book.
I can't even bring myself to throw out a terrible book.
I have all I can do [to] throw out a magazine."

—Andy Rooney, 1984. (In Andrew A. Rooney,
"Casting Out Books," *Pieces of My Mind*.)

Index